how to
write
guitar
riffs

To access the online media visit:
www.halleonard.com/mylibrary

Enter code: 8232-9413-3718-8449

how to write guitar riffs

Create and Play Great Hooks for Your Songs
Third Edition | Revised and Updated

Rikky Rooksby

Backbeat
Books
Guilford, Connecticut

Backbeat
Books

An imprint of Globe Pequot, the trade division of
The Rowman & Littlefield Publishing Group, Inc.
4501 Forbes Blvd., Ste. 200
Lanham, MD 20706
www.rowman.com

Distributed by NATIONAL BOOK NETWORK

Copyright © 2021 by Rikky Rooksby
Cover design by Paul Palmer-Edwards
Book design by Tom Seabrook

Library of Congress Cataloging-in-Publication Data available

Library of Congress Control Number: 2021945155

ISBN 978-1-4930-6109-9 (paperback)
ISBN 978-1-4930-6110-5 (e-book)

♾™ The paper used in this publication meets the minimum requirements of
American National Standard for Information Sciences—Permanence of Paper
for Printed Library Materials, ANSI/NISO Z39.48-1992

contents

This book is dedicated to Marc Bolan (1947–1977)

preface to the third edition

There is no escaping the riff: that short, supercharged musical phrase that gets into your mind and sets your pulse racing. From Johnny Kidd and the Pirates' "Shakin' All Over" (1960) to Limp Bizkit's "Rollin'" (2001) to Alter Bridge's "Last Rites" (2020), riffs have been central to rock music for over 60 years, and many great rock songs depend on them. No sooner have most novice players put fingers to fretboard than they seek a familiar riff to enjoy. For decades, guitarists have spent hours (and many a rehearsal) playing their favorite riffs. They have bent their ears working out how to play favorite riffs from scratched LPs, stretched tapes, shiny CDs, downloaded mp3s, digital streams, and YouTube videos.

Riffs excite people, whether they are musicians or listeners. Advertising agencies use riffs on television and in movie trailers. Riffs sell songs, concert tickets, and guitars. At home and in clubs, theaters, and concert halls, millions have mimed playing riffs on "air guitar." On the internet there are countless videos of guitarists demonstrating riffs. There are arguments about the correct notes or fingering for a riff, or the right tuning, or how to get exactly the right sound. Did he bend that C♯ at the end, or fret it? In the 2009 documentary film *It Might Get Loud*, much camera time is given to showing Jimmy Page, the Edge, and Jack White playing riffs.

So, how is a riff defined? How many kinds of riff are there? What makes them work? How do you write one? And how do you better use the riffs you write? These are only some of the riff-related topics this book covers.

Whether you write or play riffs, or just like listening to them, this book is an all-purpose, encyclopedic rifferama—a guided tour of the riff in all its foot-stomping, headshaking, bone-crushing, string-thrashing glory. It explains the main types of riff and the musical ingredients in their creation, with each riff type illustrated by a discussion of famous bands and songs from six decades of rock history. There are techniques that could improve the riffs you write and help you make better arrangements and recordings of them. Specially recorded audio tracks accompany 16 of the musical examples presented in the main part of the book, plus 40 more original examples from the final section.

With a good awareness of the 30 riff types discussed in this book, you'll soon figure out riffs more easily, see how they function, and move toward riffs that embody your own musical style and ambitions.

Rikky Rooksby
Oxford, England
Summer 2021

how to use
this book

Each of the 30 types of riff explored in this book has its own subsection, showing how it derives from the basic musical material. Tips point to where to find each riff on the guitar and how to fit it into a song's harmony. Musical examples are provided in notation and TAB, with the accompanying audio tracks available to download using the code printed at the front of this book. Scale patterns are given for the riffs in section 2; the patterns have been chosen as those most useful for writing riffs, so they emphasize the lower octaves and do not go high up the fretboard.

The frequent *riff galleries* offer analysis of selected famous riffs: these descriptive entries give information about the kind of riff used on the selected track, how it works musically, and even how it was recorded and arranged. As many of these famous songs fit into more than one category, the placing of these songs is not exclusive, just illustrative.

Many of these songs belong to the first waves of hard/heavy rock from between about 1967 and 1980, when the bands who wrote much of the rulebook for riffs were gigging and recording. These bands commanded very large audiences, both in concert and in record sales. These are songs that have been established as classics, so it's safer to assume that readers have heard them rather than a riff by a death metal band from the '90s (though some of these are cited too). For this third edition, there are new citations from 21st-century bands. But for as long as someone, somewhere, wants to plug an electric guitar into an amplifier and hit a distorted riff, they will look to the Who, Jimi Hendrix, Cream, Black Sabbath, Deep Purple, Led Zeppelin, Free, Queen, Van Halen, Metallica, Foo Fighters, and the like for inspiration.

It is important to stress that *How to Write Guitar Riffs* does not include any notation of famous riffs. The book's aim is to help you compose riffs, not play other people's. Music publishers issue many well-edited, authoritative guitar TAB folios for learning classic riffs note-for-note.

Although guitar riffs tend to be associated with the heavier subgenres of rock, sometimes imaginative riffs appear in other areas of popular music. For this reason, I have cited songs by groups such the Police, Siouxsie and the Banshees, the Jam, Focus, U2, Coldplay, Arctic Monkeys, and Radiohead. Sprinkled through the book are even a few riffs that are not played on the guitar.

Section 4 deals with techniques and tips for presenting riffs—in other words, what do you do with a good riff once you write it? This covers topics such as:

- writing riffs in unusual time signatures
- arranging riffs on a multitrack recording
- using detuning and open tuning
- using harmony parts
- how guitar effects change riffs.

The ideas in this section might improve riffs that come in creative moments and through jamming.

Section 5 is a masterclass with John Paul Jones, former Led Zeppelin bass player, multi-instrumentalist, and in-demand producer. It is full of insights into great riffs past and present. Here's a chance to hear about the writing, arranging, and recording of riff-based rock from a legendary player's perspective. If you thought Led Zeppelin's riffs came solely from Jimmy Page, you may be surprised. There are insights into the riffs Jones wrote for the group Them Crooked Vultures, with Josh Homme and Dave Grohl, whose debut album was released in 2009.

Section 6 provides notation for, and a guided tour of, the 40 riffs that have been specially recorded as accompanying audio examples.

How to Write Guitar Riffs is part of a multivolume series on songwriting. To find out more on chord sequences, melody, guitar chords and tunings, and writing songs on keyboards (especially if you're a guitarist), and lyrics, seek out the new edition of *How to Write Songs on Guitar* (2020), *The Songwriting Sourcebook* (2011), *How to Write Lyrics* (2021), *Chord Master* (2016), *Melody* (2005), *How to Write Songs on Keyboards* (2005), *Arranging Songs* (2007), *Songs and Solos* (2014), and *How to Write Songs in Altered Guitar Tunings* (2010). Information about these titles can be found at www.rowman.com and www.rikkyrooksby.com.

introduction

What is a riff?

The word "riff" entered the language as musical slang way back in the 1920s. The *Oxford English Dictionary* describes a riff as a "short repeated phrase in jazz and similar music." In jazz, its function was to provide a static harmonic part for soloists to improvise over—it's easier to improvise over a repeated short riff than over a whole chord progression that might require more than one scale. A riff is therefore instrumental.

In rock music, the riff soon moved to the foreground, becoming a hook—something that sticks in the memory after only a single hearing. It has been central to rock music almost since rock 'n' roll was invented, but it gained ground from the mid-'60s onward.

Much basic rock was never about the melody or the words (which is why '50s rock 'n' roll is full of nonsensical lyrics); it was about raw energy. A riff can convey this energy more effectively than anything else, especially on a distorted guitar and with the backup of drums and bass. It can be as simple as a single detuned sixth string with a couple of slides applied to it, as with Nirvana's "Negative Creep," or as meaty as the five-chord sequence (Bb–Gb–Eb–Cb–A) that appears in their song "In Bloom."

For the sake of this book, and to retain when inventing your own riffs or classifying one that catches your ear, let's take this as a working description:

> **A riff is a short, repeated, memorable musical phrase, often pitched low on the guitar, with a strong rhythmic identity, which focuses much of the energy and excitement of a rock song.**

Let's examine this description in more detail and qualify its terms.

"Short"

The majority of riffs are one to four bars in length; any longer and they begin to suggest a melody or a solo. Parts of a riff may repeat with slight variations to last 8, 12, or 16 bars, for example, but the basic material of the riff is usually about four bars. The quicker the tempo, the more likely a riff might extend further in bars.

"Repeated"

All riffs depend on repetition—it's how they fix themselves in the mind of the listener. A well-constructed riff should get under your skin and make you want to play it over and over. In rock music, the repetition of the riff fuels the energy of the song and drives the music forward, like shoveling coal into a steam train's furnace.

"Memorable"

A good riff has catchy rhythmic, harmonic, or melodic qualities. When these are exceptional, the riff may rival even the vocal chorus as the identifying feature of the song. Many classic rock numbers—think of "Layla," "Smoke on the Water," "Enter Sandman," "Smells Like Teen Spirit," "Whole Lotta Love," "Cocaine," or "Sultans of Swing"—are known as much for their riffs as their melodies.

"Pitched low on the guitar"

The majority of guitar riffs are played on the lower three strings. The E, A, and D strings have the power and musical authority generally associated with bass notes (the bass part in any music usually defines the harmony above it). As the lower three strings are denser, they have a greater resonance than the upper three (a characteristic marked by the change from the wound fourth to the unwound third string). This criterion became more important from the '90s onward, with the increased popularity of "drop D" and other detunings.

Some riffs, of course, are played on the higher strings: think of a player like the Edge, who has written fine riffs on the higher strings for U2 songs such as "With or Without You," "Sunday Bloody Sunday," and "Beautiful Day." In his case, echo thickens and sustains these phrases, allowing them to combine with the bass guitar more effectively. In songs like "Where the Streets Have No Name," the rhythmic character of the riff is created by the precise timing of the echo. As accompaniment figures, Edge-like riffs have become a standard part of the rock guitarist's vocabulary. Similar figures can be heard in songs by bands such as Coldplay and Razorlight.

"Rhythmic identity"

It is often rhythm that differentiates a riff from a chord progression or a melodic phrase. These song elements are also necessarily repeated, but riffs have well-defined rhythms that make them punchy and foreground them in a way that sequences of chords are not. Riffs will use accented notes and rests to increase their assertiveness. Rhythm is sufficiently important that a single pitch repeated with a memorable rhythm can make a riff on its own, such as the high "telegraph" figure on the intro of Tom Petty's "American Girl."

"Rock song"

This book is primarily concerned with riffs in rock guitar music. The use of guitar riffs is probably more characteristic of rock than of any other style of popular music, but riffs can be found in soul, R&B, blues, funk, pop, disco, reggae, and so on, including genres where a riff might be sampled, or a sample itself might constitute a riff by virtue of its repetition. An example would be the looped A–B notes that begin repeating at 3:50 in Tame Impala's "Let It Happen."

Riffs are also played on other instruments, such as bass guitar or keyboards, sometimes with guitar, sometimes alone. Think of songs such as INXS's three-beat "Need You Tonight"; Queen's "Another One Bites the Dust," with its I–♭III–IV progression and those much-copied first three beats; or the same band's partnering with David Bowie for "Under Pressure," where with only two notes but a memorable rhythm the bass riff defines the song. The three-beat emphasis motif is also heard in Doja Cat's "Say So."

Why are riffs important?

The strong rhythmic element of a good riff makes a big contribution to the energy of a rock performance. Riffs get audiences up and dancing. They also fill sections of a song where there aren't vocals. Instead of a progression of chords to link verse and chorus, riffs enable an arrangement to go quiet when the singer delivers the verse, then to burst out instrumentally with a loud riff.

Riffs have not only a rhythmic function but also a harmonic and a melodic function. A riff can substitute for a chord progression during a verse or chorus, or under a solo, temporarily replacing the sound of full chords. It can also be something you hum, because of its melodic qualities.

Think of this as a creative formula when writing riffs:

Riff = RHM: rhythm, harmony, melody

Check a riff for all three. Whether writing your own or learning a famous riff, being aware of its rhythm, harmonic implication, and melodic shape is useful. This provides a perspective from which to develop and refine your riff ideas.

Riffs are popular because they're often easy to play. They don't necessarily involve much guitar technique, which is why musical instrument shops resound to the imperfect execution by beginners of "Sweet Child O' Mine," "Whole Lotta Love," or "Fat Lip." Musicians love riffs because, once you've got a riff together, the whole band can get behind it, and there's an instant feeling of musical unity. Riffs are great for jam sessions: for instance, the guitar might play a riff in unison with the bass and then break away to solo while the bass continues the riff.

Jamming is also a good source of new riffs. In a live context, they're an opportunity to look up from what you're doing (because your fingers know the pattern), or to move away from the mic if singing *and* playing guitar, to interact with the audience and take in the vibe of the gig.

How many types of riff are there?

To answer this, we have to reflect on the musical materials that make a riff. According to the RHM formula, riffs can be sorted according to their rhythmic, harmonic, and melodic elements. Riffs have a rhythm, and they imply or use certain chords (harmony) and intervals (melody).

The RHM formula in this book filters riffs into three main groups, presented in sections 1–3. Section 1 includes riffs based on fundamental intervals between single notes, as found in a major or natural minor scale; section 2 gathers types of riff that draw on scales like the popular pentatonic major and minor; section 3 deals with riffs that use or are based on chords.

It's in section 3—riffs that use chords—that some problems in defining a riff are felt. There can be a fine line between deciding whether a chord change amounts to a riff or a chord progression. For example, AFI's "Girl's Not Grey" has two parts that could be considered riffs: its chorus chord turnaround is IV–I–V–VI in B, and its verse uses several intervals over a fifth-string pedal (A♭, as it is detuned) in a repeating pattern. But both figures allow the notes reasonable sustain rather than a staccato rhythm.

Then there is the chorus of Boston's mid-'70s hit "More Than a Feeling," which has a circling G–C–Em–D (I–IV–VI–V) sequence. Is it a progression or a riff? I'd argue it counts as a riff, for two reasons: first because of the repetition, and second because of its accentuated rhythm. If a chord change is repeated often enough and with a defined, punchy rhythm, it can usefully be described as a riff.

Sections 1–3 provide 30 basic riff types. Riffs could be classified in other ways, but this scheme is a tool for identifying riffs you hear, learn, or write, so you can relate like with like. If a riff doesn't obviously fit into one of these groups, asking why may be instructive. But first, let's reflect on how riffs have developed in popular music over the past half-century.

a brief history of the riff

Rock music has been around, in many forms, for about 60 years. It's not only the technology of rock that changed during that time: its musical language has undergone development and addition too.

Rock remains a music about assertion and complaint, rebellion and outsiders, living on the edge or in the fast lane (choose your cliché), and Dionysian abandon. It still has a big beat at its center, and is still in love with the sound and spectacle of loud guitars and sonic painting with a handful of chords. But rock's harmony has grown and warped, and this molds the riffs heard today. At the heart of this process is rock's relationship to one of its musical parents: the blues.

Riffs feature in rock because they were already present in jazz and blues in the years before Elvis, often in the left hand of boogie-woogie piano parts. Rock itself originated with rock 'n' roll, an accelerating of the blues format of the 12-bar progression and blues scales. The influence of scales such as the pentatonic minor and major can be heard on riff-based '50s songs like Duane Eddy's "Peter Gunn" and Jimmy McCracklin's "The Walk." The adoption of the 12-bar format meant that in the Beatles' early music you hear riffs played first where the key chord (chord I) would be, and then moved up or down to the roots of the other two chords (IV and V) of the 12-bar sequence.

In the '50s, when the electric guitar was a new instrument, players fell in love with the "twang" of the lowest strings. This particular tone—epitomized by Duane Eddy, then developed by the Shadows and the Ventures—raised the profile of the guitar via instrumental hits.

Guitar tone and musical style have always shaped each other in popular music. By the mid-'60s, "twang" gave way to a new guitar timbre: distortion. As the valves (or tubes) in amplifiers got bigger, hotter, and more overdriven, the rock guitar riff as we know it was born.

In some ways, year zero for the riff was 1964. The Beatles had a viselike grip on the upper positions of Top 20 charts the world over with the melodic, vibrant pop of songs like "She Loves You" and "I Want to Hold Your Hand" (despite the fact that they'd started out playing rock 'n' roll, and still enjoyed raving in concert through 12-bar-based '50s classics like "Long Tall Sally"). Their success meant things would never be the same again for groups like the Shadows, where the guitar was melody instrument and soloist.

The Beatles broke down a door, and in their wake came guitar-plus-vocal groups who sought commercial impact with a "dirtier," more raw sound—bands like the Rolling Stones, the Who, the Kinks, the Animals, and Them—whose songs were often driven by aggressive guitar riffs. These bands recorded some of the first, definitive riff-based songs, where guitar chords no longer supported the harmony but were the focus of interest because the riffs fused harmony to a punchy rhythm. Think of the Kinks' "You Really Got Me" and "All Day and All of the Night," the Kingsmen's "Louie Louie," the Who's "I Can't Explain," and Them's "Gloria." The continuing influence of this approach can be heard in songs such as Green Day's "American Idiot," the Vines' "Get Free," and the Raconteurs' "Salute Your Solution."

In the early '60s, the electric guitar and its portable amplifier were still new technology. The modernity of the electric guitar is nowhere more convincingly expressed than by composer/arranger John Barry's decision to give the "James Bond Theme" to Vic Flick's electric guitar (even if the guitar in question was not a solid body but a Clifford Essex Paragon Deluxe) rather than an orchestral instrument. So it was that millions across the globe who went to see *Dr. No* in 1962 heard the electric guitar claim its place in the world of film soundtracks.

As ever, technology and music-making went hand in hand. The instrument you play has a substantial effect on the music you write. Back then, guitarists were on their own, because almost no tutorial material (such as this book) was available in the early '60s. Learning guitar was a hit-and-miss mixture of word-of-mouth, lucky insights, hard graft, listening to records, imitating chord shapes from photographs, watching other players, and creative mishearing. Amps were turned up to compete with drummers and noisy audiences, tubes overheated, speakers were damaged, but in the process a key sound accessory of the rock riff was discovered: distortion. Distortion, with its saturation of overtones, made the guitar sound dangerous. It gave the notes more sustain. Distorted chords seemed less like harmony and more like battle cries. An older generation winced. Distortion encouraged a different kind of song.

By the mid-'60s, inventors figured out how to take that sound and wire it into a small metal box with an input, an output, and an on/off switch. The "fuzz box" was born, providing distortion at any volume. During this time, a significant number of hit singles featured guitar riffs and a more primitive rhythmic urgency (often, as in the case of the Troggs' "Wild Thing," and Hendrix's "Foxy Lady," with lyrics of matching sexual directness). Compared to the jazz-inflected songs of the '30s, '40s, and '50s, harmony became simpler.

The riff was to play an important role in the defining of a heavier "rock" music, which had artistic and countercultural aspirations. Rock ceased to be rock 'n' roll and had long since cast off its Teddy Boy drapes. Now it wanted to take on the world. Pop could keep the Top 20; rock wanted to make a *Big Statement*. Its main vehicle for this was the vinyl album, the 40-minute long-player, not the increasingly despised, allegedly ephemeral 45-rpm single. Songs increased in length. Instrumental prowess was looked to for revelation. Rock musicians aspired to be taken seriously as musicians—to be virtuosos like the cool dudes of jazz. What they lacked in their grasp of sophisticated harmony, melodic sense, or musical structure, they made up for with volume and power. It was an analogy to the political power dreamed of by the counterculture. Bigger amps, speaker stacks, and then powerful P.A.s provided the means of delivery. The riff held it all together.

Bigger amps and more distortion meant that a riff in which only one or two notes were played at a time could sound huge: think of Cream's "Sunshine of Your Love" or "White Room." Technology and rock's changing self-image combined to popularize riff-based guitar music in the second half of the '60s. Improved amplification and early effects pedals offered greater sustain, so a broader sound could be projected by fewer musicians. The quartet lineup of the Beatles (two guitars, bass, drums) was for a time matched in popularity by the power trio (guitar, bass, drums). Artists like Cream, Jimi Hendrix, post-1968 Who, and Free composed material based around single-note riffs instead of chord progressions. It is an odd fact to contemplate that when a band like Led Zeppelin played the intro to "Dazed and Confused" to the expectant whistling darkness of a 20,000-seat arena, often only two notes might be sounding—one from the bass and one from the guitar.

These sonic changes went hand in hand with the way rock's musical vocabulary became more linear, influenced by a fascination with static trance effects (imitated initially from Indian music), in contrast to the sequential "goal-orientated" tonality of pop. Single-note sequences were easy for audiences to remember, and often allowed players to improvise more easily than over more elaborate chords (with less risk of clashing notes).

During the blues boom and the heyday of progressive and heavy rock (1966–75), the pentatonic minor was the most popular guitar scale. There was an increase in bare fifths and fourths on the guitar (as opposed to whole chords), especially in riffs. Eventually, guitarists explored the darker, dissonant tritone interval (two notes six semitones or half steps apart, e.g., E–B♭) that had always lurked in the blues scale (E G A B♭ B).

A notable exponent of the tritone was Tony Iommi on Black Sabbath's debut LP in 1969. In 1970, songs with heavy rock riffs became unexpected hit singles, such as Free's "All Right Now," Deep Purple's "Black Night," and Black Sabbath's "Paranoid." Another example would be Badfinger's "No Matter What," which, despite being a late-Beatles-style melodic rock song, has a punchy riff in A major for its intro and its verse.

Heavy rock wasn't the only subgenre to take riffs back into the charts. In 1971 in the UK, glam rock raised its glittery head. Glam was always based around the electric guitar, and at the bottom of glam's wardrobe (beneath the satin and lurex) is the riff. Glam's best moments are often constructed around great riffs. Think of T. Rex's "20th Century Boy," "Telegram Sam," and "Get It On." Think of the Stones-based raunch of David Bowie's "Rebel Rebel," or the E–A–G riff in "The Jean Genie." Think of the opening riff of Alice Cooper's "School's Out," or the riff that runs through Roxy Music's "Street Life," or the droning detuned guitar on Gary Glitter's "Rock 'n' Roll," or many of Slade's hits.

Glam had run its course by around 1974. Its fey, androgynous sparkle was replaced by the ripped jeans and safety pins of punk. Punk rock was always more chord-based. The rock guitar riff as such was despised by most punk bands because they associated it (like guitar solos) with glam, heavy rock, and the excesses of the progressive era, although exceptions cropped up at punk's experimental edge, with bands like the Banshees and Magazine. Punk bands wanted to play fast and create a wall of noise. Both are easier to do while thrashing basic chord shapes.

After punk and new wave came the "new romantic" early '80s, when the guitar lost its place in arrangements to keyboards and synths. Riffs were still written, but in chart acts they were more likely to be played on keyboards: for example, the octave riff in Gary Numan's "Are 'Friends' Electric?" Despite the innovative guitar riffs of Andy Summers (with the Police) and the Edge (with U2), the first pronouncements that "rock guitar is dead" were made. Rumors of its death turned out to be exaggerated.

The next significant musical step for the rock riff came in the mid-'80s. Two guitar-playing movements drew the musical vocabulary of heavy rock away from its former pentatonic/blues-based habits. Players like Vai, Satriani, Gambale, Malmsteen, Morse, Johnson, *et al* looked for a new musical bag of tricks to define themselves against the overshadowing guitar heroes of the past. They played faster lead solos and sought out new scales and techniques with which to reinvent the style.

Much of this was inspired indirectly by Eddie Van Halen, whose mastery of the "tapping" technique suggested rock guitar had new territories to explore. However, these players were less successful in writing songs and forming bands to capture the wider rock audience. That was left to groups like Dire Straits, whose early triadic riffs on songs like "Sultans of Swing" would lead to the globe-spanning Les Paul honk of the "Money for Nothing" riff.

The new scales and techniques of the late-'80s speed merchants inevitably created new riffs. At the same time, heavy metal bands like Metallica, Megadeth, Anthrax, and Slayer found ways to be heavier than their predecessors. One method was to base riffs not on blues scales but on the less common modes. The Phrygian, with its lowered second (E F G A B C D), and the Locrian, with lowered second and fifth (E F G A B♭ C D), were vital in this. (There is more about these scales later in the book.) The lowered second scale degree is to 21st-century metal what the blues third was to '60s and '70s hard rock.

Some of this approach to riffs recombined with a pop sensibility in grunge bands like Nirvana, Soundgarden, and Pearl Jam, while a few years later, bands like Linkin Park and Sum 41 experimented with crossing rock riffs with rap. The use of modes for different-sounding scale-based riffs continued throughout the '90s and into the new century. Riffs became more complex, as a song such as Foo Fighters' "My Hero" shows. That riff combines octaves over open root notes, string-bending, thirds, and unison string effects. In Linkin Park's "Papercut," which is in drop C♯, octaves thicken part of the main riff as it moves to a 5/9 chord (3355xx)—a chord that has been used with greater frequency as "drop sixth" tunings have become more popular.

Widespread use of detuning and altered tunings has deepened the "heaviosity" of riffs. This was given impetus by the success of Nirvana and other grunge bands. This signifies a radical shift of thinking about the electric guitar's range. In the '60s and '70s, a tuning like drop D was a small extension to the guitar's lower pitch range, but there was no sense that it was the edge of a big new territory. The detuning that developed in the '90s rests on a very different outlook in which the assumption is that there is no reason to not continue going lower and lower, even if that crosses into bass guitar range. Further, the assumption that the detuned sixth string should stay within a standard relationship with the rest of the strings was also overturned, and the interval gap between the sixth and the fifth increased in a way that wouldn't usually happen in an altered tuning.

Seven- and eight-string guitars and five-string basses also offered new sonic possibilities to make this feasible. The note B became what the sixth string E had been to rock in the '70s, and drop C♯ and drop C tunings (C♯G♯C♯F♯A♯D♯ and CGCFAD) became the new drop D. The rumble factor of rock has strengthened dramatically, as Parkway Drive's "Dark Days" (B♭ as lowest note!) and Meshuggah's "Demiurge" make clear.

Heavy riffs in the various subgenres of metal show the following developments:

- abrupt transitions or violent contrasts of song sections, sectional discontinuity, rapid turnover of ideas (see Alter Bridge's "Ties That Bind")
- weird scales and unpredictable interval skips
- detuning, and detuned pedal notes (August Burns Red's "Paramount")
- oddly placed accents (Polaris's "Hypermania")
- shifting time signatures (Tool's "Schism")
- smudged string bends and pull-offs—especially bends on the lowest strings (see Spiritbox's "Holy Roller")
- faster tempos, with machine-gunning bars of constant 16ths reinforced by the kick drum and rapid tremolo picking
- texture effects
- less use of transposition, as riffs are more dependent on position
- being technically harder to play (Erra's "Snowblood").

Texture effects include the harmonic notes that punctuate the initial riffs in Machine Head's "Halo" and Linkin Park's "One Step Closer," the double-click muted chord in System of a Down's "Genocidal Humanoidz," and the squeal and bend in their "B.Y.O.B."

As riffs have become more complex, they have annexed bass, harmony, and melodic parts. Good examples of this are Trivium's "The Defiant," Psycroptic "Carriers of the Plague," and the main riff composed by Mark Holcomb for Periphery's "Scarlet," which implies a basic I–VI change in E minor within a Cadd9 tuning (CGCEGD), before progressing to a variety of unusual chord voicings that give the time-honored chord change a whole new quality.

The increasing asymmetry of riffs such as Mastodon's "Seabeast," while inventive and challenging for players—coupled with the particular lyrical and emotional preoccupations of metal—has meant that fewer of them have caught the public imagination. Bands have not matched riffs to songs that could rival the mainstream popularity of a "Smoke on the Water," "Message in a Bottle," or "Money for Nothing."

interval-based riffs

This section explores riffs based on a particular interval—meaning the distance between one note and another, be it a semitone (half step), tone (whole step), third, fourth, fifth, octave, et cetera—and surveys in general how intervals are used in riffs.

In this first section, intervals are considered as they occur between single notes or pairs of notes, or even chords. What matters is the underlying movement of the root note. The intervals are derived from the major scale, which arranges its notes in this pattern: tone-tone-semitone-tone-tone-tone-semitone. On the guitar, ascending a single string, this would be, in frets, 2–2–1–2–2–2–1.

The table below shows the common names of the intervals in an octave from the first note of this scale. The seven intervals that make up the major scale are marked with asterisks.

NOTES	DISTANCE IN SEMITONES	INTERVAL NAME
A–B♭	1	minor second
A–B	2	major second *
A–C	3	minor third
A–C♯/D♭	4	major third *
A–D	5	perfect fourth *
A–D♯/E♭	6	augmented fourth/diminished fifth
A–E	7	perfect fifth *
A–F	8	minor sixth
A–F♯	9	major sixth *
A–G	10	minor seventh
A–G♯	11	major seventh *
A–A	12	perfect octave *

Here's the scale of A major, in two fingerings:

Scale of A major

1 semitones

The semitone/half-step riff is the simplest of all riffs. It uses two adjacent notes, which means any consecutive frets on the same string. As a musical idea, it doesn't seem promising. But there is more to this semitone shift than meets the eye (or ear).

Take two notes a semitone apart—say, G♯ and A on string six and C♯ and D on string five:

TRACK 1

Semitone (half step) shift

Notice how, in bars 2 and 4, the slurs (hammer-on) have a slightly different effect compared to bars 1 and 3, where the first two eighth notes are picked. This type of riff was immortalized in rock 'n' roll by Eddie Cochran, who during his brief career (he died in 1960, aged 21) used it to propel hits like "Summertime Blues" and "Something Else." It enjoyed a revival in 1976–1978 during the heyday of punk, with songs like the Damned's "New Rose" and the Sex Pistols' "Holidays in the Sun."

In punk songs, the semitone riff often crops up on the bass, and sometimes in a chordal form on the guitar. You can also hear it in '90s neo-punk bands like Green Day. David Bowie's "Hang on to Yourself" deploys it in a similar rock 'n' roll fashion, combining an F♯–G single-note riff for six beats with accented D and C chords, making two bars in all. Arctic Monkeys wrote "Teddy Picker" on a semitone riff, one semitone moving up, the other down. (This riff also includes the flattened fifth, which is discussed in a few pages.)

Here's a variation on the same idea. A few rests give it more rhythmic interest:

The semitone riff often has a "delinquent" quality. A little musical analysis shows why. First, imagine that the higher note of the pair G♯–A is the keynote. In the key of A major, the scale is A B C♯ D E F♯ G♯. Notice that G♯ is the seventh note. In music, this seventh note has a special function and name: it's called the leading note.

TRACK 2

Semitone shift

Every major scale ends with a semitone step from the leading note to the keynote. This movement, especially when supported by the right chords, has the effect of asserting the key and the primacy of the keynote or "tonic." So, in a riff that repeatedly moves from G♯ to A, spending longer on the A than the G♯, A is restated as the key center. In musical terms, this is a perfectly standard, conservative idea. So how does the semitone riff generate the impression of delinquent teenage rebellion?

Strange things happen if this G♯–A single-note riff is given an upper note. In rock, the most direct way is by using fifths (nicknamed "power chords"). A perfect fifth is an interval of three and a half tones. So, a fifth comprising G♯D♯ would then move up to AE, and a fifth comprising C♯G♯ would move up to DA. (Fifths have a subsection to themselves later in this chapter.)

TRACK 3

Semitone shift

(fifths)

Here's what these fifth changes look like when notated:

But wait a minute, there's a problem. If the riff is in A major, we ought to take these upper notes from the scale of A major. Look at its fourth note: D natural, not D♯. But if we put D above the G♯ in this riff, we have an augmented fourth (G♯ to D, three tones), not a perfect fifth.

The augmented fourth is an important interval for heavy rock, as discussed later, but here it is parallel perfect fifths that are needed for the G♯–A change. For that, the upper note has to be a D♯, which is off scale. The ear, which is conditioned to hear the major-key system and all its laws as right, hears this D♯ as a "foreign" note—a note that breaks the rules. In other words, *hey presto!*—a delinquent note. So, as a band thrashes its guitar, with amps on 11, singing that the modern world is rubbish, this riff on its own terms is backing them up.

This delinquent effect is magnified if it goes a step further, with not just a fifth above the G♯–A change but a whole major chord. In this instance, that means a chord of G♯ major (G♯B♯D♯) moving to A major (AC♯E), and a chord of C♯ major (C♯E♯G♯) moving to D major (DF♯A).

Again, compare the notes in these chords with the scale of A major. The notes in the A chord blend with the scale. But the G♯ chord not only has D♯ instead of the key's D but also has B♯ instead of B, so it contains two delinquent notes, thus reinforcing the effect. Similarly, the C♯ major chord has an E♯ that's also off scale:

TRACK 4

Semitone shift
(chords)

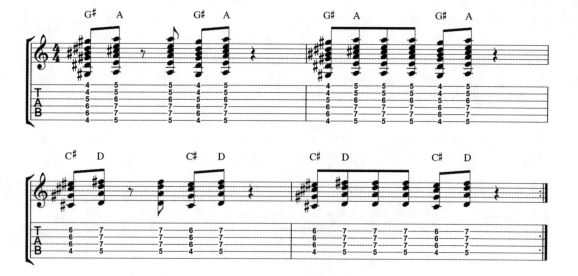

The chords of a key are generated from the seven notes of the major scale. To create basic three-note chords (triads), start with each note of the scale in turn, and miss every other note until there is a group of three. For instance, the first note would combine with the third and fifth notes of the scale (1–3–5) to create chord I of the key; the second note would be joined by the fourth and sixth (2–4–6), after which come 3–5–7, 4–6–1, 5–7–2, 6–1–3, and 7–2–4.

In the key of A, this produces the chords A major (I), B minor (II), C♯ minor (III), D major (IV), E major (V), F♯ minor (VI), and G♯ diminished (VII, G♯BD), as you can see in the musical notation. The triads are shown pitched through two octaves:

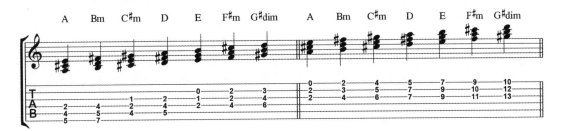

The diminished chord (VII) is neither major nor minor, and it is used very little in rock. Chord VII in any major key will be diminished. The G♯–A chord change has substituted a G♯ major for this diminished chord. The ear recognizes the G♯ major chord as being not in key. In fact, no major key has two major chords a semitone apart; there is no major key in which that inherently happens. So, with two major chords a semitone apart, the music has stepped outside the boundaries of pure major-key harmony.

Triads of A Major

In other words, the semitone riff, as a fifth or a chord shift, breaks the rules. Behind its apparent simplicity is instant musical rebellion.

More can be done with this idea. This semitone riff can develop into a song structure—imagine a punk rock 12-bar progression using the chords A, D, and E. To get the punk-style preface, play each of the chords with the major chord or fifth a semitone lower: G♯–A, C♯–D, D♯–E. Whether as fifths or full major chords, the C♯ and D♯ chords will include other "delinquent," out-of-key notes.

From a playing aspect, semitone shifts on the guitar are easy with barre chords because the movement is one fret up or down. The barre shapes for B (x2444x) and F (133211) are equally useful for this. Double the delinquent element with two semitone shifts, one after the other—as in Elvis Costello's stomping "Pump It Up," with its relentless B–B♭–A chord sequence. Gomez's "Whippin' Piccadilly" does the same in A♭ going in the opposite direction. Terrorvision made a riff out of an A♭–A7 shift in "Perseverance."

In the '90s, the semitone shift, either as single notes or as fifths, became significant in rock styles like nu-metal. Where the traditional Cochran-inspired shift is from the seventh to the root note, recent songs take the semitone shift from the root note upward—the first to the second of the scale. Linkin Park's "With You" and "Points of Authority," Limp Bizkit's "Counterfeit" and "Clunk," the Offspring's "Pretty Fly (for a White Guy)," Fear Factory's "Self Bias Resistor," and Machine Head's "Old" all have examples of this semitone shift.

In bands like Metallica and Pantera, this happens when a song uses the Phrygian or Locrian modes, where the step from the first note of the scale to the second is a semitone. (These modes are discussed in section 2.) Queens of the Stone Age's "Feel Good Hit of the Summer" uses a semitone move downward from the flattened second to the keynote, whereas their "Quick and to the Pointless" does a '50s move from a semitone beneath the keynote, changing E–F (and can be compared with the riff in T. Rex's "Jupiter Liar").

The main riff in Joe Satriani's "Nineteen Eighty," which incorporates several semitone shifts, is a good example of a reworking of traditional rock elements through using a less predictable ordering of the ingredients. These New Puritans' "Attack Music" (from their 2010 album *Hidden*) makes much use of semitones as riff and melody, an F going to B♭ and G♭ (another Phrygian idea) and in the verse the notes C–D♭.

The semitone riff as it is used in a rock 'n' roll/punk context does not exhaust its possibilities. Played as a single-note riff, the semitone can sound sleazy or exotic, particularly if a bend is used—as can be seen in the first of the *riff galleries* that follows—or deeply sinister, as with Meshuggah's detuned "Bleed," which can be related back to Black Sabbath's tone bend in "Iron Man." Cancer Bats' "Lucifer's Rocking Chair" spices up a I–♭III–IV idea by detuning to drop C and bending a GC fourth by a semitone. As an exotic bend, the semitone can be heard in the opening riff of the Cult's "Soul Asylum."

David Bowie

"The Man Who Sold the World" (Bowie)

From *The Man Who Sold the World* (RCA, 1971)

Here's a very original riff composed out of almost nothing. Progression-wise, the first chord is an A major, which goes to Dm, F, then Dm. The key is D minor (the A chord is the traditional chord V of D minor). The riff consists of an A note bent up a semitone to B♭ and an open G. In D minor, these notes are scale degrees 4, 5, and 6. The B♭ sounds exotic because of the bend, and it is dissonant against the A major chord. To hear how different these three notes could sound, play the riff against a G minor or F major. During the coda, the riff is heard against a number of different chords; listen for the varied coloring each one gives the riff.

Mick Ronson's distinctive guitar tone (probably the front pickup of his Les Paul Custom with mid-range boost) adds to the mystery. In this song, the riff is not a rabble-rousing incitement to bang heads but a sinister portrait of the twisted intent of the lyric's misanthropic character. Rarely have three notes sounded so much like the end of the world. The song was later covered by Nirvana on their MTV *Unplugged* album.

T. Rex

"Chariot Choogle" (Bolan)

From *The Slider* (T. Rex Wax Co./EMI, 1972)

"Chariot Choogle" is the great "lost" T. Rex single of 1972—Marc Bolan considered putting it out but changed his mind. The main riff is a semitone fifth B5–C5 in the key of C, supported by bass and cellos. When the vocal begins, the melody is not placed where it's expected, so there is a fascinating tension between the riff's rhythm and the melody.

Bolan may have known only a small number of chords and a few lead patterns, but he created rock magic with them. Try the albums *Beard of Stars*, *T. Rex*, *Electric Warrior*, or *The Slider*: they're full of raunchy rhythms, great riffs, and simple but inspiring lead, all played with classic guitar tones created by a Gibson Les Paul and a white Fender Strat into WEM, Vox, Vampower, and H/H amps, plus effects such as the famed Rangemaster treble boost, the Shatterbox fuzz, and the Copycat tape echo.

Led Zeppelin

"Kashmir" (Page/Plant/Bonham)

From *Physical Graffiti* (Swansong, 1975)

"Kashmir" is built on a powerful but steady drumbeat, a bass that moves in octave Ds, and a four-note riff. The guitar, in DADGAD tuning, is not particularly prominent: it has the intro riff, two verses, a bridge section on A, a chorus that moves restlessly from Gm to A, two more verses, the chorus, and the coda where an ascending scale of G A B♭ C D E F G A B C♯ appears, replete with faux–Middle Eastern trumpet flourishes.

The main riff is D5–Daug5–D6–D7. As a riff, this could be classified in several ways—for example, as a chordal riff—but I've included it here because it's really the semitone movement of the notes A–B♭–B–C that most defines it. This clever riff has the quality of a picture by M. C. Escher: every time you hear the end of the riff, it sounds as though it's a bit higher, but it isn't. This is emphasized by the descending sequence of Mellotron chords laid over the top. Sing and tap out the main riff when it disappears behind the descending sequence, and you'll be amazed how it emerges. This arrangement effect makes it unique among the hundreds of riffs in this book.

In this instance, the semitone steps are made against a single chord, but it is possible to write a riff that moves in semitones where each note has a different chord to harmonize it. The chord changes might distract from the individual notes, but the effect can be colorful.

A similar riff (based on the note A) is heard on Kingdom Come's "Get It On." The "Kashmir" riff has left its rhythmic/tempo mark on many other songs, too, such as Europe's "Walk the Earth" and the Cult's "Soul Asylum."

Sex Pistols

"God Save the Queen" (Rotten/Jones/Matlock/Cook)

From *Never Mind the Bollocks Here's the Sex Pistols* (Virgin, 1977)

The Pistols' sardonic punk anthem had all the ingredients that made *Bollocks* one of the '70s' best rock albums. The riff itself takes eight bars and is used for the verse. There is a two-bar phrase of an A chord going to a D–C♯–D change. Counting the first bar's rhythm as 1&2&3&4&, the second bar is grouped 123, 123, 12.

Experiment with playing the D–C♯–D change as fifths, then as major chords, and compare the two. After three of these phrases, the riff is completed by two bars of a G♯–A change. The emphasis in the guitars is on what sounds like fourths played on the top two strings (a fourth is a fifth inverted, as will be explained in a few pages). Extra color is gained by the muting of the A chord, taking the muting off for the D–C♯–D.

Other semitone/half-step chord shifts can be heard during the bridge. The "delinquent" effect of major chords shifting in semitones is also heard in the "no future" coda. In a pop song, the descending chords would follow those of the key: D–C♯m–Bm–A. But what it actually sounds like is D–C♯–B–A: all majors. Elsewhere on the same album, semitone shifts can be heard at the verse end of "No Feelings," and in the chorus of "EMI."

Siouxsie and the Banshees

"Nightshift" (Ballion/Clarke/McGeoch/Severin)

From *Ju Ju* (Polydor, 1981)

"Nightshift" is a doom-laden, gothic epic that was one of the highlights of the Banshees' concerts. Usually, no major key has two major chords a semitone apart; it's also true that there are never two minor chords a semitone apart in the seven chords of a major key, as is the case here.

This riff grew out of Steve Severin's unorthodox bass playing. It's made of a minor third on the top two strings (AC) over an open A-string. After two bars, the minor third slips down a fret to G♯B, creating a strange chord—an implied Am9/maj7.

Severin's picked, flanged bass continues with this riff throughout the verses, with John McGeoch's guitar restating the Am–G♯m chord change. The implication for riff writers is to try writing a chord riff on bass and work over that.

2 tones

Almost as simple as the semitone riff is the tone/whole-step riff—for instance, using two notes a tone apart, say A and G on string six at the third and fifth fret. The one-tone change is the primordial riff, immortalized in rock in the mid-'60s by records like the Kinks' "You Really Got Me" and the Who's "My Generation." It has always been a staple of hard rock and heavy metal. A more recent use would be on U2's 1991 hit "The Fly," where echo and a wah-wah pedal give it additional intensity. The tone riff has a slightly different effect to the "delinquent" semitone riff.

As described above, in A major the seventh note should be G♯, but to get a tone shift it lowers to G. This particular shift—moving onto the keynote—is more striking than the tone shifts that normally occur in the major scale (A–B, B–C♯, D–E, E–F♯). This is because lowering the seventh note undermines the major key by removing the "leading note" of traditional harmony. The scale that results—A B C D E F♯ G—is an example of the Mixolydian mode. (Modes are covered in the next group of riffs in section 2.)

TRACK 5

Tone shift

This lowered seventh is found throughout popular music. As soon as any blues influence creeps in, the seventh gets lowered, whether it's in an instrumental part on the guitar or bass or in a vocal melody. When this "flattened seventh" is sounded against the usual chords of A major, it is heard as a "blue" note. This is a different effect to when it is used on its own as single notes or fifths. If this G–A single-note riff is turned into perfect fifths, we get GD going to AE.

TRACK 6

Tone shift (fifths)

The upper notes in these fifths are already in the scale of A major, so they don't produce the "delinquent" sound of the semitone fifths. Similarly, if these notes are turned into major chords a tone apart, we get G major and A major. The G major chord thus replaces the G♯ diminished chord that would normally be chord VII on the scale of A major. This chord can, however, be derived from the Mixolydian mode by taking the flattened seventh, second, and fourth of the mode (GBD). This ♭VII is notated at the end of the scale below, in A and E Mixolydian.

The tone riff is usually found not on its own but mixed with a few other intervals. Remember that each of the riffs in section 1 often combines with other elements from sections 2 and 3. The riff for the bridge of Blind Faith's "Presence of the Lord" (played by Eric Clapton) takes A pentatonic minor and uses tone intervals: G–A, C–D, D–E, G–A.

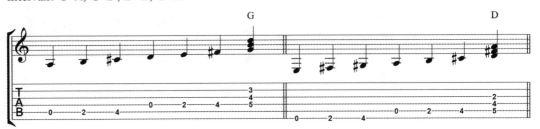

Tone riffs also feature in Clapton's version of J. J. Cale's "Cocaine," the Troggs' "Night of the Long Grass" (with an interpolated bar of 2/4 in the verse to keep things interesting), Madonna's "Erotica," Thin Lizzy's "Johnny the Fox Meets Jimmy the Weed" (with a ♭3), Jimi Hendrix's "If Six Was Nine" (with a ♭7), Deep Purple's "Child in Time" (played in octaves), and the chorus of Bad Company's "Feel Like Making Love." *Mixolydian scale in A and E, with chord ♭VII*

An A5–G5 tone shift drives the verse of the Stooges' "1969," and tone changes A–G, E–D, and D–C occur in their "No Fun." The tone shift is essential to the MC5's "Teenage Lust" and "Looking at You," the Pretenders' "Message to Love," Don Felder's "Heavy Metal," and the Vines' "Highly Evolved."

On "A House Is Not a Motel," Love insert a high single-note E–D tone-shift riff as a link from the last vocal section to the guitar solo—it's played by two electrics at 2:17, either side of the stereo image, which then break away into their solos. Tears for Fears' "Everybody Wants to Rule the World" has a tone-shift chord riff over a root pedal note.

Recent examples include Stone Temple Pilots' "Vaseline" (F–G); in Rage Against the Machine's "Renegade Funk," the first guitar riff uses C–D with a drop of an octave onto a low D, and G–A. In the Dead Daisies' "Holy Ground," the main riff switches back and forth between C and B♭ power chords, and later in the song there is a rapid tone riff between the notes G and F. (The tuning CGCFAD deepens the effect.)

The Yeah Yeah Yeahs' "Date with the Night" takes D–E and G–A from the E pentatonic minor and threads an E an octave lower in between. The Red Hot Chili Peppers' "Can't Stop" begins only with a tone alternation of D to E. When the verse starts, this idea has the root notes of an Em–D–Bm–C chord progression added underneath, showing how a riff can be stated in an elementary form before it is presented with more elaboration.

The Kinks

"You Really Got Me" (R. Davies)

From *The Kinks* (Pye, 1964)

"You Really Got Me" is a must for any history of riffs. The brutal simplicity of the opening riff contrasted with much pop of the time from other guitar bands. It was, after all, not long since the Shadows had dominated the UK charts, and the heyday of first-generation "jangle" (Rickenbackers/12-strings) from the like of the Searchers.

Unlike later heavy rock, the riff here is chordal. It's the rhythm that turns it from a chord change to a riff. Notice the way the snare drum smacks down in the space between the riffs—this rhythmic arrangement detail is vital to the sense of power. Then, as the verse develops, the riff is transposed upward several times.

The Kinks revisited this riff on "All Day and All of the Night" and "Tired of Waiting for You," extending it by adding a third chord based on the flattened chord III of the key. Another song from the same era with similar use of the one-tone riff is the Who's "My Generation," which also develops the idea by transposing it upward. Don't forget Van Halen's swaggering version of "You Really Got Me" on their first album.

Mountain

"Mississippi Queen" (West/Laing/Pappalardi/Rea)

From *Climbing!* (Windfall/Island, 1970)

"Mississippi Queen" is a riff that has unfairly slipped through the cracks of rock history. In terms of heaviness, it was a milestone.

Mountain were initially dismissed as a Cream clone, but this judgment was partly due to an over-reverent attitude to Eric Clapton and Cream, which obscured the band's musical character. The inclusion of a fourth member (Steve Knight) on keyboards gave Mountain a harmonic advantage over Cream's power-trio lineup: no more big holes in the mix when the guitarist takes a solo. The songs often contained a wider harmony than standard blues-rock, providing a rich backdrop for Leslie West's lead guitar.

The riff here is delayed by a four-bar intro moving B–A–G, as if we have entered at bar 9 of a 12-bar. This enhances the entrance of the riff when it does come in—a hammering D5–E5 change with various answering blues phrases. Transposition is used during the verse: the riff occurs four times on E, twice on A, twice on E, once on B, once on A, and then a different E phrase polishes off the 12-bar-derived form.

A famous adage states that "brevity is the soul of wit." Heavy rock is not known for either brevity or wit, so this is a timely reminder of how exciting it can be to focus your musical efforts into a truly dynamic couple of minutes. The studio version of "Mississippi Queen" (on the album *Climbing!*) clocks in at only 2:30. For a pummeling but still short live version, seek out *Flowers of Evil*.

Free

"Fire and Water" (Fraser/Rodgers)

From *Fire and Water* (Island, 1970)

Here's a classic example of the "tone-shift fifths" riff that's the blueprint for so much hard rock. Free also used these fifths on tracks like "Catch a Train." Often, they start with the first fifth being slid to the higher-pitched fifth, so the higher of the two is not struck initially but heard as a result of the slide.

In "Fire and Water," the verse starts with an A5–B5 shift and also uses D5–E5, implying a I–IV, B–E chord change. There's far more to Paul Kossoff's guitar parts than is often recognized: aside from his inimitable vibrato and wailing lead, his rhythm figures and riffs reveal he looked for sonorities to enhance Free's power-trio instrumentation. What sound like only movements of fifths turn out on closer inspection to include other intervals, such as sixths, and combinations of fretted and open strings. These aim to give more weight and/or color. In a rock quartet with no keyboard and only one guitar, every string counts.

Black Sabbath

"Paranoid" (Iommi/Butler/Ward/Osbourne)

From *Black Sabbath* (Vertigo, 1970)

In 1970, Led Zeppelin, Deep Purple, and Black Sabbath were the immediate heirs of the high-volume blues-rock of Cream and Hendrix. Of the three, it's Sabbath who were most influential on grunge and metal. Black Sabbath gave heavy metal its doomy atmosphere, its occult imagery, and the sludge-fest of Tony Iommi's (often detuned) guitar riffs. Their steady eighth-note rhythms became a hallmark of later rock, whereas some of the best rock of the early '70s had more syncopation and swing.

"Paranoid" has several riffs. The first is heard on the intro and is an E5 up at the seventh fret, with hammer-ons on the E pentatonic minor scale. The guitars settle into a chugging eighth-note rhythm on E and D, finished off with a quick Dsus4–D and an implied G. So, the verse riff isn't simply a tone-shift fifth, but there's no doubt that the essence of it is the tone shift.

Atomic Rooster

"Devil's Answer" (Cann)

From *In Hearing of Atomic Rooster* (Pegasus/Elektra, 1971)

Atomic Rooster were a minor progressive band of the early '70s who enjoyed two chart hits. Their keyboardist, Vincent Crane, played with the Crazy World of Arthur Brown (remembered for the song "Fire"), and Carl Palmer, later of '70s super-group ELP, was the drummer.

One of Atomic Rooster's hits, "Devil's Answer" is carried on a single riff. The first phrase is a two-bar change from C–B♭ and back; the second phrase goes C–B♭–F–C (a Mixolydian I–♭VII–IV). The note F in the bass under the B♭

chord each time gives the riff more variety. The rest of the song depends on the arrangement, with the guitar playing a single-note idea.

Queen
"Tenement Funster" (Taylor)
From *Sheer Heart Attack* (EMI, 1974)

"Tenement Funster," written and sung by drummer Roger Taylor, uses full arpeggiated chords for its first verse, with an emphasis on Em and Am, and an unexpected Cm7 further on. The tone-shift riff consists of fifths going D5–E5 and G5–A5, giving the chorus's first lines a slightly funky feel. But this tone-shift riff is set in a highly musical context. Listen for how the harmony opens out when a G chord appears, followed by G7, C, Cm7, D, and then Em–G for the start of the solo. An extra dimension is brought to the solo by a startling chromatic shift from G to the chords G#m and Bm. This allows Brian May to construct an elegant, mysterious solo in echoed phrases.

"Tenement Funster" suggests tone-shift riffs in fifths can be more powerful in a musical context with contrasting, fuller harmony.

R.E.M.
"The One I Love" (Stipe/Berry/Mills/Buck)
From *Document* (IRS, 1987)

R.E.M. were never what one would consider as a "riff band." From the outset, they showed a distaste for many of rock's hackneyed gestures, and this was certainly true of Peter Buck's approach to the guitar. But when they did have a guitar riff in a song, it was almost always memorable.

Buck is more renowned as a rhythm player, and for the "jangle" Rickenbacker arpeggios of R.E.M.'s classic '80s period from *Murmur* to *Document*. But the main figure of "The One I Love" has sufficient force and definition to count as a riff. It exploits the open-string resonance of an E minor chord moving to a Dsus2 (a chordal tone shift), where the top E is still sounding. It does this via a low note G, and a slide from D to E on string two, with the top E sounding at the same time. It's almost a blues riff, though it's played at a greater velocity. Guitarists should also listen to how the song ends, with a slowing up that adds dramatic weight to the highly dissonant chord, which consists of the Em shape one fret back (011000, or EB♭E♭GBE) just before the final E minor.

The Cult

"Wild Flower" (Astbury/Duffy)

From *Electric* (Beggars Banquet, 1987)

With Rick Rubin in the producer's chair, the Cult's album *Electric* set out to bang heads in an old-fashioned, no-nonsense '70s sort of way. Nothing could be simpler than "Wild Flower," a fine example of a riff that springs from an idiosyncrasy of the guitar. If you hold down a B chord (x2444x), the open-string A is now the flattened seventh so beloved of hard rock/blues riffs. To get it, all that is required is to lift the first finger off the A string while hitting the rest of the chord. Play to a mildly syncopated rhythm and repeat over a four-square, no-frills drumbeat. During the chorus and verse, Billy Duffy develops the riff by finding comparable versions of it on the chords of D, E, and F♯.

Haven

"Let It Live" (Briggs/Wason/Gronow)

From *Between the Senses* (Radiate, 2002)

Haven were a UK rock band whose powerful debut album was produced by ex-Smiths guitarist Johnny Marr. "Let It Live" comes in on a tone-shift riff based on B5, with the bass playing variations on this, and a gale force 10 lead guitar also playing a tone-shift figure through a wah-wah. This riff is felt throughout the verse, despite the fact that the harmony changes as it is adjusted to whatever the chord is. It also returns for the two-note guitar solo.

"Let It Live" is a classic English pop/rock song that sounds as if '60s group the Casuals (of "Jesamine" fame) had collided with Soundgarden, with a lovely, yearning hook line. Listen for the guitar octaves on the chorus, the hints of vocal harmony, and the sizzling, splashy hi-hat eighths.

Royal Blood

"Typhoon" (Mike Kerr/Ben Thatcher)

From *Typhoons* (Warner Bros., 2021)

Recent riff writing tends to be in fast tempos, to put multiple riffs in a single song, and for those riffs to draw on a variety of ideas. The opening riff of "Typhoon" has a fast tone-interval change following a move from the keynote to the minor third (C♯–E, then B–C♯ an octave up). The first chorus riff is based on the scale of C♯ natural minor and includes most of the notes of that scale. The second riff in the chorus is chromatic, climbing up the C♯ pentatonic blues scale but putting the major seventh after the flattened seventh (B–B♯–C♯). This gives the riff a slinky movement; it is especially effective coming out of the chorus at 2:33, when this riff is heard on its own.

3 octaves

The third type of riff is arrived at by taking a single note and playing it at different octaves. This is an economical way of writing a riff because it creatively deploys pitch to get more out of the single note. A semitone-shift or tone-shift idea could be thickened by playing the note in octaves. An octave drop or jump can also lend unpredictability to a riff.

The octave riff works independently of keys and scales because it doesn't change the note by adding a different one above or below. In this way, octaves offer flexibility: they're neither major nor minor, so a major or minor chord on the same root note can sound over them; and, if you're soloing, either the major or minor scale for a given pitch will fit. Further, a sequence of octaves used as a riff has more "air" in it than a comparable sequence of fifths. This can be heard in Ritchie Blackmore's fondness for octave-based rhythm figures during verses, as on Deep Purple's "Smoke on the Water." The octave F at the beginning of the riff on Kasabian's "Underdog" livens the sequence of three fifths (E♭5–C5–B♭5) that follow it.

Instruments with octave stringing—such as a 12-string guitar or 8-, 10-, and 12-string bass—automatically add a new dimension to a single-note riff. Bass players often use octaves to create a more dynamic effect than sticking on a single-note bass line, without altering the harmony. A riff where both bass and guitar move in octaves can have a propulsive effect. The most effective octave riffs are those that lock in with the drums in some way—so think carefully about where the notes are placed rhythmically.

Here are the finger patterns for octaves on the guitar:

Octaves

Octave riffs can be heard in the intro riff of Television's "Friction," in the bridge of Gun's "Word Up" and Deep Purple's "Woman from Tokyo," and played by synthesizer on the intro and during the verse of Gomez's "Get Miles." David Bowie's "TVC15" has a bridge and coda with a fierce octave riff running from the top down using a tone shift.

If during a riff there is a leap of more than an octave, it can add an element of surprise. This happens in the opening riff of the Black Keys' "Just Got to Be" on a B pentatonic minor scale, where a low B leaps a tenth to a bent D. (This riff is followed by a second on the B minor blues scale with a two-bar rhythm that suggests an extra beat where there isn't one.) A repeated octave leap might also be part of a riff, as with the same band's "Thickfreakness," where the fifth-string A goes up to the A above it as part of an A minor blues-scale riff, with the first A of each repeat approached chromatically, G–G#–A.

Octave riffs are common on bass guitar and therefore any style where the bass is a feature. The Red Hot Chili Peppers "Dark Necessities" brings such a bass riff in for its verse, with the octave combined with several other notes. This includes keyboard riffs, too, such as the octave combined with a fifth in Grimes' "Oblivion."

Detuned guitar gives octaves a bassier character, as is heard in the opening riff of Mastodon's "Iron Tusk," with its octave from a detuned A (the same pitch as a bass guitar's A string) up to the fifth string A of standard tuning.

Spencer Davis Group

"Gimme Some Lovin'" (S. Winwood/M. Winwood/S. Davis)

Single A-side (Fontana, 1966)

The Spencer Davis Group were a rhythm-and-blues-influenced combo blessed with the vocals of one of the UK's best singers of the '60s, Stevie Winwood. The riff here is an inverted octave on G, with the low G coming on the fourth beat of the bar. On the intro, you can hear the bass and, faintly, a guitar doubling the figure, while a piano is struck on the fourth beat G. The riff is then used as the harmonic base for smoky thirds on the organ, and features throughout the song.

The rhythmic significance of riffs is clearly demonstrated in this song. There's a similar riff in the same group's earlier hit "Somebody Help Me."

Led Zeppelin

"Immigrant Song" (Page/Plant)

From *Led Zeppelin III* (Atlantic, 1970)

Zep's third album charges in over a rising tide of tape hiss with this Viking battle hymn. Over Jimmy Page's octave F♯ riff, Robert Plant pitches an octave C♯, falling back a semitone to C (the flattened fifth). Tremolo guitars add a watery shimmer to the E–A chord changes on the verse, and the rising A–B–C chorus is underpinned by rapid bass scales from John Paul Jones. The chorus ends suddenly on the C chord, which is a flattened fifth away from F♯—an example of the dissonant chord relationships found in heavy rock. A similarly dissonant chord (Cdom9/G on guitar) is repeatedly inserted into the octave riff on the outro.

Led Zeppelin revisited this Viking theme and poked about among the scorched ruins in "The Wanton Song" on *Physical Graffiti*, which is built on a terrific G octave riff, with battering intermissions by John Bonham. Octaves are also crucial to "Trampled Underfoot," which is discussed in the section on thirds.

The Knack

"My Sharona" (Aaverre/Berrios)

From *The Little Girls Understand* (Capitol, 1979)

The Knack's brief career as purveyors of commercial US new wave began with this catchy single, which is built on a sharp-dressed octave riff. This is a good example of the "jumpy" quality in an octave riff as it goes up and down, with the bass playing the same figure as the guitars. Listen for the slide from F♯ back to the G octave at the end of bar 2 (a throwback to Cochran-type semitone-shift '50s riffs), and how bar 4 is completed with C5 and B♭5.

These fifths have a refreshing effect for the listener, in contrast to the bare octaves. They also imply a blues harmony (a IV→♭III–I change). The pentatonic minor scale (G B♭ C D F) supplies the fifths and later in the song provides some of the chords.

Jimi Hendrix

"Dolly Dagger" (Hendrix)

From *First Rays of the New Rising Sun* (MCA, 1997)

There was a late flowering of Hendrix's songwriting in the last two years of his life. Had he finished his intended album *First Rays of the New Rising Sun*, it would have shown some important crossbreeding between rock and soul. "Dolly Dagger" was slated to be the first single from it. It starts with a three-phrase riff consisting of two 4/4 + 2/4 bars (giving the feel of six quarter notes) and a bar of 4/4.

Unlike the previous examples, this is an instance of octave doubling. The opening riff is based on B pentatonic minor, but each note is doubled at the octave—listen for the fuzzy synth or bass off to one side. The first four notes are then transposed down for a repeat, and the riff concludes with a five-note blues run. On the coda, Hendrix alters the riff by extending the first phrase. Listen too for the bent thirds under the word "Dolly" on the chorus.

For a rock guitarist, Hendrix was uncommonly fond of octaves for doubling. Playing in a power trio, they helped him thicken the band's live sound. "Fire" and "Ezy Rider" both open with octaves, and in "Third Stone from the Sun" he uses them for their traditional jazz function of thickening a melody.

"In from the Storm" and "Gypsy Eyes" both feature tone-shift phrases repeated at different octaves in rapid succession. Toward the end of his concert performance at Woodstock in 1969, there is some very rapid octave playing on "Villanova Junction." "Foxy Lady" depends on an octave jump for its riff, but that song is covered in the section on fourths in this book.

Royal Blood

"Little Monster" (Mike Kerr/Ben Thatcher)

From *Royal Blood* (Warner Bros., 2014)

Traditionally, octave riffs have tended to leap up rather than down. The popularity of drop tunings has led to the deployment in riffs of an octave notes below the other notes of the riff. "Little Monster" is an example.

Somewhat akin to the White Stripes, Royal Blood are a drums/bass duo who came to notice in 2014 and won Best British Group at the 2015 BRIT Awards. Their 2014 eponymous debut album was nominated for a Mercury prize, and features songs such as "Out of the Black," "Little Monster," and "Figure it Out." Their second album, *How Did We Get So Dark?* (2017), also went to #1 with tracks such as "Lights Out" and "I Only Lie When I Love You."

Royal Blood's drum-and-bass instrumental combination serves not to emulate the dance music genre of that name but to play their own version of minimal blues-rock. The bass guitar sound on which their riffs depend comes from combination of amps with different tonal capacities, a mix of clean and distortion sounds, and harmonizers for the higher notes a guitarist might have played. "Little Monster" is based on the scale of C natural minor and has a three-note F–E♭–C riff with a C an octave down filling in between the notes.

4 perfect fifths

This interval is essential to the sound of rock, especially when played as a series of fifths. As already mentioned, a perfect fifth—colloquially known as a "power chord"—consists of two notes three-and-a-half tones apart. Here are the usual ways of playing them on the guitar:

Fifths

The fifth has a tough but slightly austere, "hollow" sound. The reason for this is evident if an A5—a perfect fifth on A—is compared to the triads of A major and A minor, or if E5 is compared with E major and E minor:

Major, minor,
neutral

Both chords contain a perfect fifth. The only note that differentiates them is the one in the middle (the so-called "third" of the chord), which is C♯ in A major and C in A minor. It's this note, the third, that carries much of the emotional content—the feelings associated with the contrast between major and minor.

In comparison with majors, minors are considered to sound sad. But if the third is omitted, this happy/sad element is removed. Like octaves, fifths are neither major nor minor, so they combine with major and minor chords on a second instrument, and major and minor scales can be played over them.

If the fifth moves up or down, it needs to move to the same notes of the scale as the lead guitar. This will often be the pentatonic minor, as shown in section 2. Fifths are the simplest way of "harmonizing" a scale for rock purposes.

Perfect fifths infiltrated rock in the mid-'60s as technology changed the sound of rock bands: amps increased in power, rock bands got louder, and the first fuzz/distortion boxes circulated. Unlike major and minor chords, perfect fifths tolerate large amounts of distortion/overdrive and remain musically effective in the rock context (this has to do with the "overtones" boosted by distortion). Played in a memorable rhythm, a single fifth can itself make a riff, as it does on A5 for the intro of the Cult's "Soul Asylum."

We've already seen how semitone (half step) and tone (whole step) riffs can be expressed as fifths. The sound of a fifth can in turn be thickened by adding the octave above the root note, as can be heard in the verse riff of the White Stripes' "The Hardest Button to Button" on an A5–C5 change, which occurs three times before adding B5–D5.

The fifth moving onto the keynote from the flattened seventh is a classic rock riff—so, in the key of E, D5–E5. Fifths are frequently heard on the lowest two strings of the guitar, and are also effective on bass guitar. Some guitarists have constructed memorable figures by using fifths on the higher strings, as with the Edge of U2. For an insight into what happens when two perfect fifths are put together (AE + EB = AEB), see the discussion on suspended chords in section 3.

Fifths can be heard in Black Sabbath's "St. Vitus's Dance" and "NIB" (in the scale of E natural minor), Iron Maiden's "The Number of the Beast," the Jam's "Billy Hunt" (an unusual punk-rock use of fifths), and Blur's "Song 2" (high on the neck on guitar in the verse). As for which intervals the fifths themselves are moved between, the minor third has always been very popular in rock. It can be heard in Public Enemy and Anthrax's "Bring the Noize," where the chorus riff moves from F♯ to A (I to ♭III).

Fifths can be linked by passing notes so that they emphasize certain points in the flow of notes, as in Dire Straits' "Expresso Love" and the Darkness' "I Believe in a Thing Called Love."

Led Zeppelin

"Whole Lotta Love" (Page/Plant/Jones/Bonham/Dixon)

From *Led Zeppelin II* (Atlantic, 1969)

Rock music was never the same after this. "Whole Lotta Love" may have owed a lyrical debt to Willie Dixon, but the musical result was something else entirely. Zep took a simple blues phrase of three notes (B–D–E, which probably occurs as a throwaway lead fill on thousands of blues songs), added an E5, and amplified it into a gargantuan riff that is undeniably raw and exciting. I recently heard a blast of it on the radio during a polite interview broadcast, and more than 50 years after its release, it still comes on like a wolf at a tea party.

The first statement of the riff is two bars of E5, with single notes added in between. The single note D, fretted on string five, is doubled by the open D string—a neat trick. The riff is then shortened to a bar just before the vocal enters. Listen for Page's harmony touch on the riff on the outro, where the last two notes, D and E, have A and G♯ over them.

The extended version on *The Song Remains the Same* (1976) ends with Page playing variations on the basic riff. The concert performance at Knebworth in 1979 featured "Whole Lotta Love" with some new riffs and variations inserted. Further live versions, with variants, can be found on *How the West Was Won* (2003) and *The Complete BBC Sessions* (2016).

Derek and the Dominoes

"Layla" (Clapton/Gordon)

From *Layla and Other Assorted Love Songs* (Polydor, 1971)

"Layla" is like an old, battered Fender guitar: familiarity has perhaps chipped off some of its lacquer, but it remains an all-time great rock riff. Rarely has a guitar riff been used with such emotional force to make a statement about a situation between a man and a woman, in contrast to the staple heavy rock lyric's litany of death, doom, and despair (and trolls, of course). "Layla" is also a fine lesson in guitar orchestration. Coming up with a great riff is one thing; finding the best presentation in a recording is another.

The opening hail of notes (several guitars at different octaves) is based on the D pentatonic minor scale. This is a blues lick with new fire in its belly. The D is left sustaining, while another guitar overdubs a sequence of fifths from D to C to Bb, which then ascend to D. The neat touch is that the root note of each of these fifths drops to a note on string six, making excellent use of the fifth shape on the guitar.

The high riff in "Layla" takes the form a1+a2+a1+a3, where bars 1 and 3 are the same D pentatonic minor phrase that opened the song, but bars 2 and 4 provide a different "answer"—bar 4 bending G up to A, instead of F up to G. Often overlooked is the wonderful counterpoint phrase midway in pitch between the extremes of the lower-string riff and the very audible high part. This accentuates the sad minor-key feel because it uses the first three notes (D–E–F) of the D natural minor scale. This guitar can be heard on the left of the stereo mix. Its first and third bars are the same as the other guitars.

Be Bop Deluxe

"Sister Seagull" (Nelson)

From *Futurama* (EMI/Harvest, 1975)

Be Bop Deluxe were a British band who flickered in the twilight of glam rock on its artier flank. Their music was defined by the vocals and fastidious guitar arranging of Bill Nelson. Like his contemporary Brian May, Nelson was an enthusiastic orchestrator of multiple lead guitars, often harmonized. Be Bop Deluxe songs tend to teem with ideas, sometimes seeming too fussy. The band never quite managed to focus themselves sufficiently to go for the commercial "jugular" in the way that Queen did, though "Ships in the Night" and the marvelous "Maid in Heaven" were chart singles.

"Sister Seagull" features a four-bar opening riff that links chorus to verse. Bar 1 is a slid fifth from D to E, heard in the center of the mix. Bar 2 answers this with a stereo lead phrase using a tumbling "cascade" scale figure on E pentatonic minor at the 12th fret. Bar 3 repeats bar 1. Bar 4 is a variation in which the scale cascade is terminated with a bend.

Throughout the song, the D5–E5 is constant, but the phrases that answer it vary. It's a fine riff precisely because it welds together fifths and lead notes. From an arrangement perspective, sometimes a riff can have its constituent parts given to more than one guitar.

Thin Lizzy

"Jailbreak" (Lynott)

From *Jailbreak* (Vertigo/Mercury, 1976)

The title track from Thin Lizzy's breakthrough album is one of their simpler riffs. It's a good example of the significance of F♯ as a key center in heavy rock because of where this key lies on the guitar. The F♯ major scale consists of the notes F♯ G♯ A♯ B C♯ D♯ E♯. In rock, it is common to find this scale in the form known as the Mixolydian mode, where the seventh note—here, E♯—is flattened to E. E, of course, is the bottom string on the guitar, which means riffs in the key of F♯ have the benefit of an open-string flattened seventh as the lowest note, which moves up a tone to F♯ at the second fret (see the start of Whitesnake's "Still of the Night" in this regard). The "Jailbreak" riff uses this idea with fifths in the sequence A5–E5–F♯5. Maximum mileage is drawn from this riff as it runs all the way through the verse and serves to link back from chorus to the next verse. Fifths can also be heard on the chorus.

Many Thin Lizzy songs have riffs in fifths, including the intro to "The Boys Are Back in Town" (A5–B5–D5), the verse of "Southbound," and "Waiting for an Alibi," where half the verse is played as fifths and half in unmistakable minor chords.

U2

"With or Without You" (U2)

From *The Joshua Tree* (Island, 1987)

Among the hard rock and heavy metal low fifths, here's an example of what can be done with a high-pitched fifth. "With or Without You" is founded on a simple four-chord turnaround of D–A–Bm–G (I–V–VI–IV), which has been used with such frequency since the '90s that it has been called "the money chords."

On the U2 song, these chords are not stated outright, only implied. Over this sequence, a couple of verses in, the Edge's high, echoed guitar plays a riff consisting of two two-bar phrases. In each case, the first half of the phrase is a G5 at the eighth fret, which "opens" into the harmonically expressive minor sixth of F♯D.

Remember that fifths are harmonically neutral, so G5 is neither major nor minor. But with a thumping D in the bass, an F♯D sixth on the guitar implies a D major chord (DF♯A). Crucially, the repeat of this sixth happens over a B in the bass, which makes us hear those notes as belonging to a B minor chord (BDF♯). Each phrase is completed by either an open string-four D and string-three G, or open string-four D and the D an octave above on string three.

It's the manner in which this riff is colored two ways that makes it so beautiful, demonstrating that it can be interesting, creatively, to repeat a riff with different harmonizing chords underneath.

> **MGMT**
>
> **"Time to Pretend"** (VanWyngarden/Goldwasser)
>
> From *Oracular Spectacular* (Sony, 2008)

Like "With or Without You," this is a riff based on a D5 shape on the top two strings moving downward. There is a complementary synth riff in the chorus that is high-pitched and moves downward from F♯ to A on the D major scale. Such riffs can be harmonized by more than one chord in a song and therefore sound as though they've changed when they haven't. They also have a clarity that cuts through an arrangement.

This riff is more decorative than an identifiable focus of the song. It is often in the back of the mix, whereas the comparable "There She Goes" by the La's has its riff right up front. A riff doesn't have to be as much the center of attention as the classic rock riff but can still function as a hook.

5 perfect fourths

Turn a perfect fifth upside-down—in other words, reverse the order of the notes—and the result is a perfect fourth (so, for example, AE becomes EA). A perfect fourth consists of two notes two-and-a-half tones apart, the distance between C and F. On all the strings except the second and third, a fourth can be held down with a single finger.

Although not as popular as perfect fifths, fourths have also been important in riff history. They also have a tough but slightly cold "hollow" sound. They sometimes feature in lead guitar breaks on the top two strings to give an "oriental" sound. Pulp's "A Little Soul," the Cranberries' "Zombie," the Vapors' "Turning Japanese," and the Beatles' "Don't Let Me Down" are good examples of exploiting fourths for their oriental feel; there are some tasty fourths in the intro to Wings' "Band on the Run," where the underlying Dmaj7 helps them fit, and in the main riff of Television's "Marquee Moon."

Chuck Berry's famous guitar break on "Johnny B. Goode" incorporates fourths. T. Rex's "Get It On" has a Berry-derived fourth riff at the top, and the same is heard in verse 2 of the Offspring's "Pretty Fly (for a White Guy)." The chunky quality of lower fourths is heard in the main riff of Supergrass's "Time."

Like fifths, fourths are neither major nor minor, so the same rules apply about chords, scales, and distortion. If they are less popular than fifths for riffs, it's because they are slightly harder to use, being more musically ambiguous. Often, the root note in a fourth is the upper note of the pair—in other words, in a fourth such as DG, G would be treated as the root note, not D.

Here are the standard shapes for playing fourths on guitar:

Fourths

Let's look at why fourths are not as straightforward as either fifths or thirds. Here is the scale of G major harmonized in perfect fourths, starting on string three (upper note) and string one (upper note), with the fourths on the fourth and second string, respectively.

Fourths in G major   This scale in fourths sounds okay, except at the 7th and 14th frets, which do not sound so good. This is even more noticeable if you play that fret position over a song in G major, or a recording of yourself strumming a G–C–D chord sequence. So why does it sound wrong?

The top note at the 7th and 14th is F♯, which is in the scale of G, so that's fine. However, the lower note in both cases is C♯, which is the correct note for the interval of a perfect fourth but doesn't belong to the scale of G major (it should be a C). To be in key, the seventh note of the scale (F♯) needs a C under it. C–F♯ is an augmented fourth, not a perfect fourth.

Slide these fourths around over a G major chord sequence and you hear that the 7th and 14th fret positions (or the second fret, the same fourth one octave down) sound horrible because of that "rogue" note, C♯. It clashes with chord I (G, making an augmented fourth), chord II (A minor, making a major third), chord IV (C, another minor second), and chord V (D, making a major seventh). It's tolerable, if exotic, over chord III (B minor) or chord VI (E minor), if the context allows. If chord VII is present in its flattened form (F), as is likely in rock, the C♯ also clashes with that.

This unpredictability is the main reason guitarists avoid using fourths in riffs beyond a few tried-and-tested patterns. One way around this is to use only certain fourths within the key. Hit both strings at frets three, five, seven, ten, and twelve (the second scale of fourths in this example) and the result is G pentatonic major on string one (the first of these pairs): GD, AE, BF♯, DA, and EB:

Notice that the seventh (F♯) has come into the picture, so we've actually used more than the normal five notes (G A B D E) of the pentatonic major. Turn this into a fret/interval pattern and it goes 2–2–3–2–3, finishing at the 15th fret, where GD is an octave above the first one.

Fourths in G pentatonic major

The practical application of the "gap" formula 2–2–3–2–3 is this: whatever the key, locate the root note on string one, move up by that formula and you'll get the same sequence of fourths. For riffs, work out the same sequence on the lower strings.

Here it is on strings five and four, and on three and two, for D pentatonic major:

Fourths in D
pentatonic major

A semitone shift on fourths is rare, and even the tone shift is not especially common. The standard arrangement approach for the "fourth riff" is to have the bass guitar play the root note or for the guitar to play the fourths over a pedal note—an open lower string on the guitar. (Drones and pedals are covered in section 3.) Low-to-middling fourths over a bass pedal note are typical of a band like ZZ Top. This tends to put the fourths over the open E or A string, although in drop D, fourths over a low D are available.

Rory Gallagher's "Secret Agent" turns a basic A–C–D chord change into a combination of single notes with fourths over A. T. Rex's "Children of the Revolution" uses a BE fourth at the second fret, going on and off the open A and D strings, with an E pedal note underneath. Van Halen's "You're No Good," "Bottoms Up!," and "Light Up the Sky" put the guitar riff in fourths over a pedal root note, with the riff transposed up a tone in "Light Up the Sky"; Buffalo Springfield's "Mr. Soul" does the same.

Ozzy Osbourne's "I Don't Know" features fourths ascending over an A pedal played in bursts of 16th notes, rounded off with a G–D chord change, and there are similar fourths in A in "Suicide Solution." There is a great run of high fourths in Wings' "Let Me Roll It," over E and F#m chords. The "oriental" quality of high fourths is heard on the main riff of Robert Plant's "Slow Dancer."

Fourths combine well with fifths and sixths. In the Cult's "American Horse," there is a tone-shift riff played first in fourths and later in fifths. (For the neat trick of using fourths on the bottom strings to make your guitar sound detuned even when it isn't, see the entry on Hendrix's "Spanish Castle Magic" in section 2.)

Although it's more of a fill than a riff, mention should be made of the grungy chromatic fourths that erupt into Coldplay's "Violet Hill" six times (at 0:47, 0:59, 1:36, 1:48, 2:25, and 2:37), offering a strong contrast to the main material.

The two notes of a perfect fourth could be played individually. The verse of System of a Down's "Genocidal Humanoidz" uses a single-bar riff that rapidly alternates the notes D♭ and A♭ (a fourth apart).

Jimi Hendrix Experience
"Foxy Lady" (Hendrix)
From *Are You Experienced* (Track/Reprise, 1967)

It's amazing how fresh *Are You Experienced* sounds on close listening. With Hendrix, there's always the danger of thinking we know what he sounds like and forgetting to listen. Nuances are missed, and Hendrix's guitar palette is reduced to a noisy E7♯9 chord. But this album is the real deal—the sheer imagination that first delivered guitar herodom unburdened by the crippling self-consciousness it now carries.

Transforming the potential of the Fender Stratocaster, from which only a few years earlier Hank Marvin had drawn his glassy, clean Shadows tone, Hendrix filtered blues, R&B, soul, Dylan, pop, and the new hard rock through his own psychedelic sci-fi vision. He conclusively demonstrated that the electric guitar was far more than merely an amplified version of the acoustic. Here, one of the great examples of feedback on a rock record establishes a raw, dangerous sexuality.

"Foxy Lady" is not a pure fourths riff, but I've included it in this section for the sheer stridency of the fourth (EA) on the top two strings, which gives the riff its power. The riff is based on an F♯ octave and the bare fourth on the top two strings, with a B chord interpolated every other bar. The implied chord is F♯m7—not F♯7♯9, as many think. (In songs where it seems Hendrix is playing the 7♯9 chord that many name after him, double check that it isn't a minor seventh.)

Listen also for the second guitar that doubles the fourth, sometimes adding a double-stop A–F♯ and other decorations. Two first inversions, on F♯ and E chords, add spice to chorus two. The feedback returns at 2:24, and it all ends with a pick slide.

Deep Purple

"Smoke on the Water" (Blackmore/Gillan/Glover/Lord/Paice)

From *Machine Head* (EMI/Purple/Warner Bros., 1972)

Deep Purple formed in 1968 in the mega-watt blues-rock rumble started by Cream and Hendrix and stoked by the Who, among other bands. As a five-piece with keyboards, they always had more musical avenues to explore than a power trio.

An all-time favorite, "Smoke on the Water" is the definitive hard-rock riff in fourths. On this track, the bass guitar supplies a string of eighth-note Gs. Listen for the two quicker bursts of fourths in the chorus, under "a fire in the sky." The fourths are based on the G pentatonic minor scale: DG, FB♭, GC, and A♭D♭ (D♭ being the flattened fifth of the scale).

To hear what the fourths give the riff, turn them into fifths and play it that way; the difference is considerable. Fourths are a musical fingerprint for guitarist Ritchie Blackmore, who put them into a number of other songs, including Deep Purple's "Burn" and the Rainbow songs "All Night Long," "Can't Happen Here," and (in 12/8) "Strange Kind of Woman."

Alice Cooper

"School's Out" (Cooper/Bruce/Buxton/Dunaway/Smith)

From *School's Out* (Warner Bros., 1972)

The focus on Alice's ghoulish imagery and *Rocky Horror* stage antics obscures the fact that Cooper albums like *School's Out* and *Billion Dollar Babies* contain some fine rock guitar, especially in the lead department. In "School's Out," delinquency is signaled from the outset by the strident garage quality of the riff, which uses high fourths (in contrast to the low fourths of "Smoke on the Water"), each riff finished off with the sulky cigarette-behind-the-playing-field phrase of E–E♭–D.

Notice how the riff changes its sound when the bass guitar settles down, going into the verse. (The choice of bass guitar note can always add extra color to a riff.) The riff carries the song through most of the verse before a series of heavily accented on-the-beat chords leads into the chorus, with its melodramatic triplets. The band found a nice variation on this with the intro riff to "No More Mr. Nice Guy," in which fourths also feature.

ZZ Top

"Tush" (Gibbons/Hill/Beard)

From *Fandango* (London, 1975)

When it comes to writing riffs in fourths, ZZ Top are in a Texan league of their own. "Tush" has fourths on strings three and four over a 12/8 shuffle in G, with a G pedal note, and a little syncopation. Riffs like this are effective in a power trio because live they make a lot of noise.

The intro is notable because the riff is heard once only in the center of the stereo mix; then the band enters (earlier than expected), and the riff splits into two guitars, panned left and right. The riff is played only three times before the vocal enters, rather than the expected four times. The verse itself is a standard 12-bar, with the riff occurring in bars 1–4 and 7–8. When the chords change to C and D, the guitars play a standard rock 'n' roll shuffle figure rather than transposing the fourths riff. This means the riff's return after the first guitar solo is fresh.

In "La Grange" (from 1973's *Tres Hombres*), the same fourths are played in A, but without a predominant pedal note on the intro—that's saved for the verse. A is probably the most popular key for this type of riff because it means the open A string provides the root note, as in Bon Jovi's "Always Run to You."

U2

"Pride (in the Name of Love)" (U2)

From *The Unforgettable Fire* (Island, 1984)

U2 have a special place in rock history. In the early '80s, they demonstrated that guitar music in rock was not exhausted, as some had trumpeted. They did this with an experimental approach born of necessity from a self-confessed lack of technique.

At the core of U2's new approach was the Edge, a guitarist who once revealingly remarked that he found little solace in blues-based pentatonic playing. Compelled to look for new guitar figures, he found the crucial stimulus to his imagination in a delay unit. This ensured that the riffs that drive U2's early music sound like nothing else in rock.

One technique central to U2 is the implied chord, as discussed in the entry on

"With or Without You." In most rock bands, guitars and bass function together: wherever the chords go, the bass follows, making sure it hits the correct root notes. U2 exploited the fact that the bass can change under a static guitar chord and create the illusion of a chord change.

"Pride," Bono's homage to civil rights leader Martin Luther King, has an implied four-chord turnaround of B–E–A–F♯m. During the first two bars of the guitar riff, the bass moves from B to E, but the Edge keeps playing the echoed figure on the top three strings. The fourths form part of the high guitar figure—a BF♯ combination and then C♯G♯. Edge's BF♯–E notes are 1, 5, and 4 over B, but they become 5, 2, and 1 over E. He then moves up and plays A–G♯–C♯ over A (1, 7, and 3), which become 3, 2, and 5 over F♯.

The Edge's delay pedal is set so there are always two versions of each note pair sounding, with the guitar and the echo in sync. The band use the same idea in the middle-eight, when a single guitar lick is played over a rising B–D–E bass line. The other advantage of U2's combination of high guitar riff with low bass is that it creates a space in the middle of the arrangement for the vocals.

6 tritones

Between the perfect fifth (CG) and perfect fourth (CF) lies an interval of importance to rock. This is the flattened fifth (CG♭), also called the augmented fourth (CF♯), depending on musical context. Its other name is the tritone, as it's an interval of three full tones. A tritone naturally occurs on the major scale only between the fourth and the seventh notes (F and B in C major).

In harmonic terms, the flattened fifth is potentially subversive, as it challenges the perfect fifth between the keynote and the fifth of the scale, on which stable harmony is maintained. In church music of centuries past, it was known by the Latin phrase *diabolus in musica* ("the devil in music") and its use in sacred music was prohibited because it was felt to have an evil quality—precisely the effect that makes it popular in heavy rock. So, the tritone has always got bad press, though it is capable of far wider musical effects than merely evoking a "black magic" vibe.

The tritone makes a vital contribution to styles of music with more complex harmony and syntax than rock. In the massive structure of a symphony (to which a rock song is like a tiny asteroid to a solar system), the tritone can stoke the long-scale energy and conflict necessary to bigger musical processes. But even in rock, it can express erotic feelings rather than satanic ones.

Play a G7–C chord change and you have what is known as a "perfect cadence" or V–I. This change has been used for hundreds of years whenever a composer wishes to establish a new key or finish a phrase, a section, or a whole piece with a powerful assertion of the home key (in this example, C major). The G7 comprises the notes GBDF.

Notice the B–F? Yes, it's the tritone, right in the middle of this most traditional of chord changes. In other words, by a profound musical paradox, the tritone is actually part of the "glue" that binds traditional harmony together. The diminished seventh chord—rare in rock but common in jazz—is also used for key-changing, and even has two tritones in it. G diminished is GB♭D♭F♭. The note pairs GD♭ and B♭F♭ are tritones. Another source for the tritone is the blues. Popular scale patterns in blues music often include a flattened fifth alongside the normal fifth. (There is more on this in section 2.)

There are several methods for making up tritone riffs. It would be unusual to link a sequence of tritones together played as intervals, though it is effective to hit a tritone in the middle of single notes or other moving intervals such as fourths and fifths. You can also make a riff that moves in single notes by a tritone. These are described in the famous songs covered in the *riff gallery* coming up.

Tritones

Led Zeppelin's handling of the tritone can be heard in the violin-bow solo in the live "Dazed and Confused," which is littered with tritones from EB♭ and FB, and in "Dancing Days" (as an augmented fourth GC♯, rather than a flattened fifth GD♭). Tritones occur in Limp Bizkit's "Break Stuff" and "Stuck" (the tritone on the chorus riff), Soundgarden's "Outshined," Stone Temple Pilots' "Down," and Korn's "Pretty." Ozzy Osbourne's "Revelation (Mother Earth)" has several riffs that use an E–B♭ change, backed up on the intro by the unsettling effect of a run based on E diminished.

On the chorus of the Strokes' "Soma," a C♯ in octaves is played against a G chord, followed by a contrasted C in octaves over an F chord. It's a long way from heavy metal, but the tritone does its job of introducing "edginess." The Dillinger Escape Plan's "Milk Lizard" has a verse riff based on an A♭ diminished triad (E♭♭–C♭–A♭) where the tritone occurs between E♭♭ and A♭; it finishes each time with an unexpected semitone shift using G5–A♭5.

Jimi Hendrix Experience

"Purple Haze" (Hendrix)

From *Are You Experienced* (Track/Reprise, 1967)

An early example of the tritone's dramatic power is Jimi Hendrix's groundbreaking, ear-bending second UK single. It is a truism of commercial music designed for radio that the first five seconds must grab the listeners' attention and make the song stand out. Hendrix's gambit was to have Noel Redding play an E octave on bass while he placed a B♭ octave across it, thus creating a tritone. I can't think of another chart single of the mid-'60s that, in musical terms, is so nakedly confrontational. The tritone's unrest expresses the psychological distress of the lyric.

This song features a riff based on E pentatonic minor (from bar 3), which is unusual because it covers two octaves and a minor third—riffs don't often fan out that much. It's a riff that signals big jumps between the notes. The main chord change is based on E, G, and A (a typical blues-derived I–♭III–IV progression). The song also features the E7♯9 chord, which has become known as the "Hendrix chord" because of his fondness for it. Its notes are EG♯DG, and its dissonance is a consequence of the tritone G♯D and the major seventh G♯G. (The chord can also be heard on the Beatles' "Taxman," as D7♯9.)

Black Sabbath

"Black Sabbath" (Iommi/Butler/Ward/Osbourne)

From *Black Sabbath* (Vertigo/Warner Bros., 1970)

This slice of pre-*Exorcist* Gothic horror scared many a young teen when they pinched the album sleeve (overgrown yard, dank old building, figure in cloak) from their elder brother's bedroom for a surreptitious listen. When I interviewed him in the '90s, Tony Iommi explained that the occult imagery of Black Sabbath's songs had arisen almost by accident. Ozzy needed words to match Iommi's evil-sounding riffs. You can't sing about flowers and love in the air over the trilled tritone riff of "Black Sabbath."

Sabbath songs often have lots of riffs. Iommi never seems to be stuck for one, producing them like an endless stream of one-ton black rabbits from a hat, to be recorded with his distinct guitar tone. The photograph on the inner sleeve of the band's fourth album shows his Gibson "monkey" SG with single-coil pickups, a customized Rangemaster Treble Booster pushing his valve amps to more distortion.

Iommi must take much credit for the introduction of the tritone into the Grimoire of Ye Heavy Ryffe. "Black Sabbath," with its famous intro of thunder, rain, and tolling bell, is built almost entirely on a tritone riff, G–D♭. Hendrix had, of course, stuck one on the front of "Purple Haze," but "Black Sabbath" is probably the defining early tritone in the realms of what became heavy metal.

The riff to Sabbath's "Children of the Grave" is also tritone-based (D5–A5–A♭5), as is "Wheels of Confusion" (the F♯–A–C–B idea at about 3:40) and "Under the Sun."

Apart from the tritone, what's hugely influential about the riff in "Black Sabbath" is its slow tempo—almost glacial by rock 'n' roll standards. Little Richard this ain't. As for the erotic quality of the tritone, Sabbath weren't that interested. It would take Jimmy Page's musical sex magick to nail that one.

T. Rex

"Rock On" (Bolan)

From *The Slider* (T. Rex Wax Co/EMI/Reprise, 1972)

At a time when pretension was cutting rock off from its fundamental energy, Marc Bolan took it back to its roots: the '50s 12-bar-based rock 'n' roll of Presley, Berry, and Cochran, filtered through a '60s post-Dylan, post-Hendrix sensibility.

You have to listen closely to hear the tritone in "Rock On," but that's kind of the point. (It's more prominent in his acoustic home demo of the track.) The examples we've looked at so far have been strident expressions of this interval, foregrounding its unmissable dissonance, but it can also subtly add a dark, sexy undertone to a chord change.

This riff begins in G major, with a high GD fourth, and then lands on a pungent B♭ as the chord changes from G to B♭. This is a I→III blues change. At the back of the mix there are several acoustic guitars, and as they strum on the B♭, an open top E-string is audible. B♭–E is a tritone.

R.E.M.

"Feeling Gravity's Pull" (Berry/Buck/Mills/Stipe)

From *Fables of the Reconstruction* (IRS, 1985)

R.E.M.'s third album opens with the most angular riff they ever recorded. To emphasize the fact, the track starts with Buck's guitar alone. What's fascinating is that here the tritone so beloved of metal bands is transferred to the top two strings and given a different slant. The first three notes are B, F♯, and F. The riff starts with a fourth on the top strings and then moves back a fret, creating a tritone between B and F. This is repeated with a few extra lower notes to extend the phrase. Then Buck hits a B on string six and intersperses this with harmonics in a sort of mutant funk rhythm.

Only when the drums come in is the sense of uncertainty about beat and time signature cleared up—notice that the drum entry indicates that the riff doesn't quite start where it seems to. This riff carries on throughout the verse, creating a remarkable, doomy backdrop to Stipe's mournful vocal.

Metallica

"Enter Sandman" (Hetfield/Ulrich/Hammett)

From *Metallica* (aka *The Black Album*, Vertigo/Elektra, 1991)

Anthrax, Slayer, Megadeth, and Metallica were the leaders of a generation of bands in the mid-to-late '80s who introduced a new brand of heavy rock. Their often-detuned riffery owed less to the blues-based hard rock of the late '60s and '70s and was played initially at lightning speed, prompting the label "thrash metal." When the dust settled, Metallica emerged as kings of the pack. Stressing the existential despair theme, they popularized a new harmonic vocabulary for metal, using a flattened fifth and flattened second in the minor scale (E F G A B♭ B C D). In came a new guitar tone to disembowel your speakers: the "mid-scooped" power chord, with its thumping top and bottom-boosted EQ.

"Enter Sandman" has since joined the list of famous guitar riffs that are played in musical instrument shops when trying out guitars, augmenting a select group that includes "Smoke on the Water," "Sweet Child O' Mine," and "Seven Nation Army." A cleanish guitar arpeggio and a touch of wah-wah start the song before drums and bass enter, and then the riff appears. Listen for the guitar on the opposite side to the riff, which initially changes from an E5 chord to A5. Both guitars play the riff at the end of this long build-up.

"Enter Sandman" is constructed on variations of a riff using an E–B♭ tritone, in which an octave leap from E up to E falls back to B and then shifts a semitone (half step) to B♭. The verses use an E–F shift, and the chorus goes up a tone (whole step) to F♯–C–B—another tritone—for "exit light, enter night," where fifths are also heard.

There is a masterful stroke with the unexpected re-entry of the rhythm section at 4:28, two riffs earlier than expected. Along with the carpet-bombing riffage, Metallica had a maniacal sense of arrangement. In rock and pop, four of anything is predictable—so make a cut. For another Metallica track with tritone and strong minor seconds, see "Of Wolf and Man" from the same album.

Sum 41

"Fat Lip" (Whibley/Jocz)

From *All Killer No Filler* (Island, 2001)

"Fat Lip" was a chart hit from the late '90s from a band who pioneered a hybrid of rap/rock. The riff is first heard in a lighter form: G♯–A–B going up to a G♯, then the same phrase but up to F♯, then the first phrase again, then a fourth phrase ending F♯–E. That gives an a1+a2+a1+a3 pattern, heard twice unaccompanied. When the rest of the band enters, they put E–B–E–A chords underneath it. This changes the harmonic meaning of the riff as first heard and deepens it, giving it more sludge and power.

The first two verse lines are sung over another riff, a neat hook that avoids the need to play the E5–B5–A5 progression on which it is based. This in turn makes the fifths that carry the second half of the verse stronger. It is like an updated version of Aerosmith's "Walk This Way."

> **Avenged Sevenfold**
>
> **"Bat Country"** (Avenged Sevenfold)
>
> From *City of Evil* (Warner Bros./WEA, 2005)

"Bat Country" is something of an epic, straddling three recognizable rock styles and employing tempo changes and abrupt transitions. It begins with an anarchic seven seconds in which one of the song's riffs is heard mixed to sound as though it is coming through a radio. Using a drop D tuning, the first riff proper has several variations on a D blues scale, emphasizing the flattened fifth note (A♭) and inserting a squiggle of fast notes during the riff's first form.

During the verse, there are fast semiquavers (16th notes) on the single pitches of D, down to A♭, and down to the low D. The song also has a variation riff with a descending A♭–G–F–D in fifths. At the chorus, the half-time tempo contrasts with the frenetic speed-metal of the verse. The song is marked by abrupt changes between sections, so it sounds like a montage of ideas spliced together.

At 1:32 and 4:06, the song suddenly changes into more of a metal ballad, with chorused electric guitar arpeggios, full chords, and a D minor feel that sounds like Radiohead doing a Brian Wilson melody. "Bat Country" raises some interesting questions about effective song structure, and also the effect of a fast tempo on the weight (or lack of) of the drums. The song reminds us that riffs can be played in octaves, fifths, or single notes for the sake of variety, without changing their basic pitches.

7 thirds

So far, we have covered semitone and tone-shift riffs, octaves, fourths, fifths, and the tritone. These are the most important intervals for riff-making. This by no means exhausts the intervals within an octave, but the others are not used as much. Major and minor seconds (two notes a tone or semitone apart) are too close together to be played as pairs in the way that fifths are. Similarly, major and minor sevenths are too discordant to be played together. So that leaves thirds and sixths.

Thirds are notes either three or four semitones apart: three semitones for a minor third (CE♭), four for a major third (CE). Thirds have a characteristically "sweet" quality, which is pleasing if fully in key. They are essential to vocal harmony singing, especially in duets. Their use as rock riffs is limited, since they don't project a tough, aggressive character without a little help. The addition of very low bass notes can make all the difference, as can be heard on the minor scale twin-lead riff of Motionless in White's "Abigail."

Where they are important in rock is as the basis of the arrangement style known as "twin lead," where two guitarists in a band play parallel melodic phrases largely in thirds. Pioneered by bands like Wishbone Ash, Thin Lizzy, and Queen, it is heard to famous effect on the coda to the Eagles' "Hotel California." Elsewhere, thirds provide the lead break for the Beatles' "Twist and Shout" and melodic interest in Van Morrison's "Brown-Eyed Girl," and there's a smooth thirds riff in Suede's "Asbestos" over a G#m–C# change. Thirds sound great on strings one and two, or three and four, and then progressively less clear on the lower strings, although they can work when played over a low pedal with distortion. (They also function well on the high strings of a bass.)

Turning away from guitar for a moment, Tori Amos's "Girl" (from her 1992 debut album *Little Earthquakes*) has a remarkable one-bar piano riff in thirds that runs hauntingly throughout the intro and verses of the song. The thirds in question are drawn from the scale of G natural minor. Around this hypnotic reiteration, Amos's vocal melody and piano make a texture of great beauty. Unlike fifths or fourths, these thirds emphasize tonality, be it major or minor. A comparable instance on guitar would be the thirds in Rory Gallagher's "Moonchild," or those played over the A minor and F chords in Fleetwood Mac's "Rhiannon."

Before tackling thirds as riffs, let's look at how they occur on a major scale. Here's the scale of D major (D E F# G A B C#), overlaid with itself with two notes out of alignment, so F# goes over the D, and so on:

The scale in thirds sounds harmonious because it is a sequence of major and minor thirds. The sequence goes major, minor, minor, major, major, minor, minor. A sequence of all major or all minor thirds would sound obviously wrong because

Thirds in D major

it would introduce notes that are not in the original scale. Play this D major scale harmonized in only major thirds to hear the effect.

Major thirds

Early vocal and guitar harmonizers created this sound because they were not advanced enough to alter the thirds where needed. Even this might be used to creative effect. Jimmy Page exploited the sound of consecutive out-of-key major thirds in "Friends," using a variant open-C tuning.

Below are the finger patterns for thirds on the guitar—minor third first, then major third:

Minor and major

thirds

Thirds do sometimes occur as riffs played on the top two pairs of strings—take the classic Chuck Berry bent thirds on the G and B strings. Thirds on these strings can be heard in the main riff of Cream's "SWLABR" and "Outside Woman Blues," Rory Gallagher's "Public Enemy No. 1," the intro of David Bowie's "Station to Station" (with a tone-shift riff), the Rolling Stones' "Can You Hear Me Knocking," R.E.M.'s "Letter Never Sent," and the Who's cover of "Young Man Blues." Guitarists like Steve Cropper and Johnny Marr play fills out of thirds on the top two strings. Marshall Crenshaw's "There She Goes Again" opens its verse with a sequence of thirds in F major.

To give thirds a bit more "edge," try chromatic (off-key) shifts up or down a semitone. To make a riff from thirds lower in pitch, put them over the open bottom E or A-string (see the discussion of pedal notes in section 3). Something like this occurs in the intro and verse of the Police's "Don't Stand So Close to

Me." "Nowhere" by Therapy? has a good example of thirds played rapidly over an A–E–F#m–D chord sequence.

The interval of a flattened (minor) third (CEb) is crucial to riff writing because it is a "blue" note. A vast array of guitar riffs uses the flattened third. The most common keys on guitar for this are A (C instead of C#) and E (G instead of G#). The effect of a riff where there is a minor third is strengthened if the key and the underlying chords are majors. This is heard in T. Rex's "Twentieth Century Boy," where the opening riff uses the notes E and G over an E major chord; in Bruce Springsteen's "Adam Raised a Cain," where the blues influence is even more noticeable; and in the Groundhogs' "Cherry Red." The Black Keys' "Lonely Boy" has an E–G minor third riff with a striking pitch shift drop to add surprise; the rest of the song has I→bIII–IV changes in both directions. The Stone Roses' "Driving South" makes hay with a riff that uses both the major and minor third through an extended 12-bar and transposes that riff up a fourth.

A more complex treatment of a minor third interval is Foo Fighters' "Rope." The main riff has four phrases, one to a bar, starting with the notes B–D, then F#–A (both minor third intervals) in the same rhythm, and then two phrases using a tone change from D to C. The sound of the riff is enriched by having high cluster chords layered on top, and by the jerky accents.

The ambiguity of using both major and minor third is easily produced when the riff is played on slide with an open tuning, as in the Stone Roses' "Love Spreads." Other riffs that mix the two thirds are the Offspring's "Pay the Man" and Gomez's "Shot Shot." The main riff in Joe Satriani's "Nineteen Eighty," first heard solo on bass and then with guitar, uses Eb and E against a tonic of C.

Less commonly are riffs that create a three-note idea with the flattened seventh, first and major third (the notes G, A, and C# in A). Examples include Nirvana's "Breed" and "Heart-Shaped Box"; Queen's "Tie Your Mother Down" has a main riff on A with a C# added, rather than the blues C that would be more common (as heard on Led Zeppelin's "Rock and Roll"). There are plenty of riffs where the blues third is followed by the usual major third, as in Zep's "Houses of the Holy" (notice the funky accented A6 chord). Thirds can also combine with fourths, as on the riff of Television's "See No Evil."

Other songs where the third is a crucial interval in the riff include Free's "Woman," which has B–B–D–B from the pentatonic minor, then slides a third DF# up to EG#. The Jam's "The Place I Love" has a riff that uses low-slid thirds from EG♯ to DF♯. Booker T. and the MG's' "Time Is Tight" depends on the warmth of low major thirds coupled with a 1–6–5–1 bass line, as does Elvis Costello's homage to it, "Temptation." There are distinctive high thirds in a funk style punctuating Dua Lipa's "Break My Heart."

Howlin' Wolf

"Smokestack Lightning" (Burnett)

Single A-side (Chess, 1956)

Chester Burnett, better known as Howlin' Wolf, was a leading figure of electric Chicago blues. "Smokestack Lightning"—covered by the Yardbirds in 1965, and a key song for the British blues boom—is a one-chord number based on a two-bar riff, dominated by Burnett's wolf-howl falsetto. At the core of this archetypal blues riff is the first change of notes: the open E and B strings (making a fourth) going onto G and D (another fourth). The two pairs are a minor third apart. The riff is completed with another third as B and D are heard in close succession, and the G–E is heard again as the scale moves downward.

Apart from the dark majesty of the vocal, much of the track's power comes from the tension created by the way the melody rides across the riff and not with it, setting up a counter-rhythm. The blues third can be heard in other Wolf songs like "Wang Dang Doodle," "Spoonful" (later covered by Cream), "Little Red Rooster," and mutated in "I Asked for Water."

Chuck Berry

"No Money Down" (Berry)

From *After School Sessions* (Chess, 1958)

"No Money Down" is a fine example of contrasting a riff with vocals. After a brief intro in which guitar and piano briefly tussle over it, the riff carries the whole verse. It's one of the most famous of all blues riffs, a five-note figure in 12/8 that starts on the last eighth note of the third beat and ends on the first beat of the following bar. In its original blues form (on songs like Muddy Waters's "I'm a Man"), it occurs as a pure pentatonic riff using notes 1–4–♭3 or the chords I–IV–♭III (in G: G–C–B♭). But Berry would often play it with a quick hammer-on that converted the blues flattened third to the normal third (G–C–G–B♭–B–G), as he does here, and the C and B notes both lend themselves to having thirds added above them.

Similar thirds mix with fourths for the main B riff of Berry's "Around and Around." The MC5's "Tonight" is another example of the minor third/major third interplay derived from Chuck Berry.

Jimi Hendrix

"In from the Storm" (Hendrix)

From *The Cry of Love* (Track/Capitol, 1971)

As mentioned earlier, Hendrix's later songs extended his compositional forms and harmonic vocabulary. "In from the Storm" is a fine example, with thirds filling out a single-note riff based on F♯ pentatonic minor. It starts with a tone shift of E–F♯, followed by thirds on the second and third strings (AC♯ and BD♯), and then a pentatonic run that unexpectedly drops onto the flattened third of the scale, an A at the fifth fret. The riff is placed by Hendrix as an "answer" to the first two lines of lyric, which themselves are sung over a single chord. Having a vocal phrase over a single chord followed by a busier riff makes a good contrast: the static chord won't distract attention from the vocal.

After a couple of verses, Hendrix starts the instrumental bridge section with a descending riff on the A blues scale at the fifth fret, which again runs down to the flattened third at the eighth. He then transposes this riff twice to reach the guitar solo. (The version of "In from the Storm" that Hendrix played at the Isle of Wight Festival, included on the *Voodoo Child* compilation, is worth seeking out.)

In a power-trio context—which is how Hendrix mostly worked—thirds take on a special significance because they sketch the harmony without the guitarist having to play block chords. If you have a riff that consists of single notes, adding major and minor thirds to some of those notes will suggest chords. This works best when neither of the notes is the root note, which can be left to the bass player.

Led Zeppelin

"Trampled Underfoot" (Page/Plant/Jones)

From *Physical Graffiti* (Swan Song, 1975)

On their sixth album, Led Zeppelin spliced their own inimitable brand of hard rock with a funk influence. "Trampled Underfoot" is a staggering display of monolithic power, complete with relentless drumming from Bonham, nimble clavinet from Jones, and another classic Page riff. The keyboard part makes consistent use of octaves on G; over this, Page plays two major thirds—AC# and B♭D—followed by a seven-note G pentatonic minor run. The C# makes a tritone against G but is softened a little by being in harness with the A. At the end of each verse, the riff is punctuated either with a B♭–C chord change or B♭–C–E♭–F, followed by a variation on the riff an octave higher.

I've never counted exactly how many times the riff is played during the track, but it must be a record, even for Zep. Such an unremitting focus on the riff is part of what gives the track its power, but it's a difficult thing to pull off without boredom setting in.

Motörhead

"Ace of Spades" (Kilminster/Taylor/Clarke)

From *Ace of Spades* (Bronze/Mercury, 1980)

Possibly rock's noisiest-ever three-piece, appealing to heavy metal fans and punks alike, Motörhead didn't so much play songs as pummel them into submission. At the core of the band's assault was Lemmy's chordal approach to bass guitar, coupled with a vocal style that made Joe Cocker sound like Cliff Richard, and drummer Taylor's double bass-drums.

The frenetic "Ace of Spades" riff is introduced by an initial phrase of E–E♭–D over an open E. The main riff is then superimposed over this at the end of the first couple of lyric lines. It consists of thirds played on the second and third strings and bent up in what most guitarists know as a Chuck Berry–type lead idea. These thirds often spice up fast passages of minor pentatonic playing. They can be heard in other Motörhead songs like "Metropolis" and "Bomber," and at a slower tempo on the Alex Harvey Band's "Swampsnake."

Nirvana

"Come as You Are" (Cobain)

From *Nevermind* (Geffen, 1991)

This riff (played on a guitar detuned by a tone) consists of a minor third moving by steps into a perfect fifth, the two notes of each pair alternating rather than being struck together. The riff is played for the intro and the verse, and under the guitar solo. What's unusual about it is its use of a third pitched so low. Notice how the vocal sits well above it, and how the guitar playing the riff has a chorus effect applied to it. A fuller guitar texture starts at 1:38 for the bridge, before the riff leads into the guitar solo. The two chords on the chorus are also a minor third apart.

8 sixths

Turn a third upside down (reverse the notes) and it becomes a sixth. Sixths are notes either eight or nine semitones apart. Eight semitones make a minor sixth (CAb); nine make a major sixth (CA). Like thirds, sixths have a harmonious quality, though the distance between the notes reduces the "sweetness," compared with thirds. The use of high sixths in rock riffs is also limited for the same reasons: they don't, by themselves, sound tough enough.

Van Halen used low sixths for the opening riff of "Women in Love," and Jimmy Page has low sixths in the main riff of "The Only One," from his solo album *Outrider* (1988). There is a riff in sixths in R.E.M.'s "Binky the Doormat." Sixths are also a trademark of guitarist Steve Cropper on his many '60s soul recordings with Booker T. and the MG's, and they are found in twin-lead guitar playing—as on the opening of Wishbone Ash's "Throw Down the Sword."

For a short riff using sixths on acoustic guitar see John Mayer's "Queen of California." Sixths and thirds combine on Jorma Kaukonen's famous instrumental "Embryonic Journey," from Jefferson Airplane's 1967 LP *Surrealistic Pillow*.

Here's how they occur on the scale of D major harmonized in sixths:

As with thirds, there is a pattern of finger movements you can learn: 2–2–1– 2–2–1–1. Harmonize a major scale with the right notes and you get major, major, minor, major, major, minor, minor.

Sixths in D major

In hard-rock styles, sixths are more likely found in conjunction with fifths and/or fourths. They can be highly effective in this way, introducing variety into a sequence of the tonally neutral intervals, because the sixth (like the third) will imply a major or a minor chord in a way that bare fourths and fifths do not.

Consider the following sequence:

TRACK 7

Mixed intervals

Here, AE moves down to GD (A5 to G5), then to GC (a fourth), and then F#D (a minor sixth). In such an instance, the sixth implies the chord of D major, though it could also be harmonized with B minor. As with thirds, this makes sixths potentially significant in any band where a single guitar is the harmony instrument.

> **Dire Straits**
>
> **"Where Do You Think You're Going"** (Knopfler)
>
> From *Communique* (Vertigo/Warner Bros., 1979)

A highly charged gem of a track and the standout on the Straits' second album, this begins with a progression of Am–F–G–E for the verse. The riff functions as a link between the verses and the coda, over which the second guitar solo is played.

Like the more famous "Sultans of Swing," this is a riff shaped by Mark Knopfler's right-hand picking technique, since it uses two strings at a time. It's built over a four-chord, four-bar sequence of Am–F–Dm–F. The first bar has thirds on strings two and three, resolving onto an F triad; the second bar has complementary sixths on strings one and three, resolving onto a D minor triad; sixths occur again in bar 3, resolving onto F in bar 4. Knopfler plays these with a sensitive touch, utilizing the Strat's neck/middle and, later, middle/bridge pickup positions.

After the last verse, the drums enter with a crescendo, the tempo increases, and more guitars play the riff than earlier. It's an exhilarating moment. "Where Do You Think You're Going" is an object lesson in what is possible with thirds, sixths, and dynamics.

9 mixed intervals

Having surveyed the important intervals for rock guitar riffs, section 1 concludes by examining how to get extra mileage out of these intervals by using more than one type in a riff. The famous songs that follow in the *riff gallery* provide examples of this. With creativity, it's possible to combine any intervals in a riff, playing them as single notes or together. Octaves, fifths, fourths, thirds, and sixths blend easily and can be comfortable to finger. Seconds and sevenths are more awkward and don't sit so well under the hand.

There are mixed intervals in the Offspring's "The Kids Aren't Alright," which has a sequence with thirds, fourths, and fifths. Wishbone Ash's "Persephone" combines thirds and fourths on the top strings over an Em–D chord change. On the coda, the riff is lengthened in a dynamic variation.

> **Led Zeppelin**
> **"Good Times Bad Times"** (Page/Jones/Bonham)
> From *Led Zeppelin* (Atlantic, 1969)

Zeppelin's recording career blasted off with the double-crunch E chord of this intro. Right from the liftoff, dynamics were top of the band's musical agenda, and long songs were not yet the order of the day. The compositional approach here is to cram as many different thrills as possible into less than four minutes. "Good Times Bad Times" is the final maturing of the type of concise rock song that the Who and the Kinks started in 1965, with clearly defined verses and choruses, and a riff.

"Good Times Bad Times" has several identifiable riffs. The first is a couple of E5s, then a fast arpeggio on D, followed by a slinky chromatic C♯–D–D♯ return to the tonic E. The underlying harmony is Mixolydian: E–D–A and back to E. At the end of the first chorus, instead of returning to the verse, Zep pull a surprise by tumbling into a contrasted section on F♯, with a riff made up of fifths and fourths. Page would use this combination of F♯ as a tonal center and fourths underneath the guitar solo again in "Over the Hills and Far Away."

Golden Earring
"Radar Love" (Kooymans/Hay)
From *Moontan* (Track, 1973)

Formed in 1961, Golden Earring were a Dutch band who scored an international hit with "Radar Love." The riff here functions as a fill after each line during verse one, almost as a musical comment on the lyric (see "Walk This Way" in this regard). The bass guitar plays a steady F♯, and above it the guitar riff plays a third (AC♯) and two fourths (F♯B and EA), hence its selection here as a mixed-interval riff.

This riff is a distant relative of a typical Chuck Berry double-stop but adapted to early '70s hard rock. Notice the effect of the riff pausing on the EA, rather than F♯B—the former implying an F♯7 chord. (The riff guitar is panned to the left.) A higher-pitched variant of this riff follows the first two lines of verse two, before the riff is heard up an octave, and finally at the original pitch. This track also has a splendid drum break, a menacing middle-eight, and an atmospheric intro with a fiery but not over-distorted guitar tone.

Dire Straits
"Money for Nothing" (Knopfler/Sting)
From *Brothers in Arms* (Vertigo/Warner Bros., 1985)

Although *Brothers in Arms* famously features a silver resonator guitar on the sleeve, on tracks like "Money for Nothing" Knopfler applied his guitar skills to a cranked-up Les Paul. The result is an interesting hybrid tone, caused by the blend of his technique and a traditional rock guitar sound.

"Money for Nothing" comes on with enough dirty guitar to appeal to those who like a good headbanging riff, though the song also has enough sweeteners—a catchy chorus, synths, and Sting's guest vocals—to appeal beyond the heavy rock audience. It is also one of the longest riffs in this book (eight bars), is in G pentatonic minor (G–B♭–C–D–F), and mixes single notes with fourths and fifths.

The first four-bar phrase ends with a B♭–C change; the second mirrors that with an F–G change. It's harder to play than it seems, because Knopfler's fingerstyle playing means it's rhythmically varied, and harmonics pop and squeak from the strings. To get this tone, his Les Paul was played through a wah-wah pedal fixed open at the right angle to boost the distinctive "honky" mid-range frequencies.

Whitesnake

"Still of the Night" (Coverdale/Sykes)

From *Whitesnake* (EMI/Geffen, 1987)

Heavy rock enjoyed revived popularity in the late '80s, as the pendulum that had swung against guitar music at the start of the decade swung back. Specifically, Led Zeppelin's reputation increased, and they became much imitated.

Enter Whitesnake's "Still of the Night," with its four distinguishable riffs. The first is a four-bar riff using the F♯ blues scale (F♯ A B C C♯ E), which has two phrases: a1 ends with E5–B5; a2 ends with B5–E5. The first two beats of bars 2 and 4 have an octave leap on F♯, making the riff sound like a welding together of Zep's "Black Dog" and "Immigrant Song."

Riff 2 is shaped by an octave, on E, with a couple of fourths at the end of it. Listen for this riff's return, after the chorus, when it is played twice in time with the drums, and twice across a continuous drumbeat.

Riff 3 comes during the instrumental bridge, over an Em–C change, and consists of a four-bar set of phrases derived from the E natural minor scale. Riff 4 follows, with triads moving downward over an E pedal. "Still of the Night" crams a whole lotta riffology into a relatively short space.

The La's

"There She Goes" (Mavers)

From *The La's* (Go! Discs, 1990)

"There She Goes" is a wonderful example of a high-pitched guitar riff, and of a riff occurring in a song that isn't hard rock. The riff is a stereo chiming figure based on a DG fourth, with other notes above and below added and taken away. The D stays constant and lends a drone-like quality, along with the chiming effect of E–D–E–D–E–D on the top two strings, one open, one fretted—an example of getting a major second from an open string with a fretted note.

At first, the riff is heard without a harmony, but notice how its harmonic value (i.e., how it sounds) changes when the chords (G, D, Cadd9) enter. The riff is extended further when the Am chord appears.

SECTION 2

scale-based riffs

In section 2 we'll explore how riffs can also be built on a scale—a set pattern of notes related to the key of a song—which could be a major, minor, or blues scale, or a Mixolydian, Dorian, or other mode. It's not as complex as it sounds...

A scale is a sequence of notes dividing an octave into a set pattern of intervals based on the semitone and the tone (half step and whole step). It is from the scale that a sense of key and that key's harmony is derived.

Riffs can also be created from a scale—in traditional rock, it's usually the pentatonic major and minor, with the two matching blues scales, and the addition of extra chromatic notes if you want to get slinky. Often, riffs use the same fretboard patterns as lead guitar—the emphasis falls on the lower-pitched areas of those patterns.

In the selected examples in the *riff galleries*, the grouping of songs and their riffs under the heading of a scale does not imply that the riff has all the notes of the scale. It only means that the riff draws most of its notes from that scale; it may be a partial expression of the scale.

10 pentatonic minor

The most important scale for rock music is undoubtedly the pentatonic. This is the scale heard most frequently in lead solos and riffs, in both its major and minor form. Pentatonic means "five notes" (the major scale has seven), and this type of scale is found in the folk music of many cultures. It can be heard when the five black keys in a piano octave are played, and is the scale most people first learn on the guitar.

The pentatonic minor can be played from any note if you move up the fretboard in intervals of 3, 2, 2, 3, and 2 semitones (or frets) on a single string. The example below shows what it looks like in A and E (with alternative fingerings).

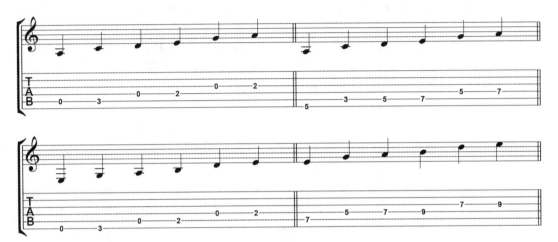

The notes are A C D E G and E G A B D. What makes it a minor scale is the interval between the first two notes: three semitones make a minor third. By comparison to a major scale, minor scales sound sad.

A pentatonic minor and E pentatonic minor

Normally, a minor scale can only be played in a minor key, and a major scale in a major key, but rock and soul share a particular musical practice, derived from the blues, where singers and instrumentalists use flattened "blue" notes against a major chord backing when such notes are not in key. The arising tension creates a musical effect associated with the blues. Played over a major chord backing, the pentatonic minor gives a distinctive "tough" sound. This colors any riffs written in the scale so they share that "tough" character.

When writing your own songs, experiment with a riff in A pentatonic minor over an A major chord backing. Then play the same riff over an A minor chord. Hear the difference? In the first instance, two of the scale's notes—C and G—are functioning as blue notes, because in A major they should be C♯ and G♯. But over the A minor chord they don't function in this way, because the scale of A minor features C and G. So, the A pentatonic minor riff sounds perfectly okay but blends in, rather than having the assertive quality it has in the major key.

Pentatonic minor riffs are the most common type of riff in rock. AC/DC's "Whole Lotta Rosie" uses a classic blues phrase sped up as a rock 'n' roll idea

(A pentatonic minor—the notes A, C, and D). Stevie Wonder's "Superstition" is an E pentatonic minor riff. The verses in Deep Purple's "Fireball" are based on single notes in B pentatonic minor (with a two-part, four-bar riff), while "Highway Star" uses G–Bb–C–Bb as chords, not single notes, in the first part of its verse. American Dog's "Last of a Dying Breed" has a fast E pentatonic minor riff that also occurs in shortened forms, with chords such as G5, A5, and D5 interspersed. Slash's "By the Sword" combines an A pentatonic minor riff with chords such as D/F# and F, so the scale phrases are threaded through the chords in a way that adds more color to the riff.

Other pentatonic minor riffs include Soundgarden's "Spoonman," Reef's "Naked," the first riff of Kansas's "Carry On My Wayward Son," Van Halen's "Outta Love Again," MC5's "Kick Out the Jams" (E5–G–A is I–bIII–IV), Ocean Colour Scene's "Riverboat Song" (with B, D, and E notes), the Sonics' "Have Love Will Travel," and Extreme's "Rest in Peace," with its Hendrix-like intro. Hendrix's own "Little Miss Lover" has a riff that uses 1–b3–b7.

Queen's "Dragon Attack" is a great example of a D pentatonic minor riff launched from the fifth string rather than the sixth when detuned by a tone, and it lies nicely under the hand. Another fresh take on the idea of a pentatonic minor blues riff is the Black Keys' "Lonely Boy," where the riff descends though an octave of the scale and finishes with an unexpected leap.

The pentatonic minor is usually implied where the root and the flat third of the scale are stated as the riff, as in the case of "Another Way to Die," Jack White's James Bond theme with Alicia Keys, which has lots of E–G single notes. Notice how the opening riff has E–F# bent a semitone to the flat third, then up to D (the flat seventh) and E.

This type of riff is heard in rap music, too: see N.E.R.D.'s "Rock Star (Jason Nevins Remix Edit)," with its 1–b3 riff played in single notes. The b3 note can also be given a slight bend, as on John Kongos's "Tokoloshe Man," with its fuzz-tone riff in C pentatonic minor.

The pentatonic minor can also be used as the five root notes for a set of major chords, out of which a riff can be made. Greta Van Fleet's "Edge of Darkness" has a riff in F# pentatonic minor that culminates in A and D chords; the D chord is the mild surprise here because it belongs to the F# natural minor scale. Arctic Monkeys' "I Bet You Look Good on the Dancefloor" is in F# and uses a chord sequence of C#–B–A–F# (V–IV–bIII–I) in that key, based on the F# pentatonic minor (F♯ A B C♯ E), with a ♭VII E chord coming in just before the chorus.

The first three notes of F pentatonic minor (F, A♭, B♭) make the riff of Booker T. and the MG's R&B classic "Green Onions," with its three-note riff transposed onto B♭ and C for the 12-bar.

Johnny Kidd and the Pirates

"Shakin' All Over" (Heath)

Single A-side (HMV/Capitol, 1960)

"Shakin' All Over" was innovative in both its use of a riff and its sense of space, which was unusual in the singles chart at that time, when many records relied on syrupy strings and massed female backing vocals. The main riff is a straight run down an E pentatonic minor scale, taking advantage of the fact that all the notes of this scale (E G A B D) are open strings on the guitar. The riff is played in first position, with pull-offs from fretted notes onto open strings. After the first burst, a chugging lower pentatonic riff takes over. This in turn is played high up, with heavy muting, alongside the vocal. The song was memorably covered by the Who on *Live at Leeds* (1970).

The Temptations

"Get Ready" (Robinson)

From *Gettin' Ready* (Gordy/Tamla Motown, 1966)

As a bass guitar riff, "Get Ready" seems straightforward: a D pentatonic minor riff with the bass sometimes doubled by brass. But the song has a strongly contrasting verse and chorus: the verse has the riff, while the chorus has a four-chord sequence in F major (F, B♭, Gm, C), with James Jamerson switching the bass line to an F major scale (F G A B♭ C D E) in running eighth notes.

Things get a little more complex when the arrangement of the riff is scrutinized. The riff is accompanied by a piano part that appears to be hitting a D major chord over much of the riff and adding major thirds above some of its notes. This leads to the notes F♯ (the major third of D) and the blues third F sounding in close proximity.

The bridge (at 1:41) brings in the D blues scale by using an A♭. This track is a good example of a riff driving an up-tempo soul number.

Free

"The Stealer" (Fraser/Rodgers/Kossoff)

From *Highway* (Island/A&M, 1970)

"The Stealer" is an excellent example of an A pentatonic minor single-note riff. It breaks into three parts: there's A–G–A in the bass, then C–A and up an octave to A, and finally a C slid to D, with the open D string also hit. Doubling a fretted note with an open string was one of Paul Kossoff's guitar trademarks. The riff has an effective rhythm (punctuated by Fraser's typically loping bass), unexpected changes of direction, and resonance. It was either recorded in stereo or double-tracked.

Listen for the overdubs during the verse: the riff continues, but its effect is altered by the high guitar chords on top, which add a new dimension. The second chord riff on this song uses the chords I–IV–♭VII–IV. Other pentatonic minor Free riffs include "Mr. Big," with its memorable Em7 chord (022033).

The Temptations

"Ball of Confusion (That's What the World Is Today)" (Whitfield/Strong)

From *Greatest Hits II* (Gordy/Tamla Motown, 1970)

Much of this book concentrates on rock riffs, but riffs also feature prominently in soul, funk, and R&B. "Ball of Confusion" gives a profound insight into what happens when a pentatonic minor riff is contrasted with major harmony. It's a typical Norman Whitfield "groove" song, with a repetitive two-bar C pentatonic minor bass riff churning beneath the C major harmony. On top, guitars add strange arpeggios with echo, notably on the dramatic intro, with Dennis Edwards's arresting count-in (on headphones, you can hear the amps buzzing), while the brass section gives the occasional jazzy flourish. Verses end with an arpeggiated bridge of C, F, and G, with a punchy James Brown–type link, but the rhythmic drive of the riff is relentless. The music can afford to be simple because of the clever division of the lyric among the Temps' contrasting voices.

The lesson here is that a riff placed in the bass doesn't quite collide with the vocal as it might if it were pitched higher, on guitar. Whitfield and Strong used similar riff ideas at Motown, drawing on the root, flattened third, fourth, and flattened seventh notes of the pentatonic minor in "Psychedelic Shack," "You

Make Your Own Heaven and Hell Right Here on Earth," and "Papa Was a Rollin' Stone." A distant relative of this type of pentatonic minor riff on the bass occurs in Gomez's "Get Myself Arrested," the Stone Roses' "Daybreak" (on bass), Black Rebel Motorcycle Club's "White Palms," and Living Colour's "Middle Man," which is in C minor but with B as well as B♭ in the riff.

Black Sabbath

"The Warning" (Iommi/Butler/Ward/Osbourne)

From *Black Sabbath* (Vertigo/Warner Bros., 1970)

Tony Iommi found his own variations on the pentatonic minor riffs that were common in late-'60s hard rock. The Sabs' debut has "The Wizard" (A pentatonic minor, with a semitone A5–B♭5 change for the verse), "Behind the Wall of Sleep" (A pentatonic minor, A5–B5 riff on bridge), "Evil Woman" (centered on G, with blues-derived flattened seventh and flattened third notes), and "The Warning" with its D–F (I–♭III) riff. "The Warning" uses a popular rock formula of the time: in a 12-bar sequence, play four riffs on the keynote, two riffs transposed up a fourth, two riffs on the keynote again, and then, where chord V would have been in bar 9, add something else. Sometimes, riffs are transposed up a fourth, or, as in "Evil Woman," a sixth.

Free

"Wishing Well" (Rodgers/Kirke/Yamauchi/Kossoff/Bundrick)

From *Heartbreaker*, (Island/A&M, 1973)

Taken from Free's last studio album, "Wishing Well" was one of their heaviest tracks. By 1972, guitarist Paul Kossoff was in poor health and apparently did not play on the track, although he received a writing credit. It was singer Paul Rodgers who did a very passable imitation of Kossoff's patented lead wails, achieved here by running a guitar through a Leslie speaker.

The riff is a descending E pentatonic minor scale, divided into two parts: E–D–B–A, B–A–G–E. The first four notes are repeated before it comes to rest on a G5 chord. Later in the song, the riff is transposed to A pentatonic minor by shifting the fingering across one string. Transposition by a fourth is one of the most common riff shifts in guitar rock.

Free

"Heartbreaker" (Rodgers)

From *Heartbreaker* (Island/A&M, 1973)

From the same album as "Wishing Well," the title track (not to be confused with Led Zeppelin's "Heartbreaker") makes fine use of a heavy, multitracked D pentatonic minor scale. The interesting point is the way the riff starts not on D but on A and then works up the scale, A–C–D–F–G–A, before dropping to D. In other words, the keynote is displaced into the middle of the riff. Timing also plays a significant role: the riff starts on the second beat of a slow 4/4 time and arrives on D in the second bar, but the phrasing makes the riff sound more like one bar of 3/4 and one of 5/4, rather than two bars of 4/4. The slow groove is typical of Free, though the thickened guitars and ambient sound are more impressive here than on their earlier songs.

Compare this with Ten Years After's "Love Like a Man" (B–D–D♯/E–D–B–D♭–G–E), which is a tone higher and has the same finger pattern with the root on the fifth fret and in the middle. The riff occurs throughout the verse. Other relevant Free songs here are "The Hunter"—which has a G pentatonic minor riff with a G major chord on the third beat of each bar of G from time to time, reminiscent of Cream; and "I'll Be Creeping," in which the first part of the riff is in B pentatonic minor but the second part is a major chord with a D–D♯ hammer-on.

The Strokes

"Alone, Together" (Casablancas)

From *Is This It* (Rough Trade, 2001)

The Strokes offer an A pentatonic minor riff in a very different musical style to hard rock. This is spiky New York new millennium new wave. The one-bar riff is played for a mere four times and ten seconds, and then we're into verse one. It crops up twice after two lines of lyric, and four times after the next two lines.

During the chorus, the guitar that played the riff follows the vocal melody while the second guitar plays chords in straight eighths. When the riff is playing, it isn't doubled by either the second guitar or the bass, so the arrangement has more breathing space. At about 1:45, the riff is heard with an A minor chord, making the minor tonality explicit. Listen for the minimalist guitar solo toward the end. The riff makes two more appearances at 3:00 before the song abruptly finishes. There's no attempt to extend the riff for any serious head-banging.

The White Stripes

"Expecting" (J. White/M. White)

From *White Blood Cells* (Sympathy for the Record Industry/V2, 2001)

In the period following the publication of the first edition of this book, few rock bands created as much of a splash as minimalist Detroit duo the White Stripes, possibly rock's first ever power duo of guitar and drums but no bass player.

Jack White is a man obviously in love with the primitive sound of an electric guitar. "Expecting" comes across as a garage-band homage to Black Sabbath. The main riff, played in fifths, uses the root, flattened third, and flattened seventh of the pentatonic minor (D–F–C) and transposes it down a fourth onto A (A–C–G). The Stripes' idea of recording as live as possible is evident in the delightful fluctuations in the tempo. No click tracks here!

Audioslave

"Cochise" (Commerford/Cornell/Morello/Wilk)

From *Audioslave* (Epic, 2002)

"Cochise" comes in with a glam drumbeat and noise before the riff enters in a classic a1+a2 form, where a2 has a slight syncopation, the riff anticipating itself by coming in earlier (rather like the syncopation in Led Zeppelin's "Misty Mountain Hop"). It's based on E pentatonic minor, descending like a heavier version of Free, with a loping movement, though the verse ends with a chromatic D–D♯–E movement.

There is another riff in the chorus that rises on E, G, A, and B. An octave riff on the notes B and E provides the bridge. It's a good example of breathing life into an old riff idea through rhythm and timing. During the first lead break, it falls to the bass guitar to keep the riff going. Additional color is created by the appearance of a G♯ in the vocal melody on the phrase "take it on me," in contrast to the G of the E pentatonic minor scale.

11 blues scale

There's an important variation on the pentatonic minor, known as the blues scale, when the flattened fifth is added between the fourth and fifth. This note was discussed in the section on the tritone in section 1.

Here are two blues scales on A and E:

A blues scale and
E blues scale

The notes in A are A C D E♭ E G. In lead playing, the extra note (E♭) is often heard when the D is bent up a semitone, but it can also be fretted as a note in its own right. Add it to the pentatonic minor for a riff with a bit more color, and to facilitate more stepwise movement. The flattened fifth is an example of a chromatic passing note. Chromatic means "relating to color," or, in music, a note that does not belong to the home scale (of A pentatonic minor, in this instance). Using the A blues scale, this is the opening riff of AC/DC's "Black Ice," where the riff is thickened by an open fifth string and several double stops.

Twinned with the pentatonic minor, the blues scale is everywhere in rock. Mountain's "One Last Cold Kiss" has an A blues-scale riff, structured a1+a2+a1+a3, with the flattened fifth achieved via a bend. The same band's "Never in My Life" opens with a Mixolydian riff in D and then a distinctive slithering blues-scale riff in G minor, the first three notes being the fourth, flat fifth, and fifth on the scale (C–D♭–D). That riff is also memorable because of the effect of displacing the keynote G from the start or end of the riff.

The same displacement can be heard on Blind Faith's G pentatonic minor "Had to Cry Today," and in one of the riffs in Clutch's "50,000 Unstoppable Watts," where the note G is repeatedly stressed during an E pentatonic minor riff. "Tired Angels" is another great Mountain riff featuring a superb tone bend on the fifth string with a quasi-vocal sound, its second riff being on the E blues scale.

Queens of the Stone Age's "Leg of Lamb" has a bend from A♭ up to A, with a low D sounded underneath the A♭ (a tritone), and finishes off with the lower part of the D blues scale. Accept's "Undertaker" has a heavy, accented descending E blues-scale riff that doesn't appear until after the song's first chorus. Black Sabbath's "Rat Salad" is a kind of "Moby Dick" drum solo/riff number based on a G blues scale (G Bb C Db D). The Eagles' "Life in the Fast Lane" starts with an E blues riff that makes good use of variation of the initial idea. Muse's "Supermassive Black Hole" has the E–G flat third riff in a1+a2+a1+a3, with the last of the four phrases being a hammered-on flat fifth. A riff with clear precedents in Prince and Jimi Hendrix, it is harmonized at the octave.

Greta Van Fleet's "When the Curtain Falls" has a riff on the G minor blues scale that's launched by an octave shift from F to G and then a contrasting burst of notes on the upper strings harnessing a phrase more often encountered in a guitar lead break. The overall effect is energetic and busy.

To demonstrate how this scale doesn't have to culminate with a heavy rock riff, listen to Elbow's "Grounds for Divorce." There, the D blues-scale riff with the flat fifth bent is integrated into a more mainstream song. The riff is played in octaves.

Avenged Sevenfold's "Afterlife" and "The Beast and the Harlot" have riffs that show how there can be ambiguity as to which scale or mode is being used, since different types will share notes. In "Afterlife," there is a distinctive riff, with several 16th-note triplets on the notes D, F, D, and Ab over a drop D on the sixth string. These notes belong to the D minor blues scale, and D Phrygian and Locrian modes. The simplest analysis that covers the notes played is the best, taking into account the remainder of the harmony, so in this instance I would use the D minor blues scale as the label.

Cream

"Sunshine of Your Love" (Bruce/Brown/Clapton)

From *Disraeli Gears* (Atco/Reaction, 1967)

Cream were rock's original power trio, linking high-volume, blues-influenced riffing with live improvisation and Pete Brown's poetic lyrics. "Sunshine" is one of the most played rock riffs: it's based on a D blues scale (D F G Ab A C) and terminates with a D–F–D phrase that is either above or below the riff, depending on where in the song it is.

After its initial statement in single notes, the first D–D–C–D is turned into dominant seventh chords. This is a good example of how a single-note riff can be partially harmonized. During the verse, the D riff is played four times before it is transposed onto G.

Some riffs like "Sunshine of Your Love" are famous not only for the notes but for their guitar tone. Clapton's mellow front-pickup "woman tone" distortion is the icing on the cake.

Cream were one of Hendrix's favorite bands. The Jimi Hendrix Experience's *Live at the Winterland* album has Hendrix lamenting, in his best stoned drawl, that Cream are splitting up, by way of introducing his own version of "Sunshine." "It's not saying that we're better than them," he begins with an amused smirk, "but we'd like to do it in our *own* way, which is an instrumental, loose-jam-type scene"—at which point the Experience plough into a version that's faster than the original, with Jimi performing his usual minor miracles in keeping the riff going and interjecting scraps of the melody. Seek it out.

Jimi Hendrix
"Fire" (Hendrix)
From *Are You Experienced* (Track/Reprise, 1967)

"Fire" is another jewel of a riff from the Crown Prince of the Strat. This gem of wisdom from the guitar works of Jimi concerns visible techniques and "invisible" ones. A visible guitar technique is one people notice, like playing squillions of notes a second, dive-bombing with the tremolo, or playing behind your back. An invisible technique is noticed if you get it wrong, but not when it's executed correctly. Into this category falls string-muting.

At the high volume at which he played, Hendrix had to be very good at string-muting. A highly amplified electric guitar is quite a beast to tame. He needed to be adept at positioning his fretting fingers so they would hold down notes and mute unwanted strings at the same time.

This technique is necessary in a song like "Fire" because the riff is a D blues scale at the tenth position, coming in on the flattened fifth (A♭) but played in octaves on strings five and three. By muting the other four strings, Hendrix was able to whack the whole lot and only have the octave pair ring (the rest gave a percussive noise).

The riff itself is four bars long. The octave phrase occurs in bars 1 and 2; bars

3 and 4 use the notes A–C–D twice, while this phrase also supports the verse. (Hendrix was fond of octaves, as heard on "Purple Haze" and "51st Anniversary.") Notice that Hendrix transposes the chorus chords up a tone for the two guitar solos but doesn't transpose the riff itself.

Jimi Hendrix
"Voodoo Chile (Slight Return)" (Hendrix)
From *Electric Ladyland* (Track/Reprise, 1968)

Even in its shorter, hard rock arrangement, "Voodoo Chile" reveals its origins in the blues. Rock guitarists are familiar with the three-chord 12-bar format, but there are plenty of blues songs that never stray from their initial chord. "Voodoo Chile" may not have the same definition as some of Hendrix's own riffs, but the basic idea of the guitar accompaniment can still be considered a riff.

Hendrix splits up the strings of the E chord, creating a bass line with a minor third E–G–E climb, a stab of harmony every time he hits the fretted notes of the chord, a strident fourth from the top two open strings, and a blues-scale lead lick at the end of the bar. He makes many subtle rhythmic and tonal changes to this single-bar idea. The longer version of "Voodoo Chile" makes the blues element more overt. If you enjoy Hendrix in this vein, seek out what, in my opinion, is his deepest blues, "Hear My Train A Comin'." The live version on *Jimi Hendrix Concerts* (1982), from the second show at the Winterland, San Francisco, October 10, 1968, is especially fine.

The British Blues Boom of 1965–1969 produced plenty of songs with this kind of riff, for instance the Groundhogs' "Mistreated," with its naked debt to Muddy Waters's "Catfish Blues." A rougher version of the tradition survives in bands such as the Black Keys, as on "Stack Shot Billy," where a pentatonic minor melody is sung and played at the same time.

Fleetwood Mac
"Oh Well (Part 1)" (Green)
From *Then Play On* (Reprise, 1969)

Before evolving into mid-'70s AOR giants with West Coast harmonies and platinum hooks, there was another Fleetwood Mac, spoken of in reverential tones by people who bought their records in the late '60s—when, at one point, it was said they were outselling the Beatles and rivalling Led Zeppelin in the polls. This was the band's first incarnation—a triple-guitar blues-orientated lineup led by Peter Green.

It was Green who made Fleetwood Mac a band to be remembered. Blessed with a fine voice for understated blues, his lead playing had a finesse to match anything by Beck, Clapton, Kossoff, Page, or Bloomfield. His distinctive sensitivity is heard on "Need Your Love So Bad," "Love That Burns," the minor-key "Black Magic Woman" (later popularized by Santana), and the hit "Albatross." Few rock bands have played so poetically as the Mac on these numbers.

Their best album is *Then Play On*, from which "Oh Well" is taken. The shuffling rhythm suggests it might have been initially written on acoustic guitar and then arranged for the band. The somewhat African feel of the rhythm is something the Mac were good at, and it recalls the Who's exotic percussion on "Magic Bus," as well as Santana.

Riff 1 enters on acoustic guitar and is then doubled by lead guitar and bass. It's made of four phrases that draw on the E blues scale, starting with E pentatonic minor, and then bringing in additional notes to the scale. Riff 2 is a tone-shift single-note riff, D–E. Riff 3 is a 1–♭3–♭7 that culminates in an ascending scale. There is considerable doubling of the guitars throughout.

Led Zeppelin
"Heartbreaker" (Plant/Page/Jones/Bonham)
From *Led Zeppelin II* (Atlantic, 1970)

Originally blasting off the second side of the vinyl *Led Zeppelin II*, "Heartbreaker" is a classic example of how to develop a riff's potential by transposition. It has an A blues-scale riff of two one-bar phrases; the second has four 16th-note A's instead of a single A. The riff is transposed up a tone to B and back to A, and for the middle-eight transposed to C, D, and E in succession. The effect of these rapid transpositions is one of mounting excitement, culminating in the crescendo to E. The riff is reinforced by John Paul Jones playing a bass distorted through a Leslie speaker.

"Heartbreaker" is inventive and condensed hard rock. Put alongside comparable material on *Physical Graffiti*, it's noticeable how many more ideas are crammed into this earlier song. For example, there are several other riffs after the guitar solo, one of which is based on the scale A–C–C♯–G–F♯–E, before the original riff returns.

Led Zeppelin

"Bring It on Home" (Page/Plant/Dixon)

From *Led Zeppelin II* (Atlantic, 1970)

Sometimes it's not how good a riff you have but how well it is introduced. "Bring It on Home" reproduced Sonny Boy Williamson's version of a Willie Dixon song as its intro and outro, but Led Zeppelin don't owe a debt to anyone for the middle section ("Bring It on Back") or the sheer drama with which the main body of the song kicks off, with a blast of harmonica and the explosive first plays of this E blues-scale riff.

The basic notes are in E pentatonic minor, with the blues flattened fifth coming in as a bend from A. The riff also cleverly contrasts the blues flattened third G with the major third G♯. It's also a great example of harmonizing a riff, since Page doubles it two octaves up—as in the film *The Song Remains the Same*, where Page is shown harmonizing the riff several octaves plus a third above the bass. The vocal sections of "Heartbreaker" use a ♭III–IV–I progression.

For other examples of a I–♭III–IV chord riff, listen to Rory Gallagher's "Cradle Rock," Red Hot Chili Peppers' "Higher Ground," Black Rebel Motorcycle Club's "Spread Your Love," and Norman Greenbaum's "Spirit in the Sky."

Aerosmith

"Walk This Way" (Tyler/Perry)

From *Toys in the Attic* (CBS/Columbia, 1975)

The virtues of this classic riff, later recycled by Run-DMC in the late '80s, are not so much the choice of notes (E blues scale: E G A B♭ B) or the octave drop from E, but its rhythm (quick little bursts) and the rude flickers of damped guitar strings that punctuate it.

The most telling feature from a harmonic angle is that the verse and chorus are in C major, with a C–F change, but the riff is in E. The first solo is also in C, hence the shock of the abrupt shift back to E major at 1:23. Near the end, at 2:43, there's another switch back to E. The riff is invested with extra innuendo because the lyric introduces its appearance with the phrase "like this."

Van Halen

"Jamie's Cryin'" (E. Van Halen/A. Van Halen/Anthony/Roth)

From *Van Halen* (Warner Bros., 1978)

Van Halen's debut album is dominated by the guitar-playing of Eddie Van Halen, especially the lead dexterity and tapping of tracks like "Eruption." No surprise it was so influential. But there are mighty riffs present, too. Tons of bands had covered "You Really Got Me," but Van Halen provide a chunky take on the chord riff on their version of that Kinks classic, which was also their debut single.

"Jamie's Cryin'" features a single-note riff descending the E blues scale (using the notes E, G, A, and B♭) and a variation with a cleverly voiced E7 in which both D and B are fretted and doubled by an open string. The sonority of this chord is projected by Van Halen's amp distortion/phasing setup. Notice how the descending four notes are shifted forward one eighth note during the variation (at 0:12), and the triplet arpeggio figure at 0:33 on the phrase "so sad." This type of triplet arpeggio always puts breadth into a single-note riff. Create variation in a riff by moving some notes backward or forward a beat or portion of a beat.

The riff is the basis for the guitar solo, too, with Eddie supplying one outrageously "vocal" bend at 2:02.

Kingdom Come

"Living Out of Touch" (L. Woolf/M. Wolff)

From *Kingdom Come* (Polydor, 1988)

Kingdom Come caused a ripple in heavy rock circles with their debut in the late '80s, with its audacious attempt to recreate the sound of Led Zeppelin. "Living Out of Touch" is a half-decent hard rock number that starts with an A pentatonic minor riff structured a1+a2+a1+a3, with a3 bringing in the flattened fifth of the blues scale. Underneath, the bass moves from A to G.

The verse mostly works an Am–F change, with a well-placed four-note fill to wake up anyone in the back row. During the guitar solo, the verse's chord change is transposed to Bm–G, and later to C#m–A. Toward the end, the first riff is transposed up a tone to B.

The best part is the second riff in the coda. This uses A, B♭, B, and D from the E blues scale, with the flattened seventh D heavily weighted by repetition and ably supported by back-leaning, Bonham-esque drums. The D note occurs as an open string and held at the fifth fret on the fifth string—a touch Jimmy Page used in "Whole Lotta Love." A similar riff in the same key can be heard on the Alex Harvey Band's "Midnight Moses" (*Framed*, 1973), and in Jeff Buckley's "Last Goodbye."

Lenny Kravitz

"Are You Gonna Go My Way" (Kravitz/Ross)

From *Are You Gonna Go My Way* (Virgin, 1993)

This may not be the world's most original riff, but it certainly hit the right spot for many, including guitarists, as "Are You Gonna Go My Way" has joined the list of "must learn" riffs. There are some useful tips to gain from the arrangement here, too.

The main riff is on the E blues scale, the B♭ created by a bend from A. The riff is in two bars, with bar 2 as an answering phrase that ends with a strident fourth (DG) on the top two strings. Notice that since there isn't a G# anywhere to be heard, the implied chord is Em7, not the Hendrix chord of E7#9. When the vocal comes in, that fourth disappears from the riff (it would have obscured the words).

The first neat touch is a transposition of the riff from E minor up a minor third to G minor. The riff finds its way back via accentuated chromatic notes. The hook line is supported by a short chord riff higher up the neck using a tone shift of E to D to E, and then a minor third E to G to E. A Mixolydian chord sequence of E–D–A is used for the guitar solo.

When you have absorbed the guitar part, listen to the rhythm section. The drums and bass provide the right backing to give the riff maximum "bounce," with the bass omitting notes, for example. Another Kravitz song, "Rock and Roll Is Dead," has a riff on the A blues scale (A C D E♭ E G) and starts with a chromatic approach to the A by way of G and G#; during the guitar solo, the riff is transposed up a fourth to D.

12 **pentatonic major**

There is also a major form of the pentatonic from which you can create riffs. In A, its notes are A B C♯ E F♯. Here it is on A and E:

A pentatonic major and E pentatonic major

Notice that the first three notes are each a tone apart. This scale is the first, second, third, fourth, fifth, and sixth of the ordinary major scale. A riff based on the pentatonic major over a major chord backing won't give the same "tough" sound as the pentatonic minor. This is because none of these notes are "blue" notes; they're contained within the harmony and blend in. If you play this scale over minor chords in A minor, it sounds fairly horrible.

The pentatonic major scale is good for riffs that are bright and upbeat. Popular in '50s rock 'n' roll, it lends itself to 12/8 or triplet-type rhythms, and to an arpeggio-style riff using A–C♯–E–F♯ and up to the octave A. Like the pentatonic minor, this scale has a blues variant where the flattened third (here C) is added to the scale, giving A–B–C–C♯–E–F♯. Suede used this variant for the riff of "Elephant Man" in E (E–F♯–G–G♯–B–C♯, transposed up a tone to F♯ for the last chorus).

The archetypal major pentatonic riff is Jimmy McCracklin's "The Walk." Other related riffs include T. Rex's "Thunderwing" (in A), "Beltane Walk," and "Baby Boomerang" (both E); Dire Straits' "Walk of Life"; the Beatles' "Dig a Pony"; and Free's "Ride a Pony" (E–G–G♯–B–C♯–E), where the blues riff is transposed onto A in the verse. David Bowie's "TVC15" has a pentatonic major riff consisting of an upward run with a third hammer-on at the top, over a I–VI chord change. The first riff in Pearl Jam's "Alive" is on A pentatonic major (A B C♯ E F♯), with the note B bent a semitone to C. The intro phrase of the Sports' "Suspicious Minds" (not the Elvis song) uses the same five notes in D major (D E F♯ A B). The opening riff of Badfinger's "No Matter What" is also derived from A pentatonic major.

The Temptations

"My Girl" (Robinson/White)

From *Temptations Sing Smokey* (Gordy/Tamla, 1965)

After several years of simmering, 1964–1965 was when Motown came to the boil in the charts. One of the company's biggest early hits was this gentle love song, penned by Smokey Robinson as a pairing to "My Guy," and sung impeccably by David Ruffin, one great voice of five in the Temptations. Motown records were not often arranged around guitar riffs, and where they do occur, they have more of a supporting role than in rock. But sometimes the guitar does contribute a hook, as with the Four Tops' "Something About You," and here in "My Girl." The verse works a I–IV chord change in C (C–F), and over this the guitar plays a C pentatonic major run (C–D–E–G–A–C) and then a similar pentatonic major run on F (F–G–A–C–D–F). For the last verse, the song modulates to D major, so the figure gets pushed up a tone. The guitar is remarkably clear and bright on the first verse, but it's pulled back for the second, when the strings take over.

Jimi Hendrix

"Spanish Castle Magic" (Hendrix)

From *Axis: Bold as Love* (Track, 1967)

"Spanish Castle Magic" is a great piece of riff writing for several reasons. For a start, there aren't as many fine rock riffs on the pentatonic major as on the pentatonic minor. Hendrix wrote this in E, with the main notes being the bottom open E-string, C♯, and the E an octave above. He fills in the musical space by hitting a BE fourth with the top two open strings, with the B doubled on string three at the fourth fret to get more resonance. For the chorus, instead of coming back to the E riff, Hendrix transposes up a fourth to A, twice, before returning to the E riff. This unexpected transposition creates a sunny, uplifting emotion. The riff has another transposition, up a tone to F♯, where it's given a simplified form for the guitar solo.

This song's other riff feature is the use of fourths as inverted fifths during the verses, making it sound as though Hendrix has drastically detuned to get notes that seem so low. The first two chords of the verse are fifths, but the next two are fourths (at 0:17 and 0:26 in verse one). The choice of notes makes them seem lower than they really are. Try this fingering for a D5: 5577xx. This type of chord was a key feature of early '90s grunge.

Marmalade

"Radancer" (Nicholson)

Single A-side (London/Decca, 1972)

As well as a UK #1 with their cover of the Beatles "Ob-La-Di, Ob-La-Da," and a US Top Ten hit with "Reflections of My Life," Marmalade also had the pleasure of knowing that their single "I See the Rain" was one of Hendrix's favorite records of 1967. Their 1972 single "Radancer" sounds like an emulation of the then chart-dominating T. Rex, in particular "Telegram Sam" (a UK #1 in January that year), though the vocal delivery resembles a watered-down Beach Boys.

The riff is a two-bar figure using a 1–6–5 (A–F#–E) sequence in A major on the bass strings, the second bar offering a rhythmic variation of the first. During the verse, the riff is transposed up a fourth to D, while another figure is used when the 12-bar-derived verse reaches the obligatory E chord. Unfortunately, the song itself doesn't live up to the riff or title. But those opening 15 seconds are exquisite, with a funky rock 'n' roll guitar tone. Maybe one day someone will sample it.

T. Rex's "Ride a White Swan" has a similar pentatonic major riff on the top two strings (Ab, with a capo at fret four). Van Halen's "DOA" contains a detuned, heavier version of the "Radancer" idea. Slade's "Gudbuy T' Jane" reverses the direction of the 5–6–1 idea on an A chord.

Roxy Music

"Street Life" (Ferry)

From *Stranded* (Atco/Island, 1973)

The early Roxy Music albums are a far cry from the sophisticated sheen of their '80s output, such as *Avalon*. Odd lyrics delivered by Bryan Ferry in a distinctly un-rock, quasi-crooning style were set to weird structures and quirky parts supplied by Brian Eno and Phil Manzanera. Manzanera's guitar work was shaped by his lack of schooling in the typical blues-rock of the time—a lack he turned to creative advantage.

The riff of "Street Life" is sung through the verse. It consists of notes taken from a B♭ pentatonic major scale (B♭ C D F G), played over the chord sequence B♭–E♭–A♭–F. The initial note B♭ of the riff is held over the first three chords, and then the other notes are played over the F. Manzanera thus avoids distracting from the vocal, because the runup falls when Ferry is usually between phrases. On the fourth time around, there is an extra C note.

At 1:25, Manzanera transposes and alters this run, starting on D♭, to lead into the next verse. It's a fine example of "part-playing," where the guitar line complements the arrangement, rather than wanting the spotlight. A riff can be an accompaniment and still be a hook.

Kings of Leon

"Sex on Fire" (C. Followill/N. Followill/J. Followill/M. Followill)

From *Aha Shake Heartbreak* (Handmedown/RCA, 2004)

Kings of Leon first came to international recognition with the album *Aha Shake Heartbreak*. This is a typically earthy but inventive track. Sometimes with a riff, it's not the notes but where you play them on the guitar that matters.

This song has two riffs. The riff proper comes in the intro and verse on an E–C♯m change. It consists of an E on open string six, with the notes C♯ and B fretted on the fifth string at the 16th and 14th frets. This place on the neck on the lower strings has a distinct timbre. It is heard most clearly on the intro, before the other instruments enter. When they do, the riff is refreshed by the off-kilter nature of the rhythm and arrangement, which disguises the beat. The beat doesn't settle down until about halfway through the verse. This E6 idea with a typically sunny feel moves down to the note A and G♯ over a fretted C♯. The chorus has a very U2 feel, with a soaring vocal and an Edge-like guitar figure in E major on the top two strings, with string one open.

Deftones

"Ohms" (Moreno/Carpenter/Cunningham/Delgado/Vega)

From *Ohms* (Reprise, 2020)

The alternative-metal band Deftones have nine albums, several of them platinum sellers, to their credit, and have built a reputation and won Grammy awards for their experimental heavy rock. "Ohms" hovers between the keys of C♯ minor and its relative E major, whose respective pentatonic scales share the same notes. The opening riff is a descending pentatonic major grouped in a triplet rhythm, which covers an octave from E down to E. This riff returns at the end of the song, but in a neat twist not before a reversed version of it is heard, ascending, at 3:21.

At 0:20, a second riff comes in based on low thirds of BD♯ moving to C♯E, suggesting C♯ minor, and a repeated tone movement between F♯ and G♯. A third riff appears after a static passage on an E chord, implying A and F♯m chords. The song shows how a group of riffs can replace the notion of a chord progression. In the accompanying video, Stephen Carpenter can be seen playing an ESP nine-string guitar.

13 major scale

The major scale has been the basis for most Western music for about four centuries. It consists of seven notes arranged in a sequence of intervals: tone, tone, semitone, tone, tone, tone, semitone (whole step, whole step, half step, whole step, whole step, whole step, half step). In frets, this is 2–2–1–2–2–2–1.

Hold down any note on any string below the tenth fret (assuming a 22-fret electric guitar). Play it, then move up the string according to the 2–2–1–2–2–2–1 pattern, playing each note, to hear a major scale.

The notes for the scale of C major are C–D–E–F–G–A–B. The semitone gaps between notes three and four, and seven and eight, coincide with E–F and B–C, the two pairs that need to be a semitone apart. A start on any other note in the scale requires notes to be lowered or raised to preserve this pattern. Thus, in the scale of E major (E F♯ G♯ A B C♯ D♯), four sharps are required to get the right "gaps":

A major and
E major

Though not as popular for riffs as the pentatonics, the blues scale, or the Mixolydian mode, the major scale is vital as a fundamental musical reference. In fact, because it isn't used as much for riffs, it offers a chance to make riffs contrast with the majority of those played by rock bands. Examples include the Offspring's "Walla Walla," the intro riff to Sum 41's "Fat Lip," and the Strokes' "Barely Legal," where notes from the G major scale are played on the intro over G and C chords.

Bruce Springsteen's "Born in the USA" has a three-note keyboard motif using E, F♯, and G♯ from the scale of B major (the fourth, fifth, and sixth), which is then heard against an E chord. Marshall Crenshaw's "Whenever You're on My Mind" opens with a guitar figure that uses most of the scale of A major.

Another approach to the major scale, as used by the Smashing Pumpkins on songs like "Mayonnaise," is to harmonize the major scale in fifths and make riffs out of those fifths. This creates interesting effects such as the occurrence of fifths on the major third and seventh, instead of the blues flattened third and flattened seventh.

A major scale riff may well be easier to sing along with than other types of scale. Genesis made a four-note riff of the first four notes of G major for "Follow You, Follow Me," which became the chorus melody.

Them

"Here Comes the Night" (Berns)

From *Them* (Decca/Parrot, 1965)

Singer Van Morrison first came to fame with the band Them, lending his vocals to hits like "Baby Please Don't Go" and "Here Comes the Night." Over the opening E–A chord change, a five-note riff is played that owes something to Duane Eddy. It's pitched low on the guitar, with a "woody" tone and the notes B, E, B, C♯, and A (derived from E major). The fifth time, a variation is introduced to fit the underlying B chord that leads into the verse, with its change of rhythm. A distant relative of this riff crops up on Bruce Springsteen's "Born to Run."

The Four Tops

"I'm in a Different World" (Holland/Dozier/Holland)

From *Yesterday's Dreams* (Motown, 1968)

This Four Tops single, the last written for them by the Holland/Dozier/Holland team, features remarkable changes of key and some beautiful guitar chords. But the aspect to focus on here is the two-bar guitar riff in the bridge section at 0:37, mostly doubled by the bass, and again at 1:47 and 2:20. The scale is G♭ major with the seventh omitted, and the guitar tone is clear. The riff is supported by a I–IV–VI chord sequence in G♭ (G♭–C♭–D♭; or, if you prefer to think of it as F♯, F♯–B–C♯). The major scale is crucial to making this riff express the optimistic, joyful emotion in the lyric.

Amen Corner

"Bend Me Shape Me" (English/Weiss)

From *Around Amen Corner* (Deram, 1968)

Amen Corner were a '60s pop outfit whose songs were characterized by the feathery vocals of Andy Fairweather-Low. This bubblegum song with a hint of Motown (a US hit for the American Breed in 1967, paid homage to by Badly Drawn Boy on *The Hour of Bewilderbeast*) is driven by a superb descending riff on the intro and through most of the verse. The first four notes are E, C♯, B, and G♯, which could have come from a '50s "The Walk"–type riff. Instead, they're rounded off with an A and F♯. The only note omitted from the E major scale is D♯.

The riff fits over a chord sequence of E–B–A–F♯m. On both the E and B chords, the riff moves to the note that implies the relative minor of these chords—C♯m and G♯m are relative to E and B. The riff is carried by the piano, bass, and brass instruments to give a strong ensemble performance. At about 1:43, the riff is played by trumpets. The tip here is to write a riff that can run through a strong chord sequence.

George Harrison

"What Is Life?" (Harrison)

From *All Things Must Pass* (Apple, 1970)

It was George Harrison, of all the Beatles, who made the boldest and most successful start to a solo career following the group's break up in April 1970. He had stockpiled enough songs for a double album, with several becoming #1 singles. "What Is Life?" was the B-side of "My Sweet Lord" in the UK, but a hit in its own right in the US. It opens with what film critic Owen Gleiberman in *Entertainment Weekly* memorably described as "a sassy, jagged lightning bolt" of a riff, constructed from two overlapping four-note phrases down the E major scale, using a fuzz- and treble-boosted tone. It has some syncopation and a contrasted ending every other time, so it sounds as though it is resetting itself. The riff is arranged with the bass playing an octave below, and it returns for the chorus. The production is classic Phil Spector everything-and-the-kitchen-sink, deep and reverby, with multiple layers of instruments.

Status Quo

"Paper Plane" (Rossi/Young)

From *Piledriver* (Vertigo/A&M, 1973)

Status Quo emerged riding the coattails of psychedelia, reaching the Top 20 with the mildly lysergic "Pictures of Matchstick Men" in 1968. But, by the early '70s, they had turned into a blue-denimed, eight-armed, four-headed, hair-shaking, Telecaster-thrashing beast of deafening 12-bar boogie. In the context of a Top 20 dominated by Donny Osmond, David Cassidy, and the Sweet, Quo were a fresh breath of stale, sweaty air.

Status Quo were not really a riffs band. They didn't believe in breathing spaces, for a start. Most of their songs featured the rock 'n' roll "fifth-sixth" shuffle figure—alternating root note + fifth with root note + sixth—with precious few gaps. "Paper Plane" earns its citation here with a clever variation. The riff is a B♭ shuffle at fret six, lasting two bars. In bar 2, from the third offbeat, three eighth notes suddenly flash into view (E♭–D–C) and flow into the B♭ that starts the next bar. These notes imply the B♭ major scale. The transition between the boogie shuffle pattern and these notes is seamless—a fine bit of guitar fingering.

Queen

"Bohemian Rhapsody" (Mercury)

From *A Night at the Opera* (EMI/Elektra, 1975)

This riff was later immortalized in the movie *Wayne's World* in a sequence where an outbreak of headbanging takes place in a car, but for its first-generation audience it evokes the winter of 1975, when "Bohemian Rhapsody" took up what seemed like a permanent position at the UK #1 slot.

Sometimes with a riff, placing is everything. The riff comes after the mock-operatic middle of the track, which climaxes with a B♭ chord topped with a note (sung by Roger Taylor) that's so high it can induce altitude sickness. With a crash, the band re-enter playing a four-bar riff in E♭. The key is unusual, since the guitar is not usually given to flat keys like B♭ and E♭, where its open strings are ineffectual. This was a consequence of the song being composed by Freddie Mercury on piano. However, from a creative perspective, writing a riff in a less guitar-friendly key may result in something different, or make unusual use of open strings.

Anyone who's played the riff on guitar finds that it doesn't sit comfortably under the fingers. It's also unusual because it's based on the major scale and lacks the flattened seventh so often used in rock. The first bar drops from E♭ to G (an idea familiar to bass players) and then ascends the E♭ major scale (only the F note is missing). Bar 2 has a variant that stops halfway up on the fifth, B♭. Bar 3 repeats bar 1. Bar 4 transposes the idea of bar 2 onto F major.

The Jam

"Going Underground" (Weller)

Single A-side (Polydor, 1980)

The Jam were not a band for riffs. Because of his early fixation with the Who and Pete Townshend, Paul Weller's approach was always rhythmic and chord-based— and, after all, who feels like playing low-string, heavy riffs on a Rickenbacker? Like the Edge, though for different reasons, Weller rejected the blues/rock vocabulary of the '70s guitar hero. It took until the mid-'90s before his solo work drew selectively on British rock of the 1968–1973 era. Yet, scattered through the Jam's output there are some memorable guitar figures that count as riffs.

"Going Underground" starts with a multitracked riff that initially works the old rock 'n' roll D5–D6 idea. The twist is that the riff culminates with a quick D–C♯–B phrase—notes taken from the D major scale—when we might have expected a flattened seventh (C natural). This riff is the first part of the verse, before a shift to B major for the rest. Alternation of keys (further developed by a lift to C♯ major for the guitar solo and final chorus) is an important structural feature of the song.

"It's Too Bad" (from *All Mod Cons*) is another example of a major scale–based riff, on the chords G, C, and D. Compare this with Supergrass's "Tonight" or Fountains of Wayne's "Radiation Vibe," where rock 'n' roll shuffle figures use the major seventh instead of the blues flattened seventh.

14 mixolydian

After the major scale and the minor and major pentatonics, we come to a group of scales known as modes. There are seven main modes, which date from ancient Greece and have always been present in Western music.

Modes are simply scales that use a different pattern of intervals to the major scale (the Ionian mode is equivalent to our major scale, so that's already been covered). To get the interval pattern for the main modes, play from any "natural" note (i.e., any white key on the piano—C, D, E, F, G, A, or B) to its octave using no sharps or flats. This same interval pattern can, with the addition of the right sharps and flats, be generated from any initial pitch.

Before the invention or discovery of the major/minor tonal system, where a given scale leads not only to melodic ideas but to a set of related chords, modes were primarily melodic devices. They were not treated as though they could generate harmony. One of the challenges of using modes as if they were a substitute set of keys or tonalities lies in this. Modes are often unstable. Given the chance, a listener brought up with the major/minor system will tend to hear modal harmony as the nearest equivalent key.

A Mixolydian chord progression easily dissolves into sounding like the previous major key on the circle of fifths, because its notes are the same as that key's scale. An example would be C Mixolydian, whose notes are C D E F G A B♭, which is the same as F major (F G A B♭ C D E). For this reason, modal riffs—especially the Phrygian, Lydian, and Locrian—won't be pure examples, but they bring in other notes when their riffs become more than single-note riffs.

Think of the Mixolydian as being a variation on the major scale, because it is the same except for the seventh note, flattened by a semitone. Since rock music has flattened sevenths everywhere, the influence of the Mixolydian mode is common. Rock singers habitually sing melodies with the seventh note of the

A Mixolydian and E Mixolydian

major scale flattened, and it's also a common note alteration in riffs and lead guitar. To introduce them into your playing, take any major scale fretboard pattern, find the seventh note, and move it back a fret (or semitone). This flattened seventh gives a Mixolydian riff a "harder" quality than the straight major scale riff, but the presence of the rest of the major scale makes for a more sophisticated sound than the pentatonic. So, for stepwise movement in a rock riff, use the Mixolydian.

For a funky E Mixolydian riff, try Lenny Kravitz's "Always on the Run," where there are plenty of blues thirds added as well (in single notes and in the G chord on the chorus), or Ian Dury and the Blockheads' "Sex & Drugs & Rock & Roll." Ashton, Gardner, and Dyke's "Resurrection Shuffle" has piano and brass playing the G riff, which ascends G–Bb–B–D–E–F–G: the Mixolydian with both minor and major third.

In David Bowie's "Panic in Detroit," the verse chord change of D–E is threaded by a descending D Mixolydian scale that stops on E; that note is treated as the root of an E major chord, rather than the expected E minor. Led Zeppelin's "Custard Pie" takes a classic rock 'n' roll shuffle figure in A and extends it to the octave, with a partial Mixolydian run of E–F#–G–A over A. Smokey Robinson and the Miracles' "Tears of a Clown" is driven by a Mixolydian bass line in Db, using all the notes of the scale.

Primal Scream's "Rocks" and "Jailbird," Green Day's "Warning," and Ike and Tina Turner's "Nutbush City Limits" all have Mixolydian riffs. AC/DC's "Thunderstruck" opens with B major and E minor arpeggios, and then a fast sequence of notes on the B string drawn from the B Mixolydian scale. Here, the scale functions as a riff partly through the repetition of it. The Beatles' "Birthday" uses the A Mixolydian in a classic '50s rock 'n' roll approach, transposing the riff through the 12-bar pattern.

Radiohead's "Morning Mr. Magpie" gives the Mixolydian riff a more experimental feel, with the notes G–Bb–A (covering a minor third) being repeated in short durations over a C bass. This implies a C7 chord in the key of C, which is the correct seventh for C Mixolydian. (In traditional harmony, pre-blues, C7 is a chord in the key of F, not C.)

The Animals

"We've Gotta Get Out of This Place" (Mann/Weil)

From *Animal Tracks* (MGM, 1965)

The Animals' most famous guitar moment is obviously "House of the Rising Sun," but that is an arpeggio accompaniment and lacks the rhythmic definition that turns a chord sequence into a riff. Instead, take "We've Gotta Get Out of This Place," propelled by a C Mixolydian bass riff (C–D–E–F–G–A–B♭) in which only the D isn't used.

The riff carries much of the first verse, along with only a cymbal and the voice. Other instruments enter, but the bass keeps going all the way to the first chorus at 1:11, where the chord changes to F. Notice also the second riff that comes in as a link to verse two, after chorus one, which goes 1–♭7–4–5 twice. The lesson of the arrangement is: keep a riff going with different things happening on top to create tension.

The Animals' bass player, Chas Chandler, went on to manage a guitarist who had quite a flair for riffs—see under "Hendrix, Jimi."

The Rolling Stones

"(I Can't Get No) Satisfaction" (Richards/Jagger)

From *Out of Our Heads* (Decca/London, 1965)

The riff for "Satisfaction" came to Keith Richards in the middle of the night—he managed to get it down before falling asleep again. Originally conceived as a Stax-type horn line, then played on guitar over a stomping four-to-the-bar drumbeat with sardonic flickers of tambourine, it was the perfect accompaniment for one of the '60s' seminal tales of teenage frustration.

The riff consists of only three notes—B, C♯, and D: the fifth, sixth, and flattened seventh of E major. Its innovation lies in starting on an E chord with a B rather than the root E. The sound of the riff is defined by the supporting chords: D major under the D, A under the C♯. The guitar line also stuck out at the time because of its Gibson Maestro fuzz tone. A similar figure with a cleaner guitar sound can be heard on the Four Tops' "Something About You" and Buffalo Springfield's "Mr. Soul."

The Beatles

"Taxman" (Harrison)

From *Revolver* (Parlophone/Capitol, 1965)

"Taxman" has a bass figure consisting of the notes 1–8–4–5–♭7–8 in D major (D–D–G–A–C–D). During the verse, this figure is transposed to the chords of C and G. The guitar doesn't double the riff (as it would with such a riff in later heavy rock) but plays pungent slashing chords. In the absence of a third from the riff—which would determine if the riff is in D pentatonic minor or D Mixolydian–it's these guitar chords, clearly major, that make us hear the riff as Mixolydian.

This riff was later subject to an homage by the Jam, when they adapted it for "Start," and a similar one occurs in Jeff Beck's "Rock My Plimsole," though there it has an additional note—the flattened fifth inserted between fourth and fifth—and is slower. Variations on this Mixolydian pattern, with the octave leap and no open strings, lend themselves to 12-bar blues because they are so easily transposed around the fretboard.

The Beatles

"Paperback Writer" (Lennon/McCartney)

Single A-side (Parlophone/Capitol, 1966)

"Paperback Writer" has one of the Beatles' heaviest intros, thanks to the opening riff, marking a significant change away from the beat-pop of their early hits. The song itself is little more than a G–C change supporting a clever lyric. The riff is on the chord of G7, using notes 1–4–5–8–5–♭7 (G–C–D–G–D–F), with several hammer-ons.

After the complex vocal counterpoint, the riff kicks in with maximum dynamic contrast, even without bass. Its power is evident despite the original eccentric '60s mix, which squashes it over to the left of the stereo image. The riff is comparable to the earlier "I Feel Fine," though that had a noticeably cleaner guitar tone. As with "Taxman," the rhythm guitar chords color the riff as Mixolydian, not pentatonic, despite the lack of a third in the riff.

The Rolling Stones

"Jumpin' Jack Flash" (Richards/Jagger)

Single A-side (Decca/London, 1968)

Here, the Rolling Stones develop their mature riff style. "Jumpin' Jack Flash" starts with an emphatically struck B major chord and then a passage in single notes using 4–5–♭7 of the scale (E–F♯–A) played three times.

The effect of the riff lies in the harmonic "drag" caused by the thrice-repeated emphasis on the flattened seventh, which is like a sulky child who has to be dragged back to the tonic B major chord. Jagger's drawling vocal only strengthens the impression.

The remainder of the song uses E, D, A, and B—in B major, chords I, ♭III, IV, and ♭VII—so the Mixolydian influence is also felt at the level of the chords.

Deep Purple

"Speed King" (Blackmore/Gillan/Glover/Lord/Paice)

From *Deep Purple in Rock* (Warner Bros./Harvest, 1970)

The verse here is built on a F–G–C–B♭ chord sequence (♭VII–I–IV–III), but the interesting moment comes on the chorus, where there's a riff using the notes C–B♭, alternating several times, then dropping from the C down to the E (not E♭, the blues third), which implies the major scale, as B♭ implies the Mixolydian. As the riff ascends, we hear E–F–F♯–G, with the flattened fifth F♯ inserted as a chromatic passing note.

The drop to the E from C (a sixth) makes the E sound lower than it actually is. This is a well-known trick among bass players, but one that guitarists have not taken as much advantage of as they might in constructing riffs. Hendrix does the same drop in "Hey Joe," toward the end of the song, when he brings in a single-note run over the chords C–G–D–A–E. For a really funky riff, chain together several of these sixth drops in a rising phrase, but be mindful of where the accents fall.

Queen

"Now I'm Here" (May)

From *Sheer Heart Attack* (Elektra/EMI, 1974)

Inspired by guitarist Brian May's reaction to his band's first tour of the US, "Now I'm Here" is one of the best hard rock tracks Queen ever recorded, and it pays tribute to Chuck Berry with its "go, go, little Queenie" reference on the coda. It starts with muted fifths by May (possibly three guitars, left, center, and right) and then a descending sequence from D to C to B, similar to that in Cream's "Badge."

After Mercury's echoed vocal phrases, the song erupts on a Who-like Asus4–A–Bsus4–B chordal roar, and then crashes into a "Black Dog"–like convoluted four-bar riff. This riff is unusual because of its length—it actually takes four bars to play it, as opposed to the standard practice of dividing the four bars into two answering phrases, or smaller single-bar units. May takes the notes from E Mixolydian but adds G and B♭ as passing notes, giving a blues feel. In addition, some of the riff's notes are harmonized as fifths. When the riff appears at the coda, it's cleverly altered to lead into the Mixolydian B–E–A chord changes.

For a hard rock song, "Now I'm Here" has plenty of musical ideas to match its big arrangement. It makes much use of transposition—taking phrases and moving them up in pitch. The verse daisy-chains a sequence of V–I cadences, with a chord sequence of G–C–A–D–B–E–C♯–F♯.

Siouxsie and the Banshees

"Fireworks" (Ballion/Clarke/McGeoch/Severin)

Single A-side (Polydor, 1982)

This single dates from a period when the Banshees were truly flowering from their crude punk origins into a band that delivered a dark and gothic psychedelia with brutal force. The track opens with the sound of a string section tuning up. Called to attention by the tap of a conductor's baton, the strings launch into a staccato scale riff on the notes A–G♯–F♯–G♯–G♯–F♯–G♯, played three times, with A–G♯–A–B as a fourth completing phrase. Initially, as there is no chord behind this, it seems the keynote is A, but when the band thumps in, it does so on an E chord, making the riff 4–3–2–3 on the scale of E major.

After two bars, the bass moves down to D, which does two things: it implies E Mixolydian and generates a tense tritone between D and G♯. When the vocal verse starts, the music goes to an Am–Dm change, revealing that the key is actually A minor, and the riff is transposed onto the notes D–C–B–C.

"Fireworks" demonstrates that a riff sometimes benefits from being voiced by a different instrument than the guitar, and that music involves active listening, where in subtle ways we revise our understanding of what we hear from bar to bar.

Foo Fighters

"Times Like These" (Grohl/Hawkins/Mendell/Shiflett)

From *One by One* (Roswell/RCA, 2002)

This riff shows a number of features typical of riffs composed after around 1990. It begins with the rhythmic playing of a single unusual chord voicing: x50505, which is DDCBA. This could be interpreted as a Dm7add13, except it doesn't have the third (F), nor the F♯ that would identify it as a major. The voicing has a unison (DD), a semitone (CB), and two minor seventh intervals: D to C and B up to A. Then a second riff comes in which is D Mixolydian, where you hear the flattened seventh (C) in close proximity to the major third (F♯). (Compare this choice of notes with the riff on John Kongos' "He's Gonna Step on You Again.") This is played in a bar of 7/4, or alternating bars of 4/4 and 3/4. This second riff sounds different each of the three times it is played because the bass line descends D–C–B, implying a different harmonization.

Wolfmother

"Joker and the Thief" (Wolfmother)

From *Wolfmother* (Interscope, 2006)

"Joker and the Thief" is something of an homage to bands like Deep Purple, Atomic Rooster, and Argent. The arpeggiated intro gives this track something of a '70s prog-rock sound.

The Mixolydian flavor comes through at several points. The intro is played over a series of chords, D–C–D–C–F–G, which make it sound different each time. In the verse, riff 2 is a I–♭VII in D5–C5 on the guitar in a punchy style. After the second chorus, there's a descending riff played on D and C on a Mixolydian scale.

Greta Van Fleet

"Highway Tune" (Daniel Wagner/Jacob Kiszka/Joshua Kiszka/Samuel Kiszka)

From *Greta Van Fleet* (Republic Records, 2017)

Greta Van Fleet are the most recent band in rock history to arouse comparisons with Led Zeppelin, in a controversy reminiscent of the one ignited by Kingdom Come's first album in 1988, although Greta's initial sound was less coiffured than that of their '80s predecessors, with a rawer feel.

"Highway Tune" is based on E, A, and B chords, and has a riff accessible enough to be heard in music instrument stores. It can broadly be described as Mixolydian (E–F♯–G♯–A–B–C♯–D), but the term "Mixolydian blues" might be more accurate, since the riff plays off the G♯ against a blues flattened third (E F♯ G G♯ A B C♯ D). However, the Mixolydian blues scale is usually defined as a nine-note scale with a flattened fifth (in E, a B♭).

This riff is enlivened by semitone string bends and a descending figure using the A–G♯–G on the sixth and the open D string. Incorporating such bends was a feature of some Jimmy Page riffs, such as "The Rover." The "Highway Tunes" riff also has a pentatonic minor blues turnaround phrase across the top.

15 aeolian/natural minor

The most common minor scale for soloing in popular music is the natural minor or Aeolian mode. In A minor, this would be A B C D E F G:

A Aeolian and E Aeolian

In A, no sharps or flats are needed to match the interval pattern, which is 2–1–2–2–1–2–2. The Aeolian mode in A differs from A pentatonic minor in adding two notes: B and F, the second and sixth of the mode. These notes can be very expressive, and they bring a new dimension to any pentatonic minor ideas. Listen to Green Day's "Revolution Radio," which emphases the two notes on the top two strings over an Am–F chord change in a way that momentarily triggers the dissonant tritone between F and B. The Aeolian sixth (F against an Am chord) can be heard in the opening riff of Europe's "Days of Rock 'n' Roll." The presence of either of these notes reveals a riff is in the Aeolian mode rather than merely pentatonic minor.

An example drawing on the scale of E natural minor is the White Stripes' "Seven Nation Army," with its bass note riff of E–G–E–D–C–B. These notes are turned into major chords by the guitar part. Weezer's "Hash Pipe" makes a riff from pounding the first three notes of A natural minor, and later turns them into fifths.

Gorillaz's "Feel Good Inc." has a four-bar bass riff in the verse on a natural minor scale that goes up and down an octave and ends with a leap. Its first phrase is powerfully answered by its second. This riff has a '70s funk feel but is rapped over. It implies the chord sequence E♭m–B♭m–A♭m–E♭m, like an updated Curtis Mayfield. The vocal melody over the ethereal chords partly matches the riff.

Bloc Party's "Hunting for Witches" uses F♯ natural minor for the opening, almost arpeggio riff, which is harmonized in octaves, putting a new slant on a I–VI–VII–I–IV–V minor chord sequence. Insomnium's "Weather the Storm" creates a fast scale-riff on the top string using pull-offs in D natural minor.

The natural minor can be given a twist if the flattened fifth is included, as happens in the second riff following the second chorus of Accept's "Undertaker," where the note contributes to the sinister feeling.

Another type of minor scale—the harmonic minor—can generate more exotic-sounding riffs. This involves one note change from the natural minor—the seventh note is raised a semitone to G♯, leaving a large one-and-a-half-tone jump between notes six and seven (F–G♯), giving the scale an unusual flavor.

A harmonic minor and E harmonic minor

The harmonic minor is heard in the riffs of Queen's "Death on Two Legs" (and listen for the tritone on the "false" intro) and "Flick of the Wrist" (the notes B, C, D♯, E, and F♯, taken from the E harmonic minor scale of E F♯ G A B C D♯ E); and Robert Plant's "Wreckless Love," which takes E–F–G♯–A (the last four notes of an A harmonic minor) and plays them over an A5–G5 tone riff.

COMPARING SCALES							
Minor scale	1	2	3	4	5	6	7
E pentatonic minor	E		G	A	B		D
E natural minor	E	F♯	G	A	B	C	D
E harmonic minor	E	F♯	G	A	B	C	D♯

There is a "classical" feel to some of the British band Muse's songs because of guitarist Matthew Bellamy's fondness for the harmonic minor: E harmonic minor on "Sunburn" and "New Born," F♯ harmonic minor in "Muscle Museum" (an F, or strictly speaking E♯, is clearly heard at 1:54–2:00), and D harmonic minor in the solo of "Micro Cuts" (2:42–3:06) and in "Darkshines." Muse's chord sequences often imply the harmonic minor by having the major chord V in the minor key. "Feeling Good," for example, is Gm–Gm/F–E♭–Dsus4–D, implying G harmonic minor.

Wishbone Ash

"The King Will Come" (M. Turner/D .Turner/Powell/Upton)

From *Argus* (MCA/Decca, 1972)

Wishbone Ash were a staple of the UK rock circuit in the early '70s, enjoying reasonable album sales while never moving into the top league. For a rock band, their albums have a very English character, and their lyrics avoided aping the standard American rock themes. Although this might be a weakness for those who like their rock 'n' roll "red in tooth and claw," it was part of their particular charm. Before Thin Lizzy and Queen, Wishbone Ash pioneered the harmony lead guitar approach, where improvisational solos would alternate with carefully arranged stretches of melodic playing.

First heard at 1:04, after the slow crescendo of the intro, the double-tracked riff of "The King Will Come" is intriguing because it leaps an octave plus a minor sixth from a D on the fifth fret of the A-string to a clipped B♭ on the sixth fret of the top E. The underlying scale is D natural minor (D E F G A B♭ C). Each time this low D receives a marked and expressive vibrato.

After the verse ends, there is another riff on the same scale answered by high fourths, then a descending C–G/B arpeggio. During the first guitar solo, the rhythm guitar and bass play a chordal version of the first riff. The track is full of pleasing guitar ideas, such as the almost John Renbourn–like snap 'n' roll folk guitar lick from 4:25.

Two other tracks on *Argus* are worth attention for their riffs: "Blowin' Free," with its top-string triads over a D pedal note; and "Throw Down the Sword," with its riff harmonized in sixths.

Paul Kantner, Grace Slick, David Freiburg

"Flowers in the Night" (Kantner/Slick)

From *Baron Von Tollbooth and the Chrome Nun* (Grunt/RCA, 1973)

In the '70s, the two leading lights of Jefferson Airplane, Paul Kantner and Grace Slick, made several spin-off albums, of which this was the second. It's a fine set of melodic songs with many Airplane trademarks and a dense production that ensures hours of pleasure discovering instrumental parts you previously hadn't noticed. This album dates from an era when musicians jammed lead guitar all through a track if they wished.

Solo drums kick off "Flowers in the Night," and then, on the left, in comes a wonderful guitar riff that takes four bars to unfold its three phrases. The first phrase is two bars long; it starts on the bottom E and uses the E blues scale but ends with G–F♯–G. The second phrase is a rapid D major arpeggio (using the notes D, F♯, and A). The third is a descending phrase starting on string one and ending with a bluesy A–B slide on string three.

The full riff spans just over two octaves (over the chords Em, G, D, and Em), has superb upward motion, is played through much of the verse, and does slightly unexpected things en route. The underlying scale is E natural minor/E Aeolian (E F♯ G A B C D).

As a historical comparison, this riff should be compared to Billy Talent's "Devil in a Midnight Mass" from 2006 (drop D, D Aeolian) to show how such riffs have got much faster, and also with a more expansive combination of notes.

The Police

"Walking on the Moon" (Sting)

From *Reggatta de Blanc* (A&M, 1979)

And now, a natural minor riff played on bass. Few chart singles have used space as imaginatively in an arrangement as "Walking on the Moon." Alone in the reverb, with Copeland's rattling percussion hitting all kinds of accents unknown to rock 'n' roll, Sting's bass plays the simplest of two-bar riffs, taking notes from D natural minor (C–C–D, F–E–C). In between the two phrases of the riff, the guitar sends a Dm7add11 chord floating into the distance (its sustain enhanced by a short delay and chorus).

This soundscape was the perfect aural evocation of a metaphor: white-suited men slowly bouncing over moondust, weightless against black; a young man intoxicated by love, walking back from his girlfriend's house, having presumably missed the last bus. Proof that a riff doesn't have to be chained to the usual rock 'n' roll imagery.

Papa Roach

"Last Resort" (Shaddix/Esperance)

From *Infest* (Dreamworks, 2000)

Though it is in drop D, much of "Last Resort" is based on a descending figure of E5–D5–C5–B5 (I–VII–VI–V) in E minor. Notice how the fifths are played with clear beats between them. Often, it is these spaces that make all the difference to the punch of a riff. During the verses, there is a rapid 16th-note riff based on the scale of E natural minor, which has precedents in Whitesnake's "Still of the Night" and Iron Maiden's "The Number of the Beast."

"Last Resort" also includes a chord voicing that has become more popular since the '90s: the inverted fifth. This is a power chord with the fifth note doubled at the octave below. Thus, in this song, E5 (EB) becomes (BEB), which is 979xxx in drop D.

System of a Down

"Toxicity" (Tankian/Malakian/Odadjian)

From *Toxicity* (Sony, 2001)

The main riff here is in a detuned form based on C5–A♭5–G5, with a fast set of five notes taken from the C–D–E♭ notes of a C natural minor scale. This rapid run of notes, almost in a machine-gun effect, is repeated and extended at the end of the chorus. Its speed contrasts with the bar allotted to the A♭5–G5 change. The verses use a higher-pitched arpeggio Cm–E♭ change, staying away from the low bass frequency of the main riff.

After the second chorus, the break has first a C–D–E♭ riff four times—the second the same doubled an octave lower, and then with a change of rhythm and a distinctive and very grungy bend D–E♭. After another verse and chorus, this variation of the riff returns, with the vocal singing the same pitches but two octaves higher. It's a distinctively '90s-sounding riff based on a minor scale, detuned, with rapid percussive picking.

Arctic Monkeys

"Do I Wanna Know?" (Alex Turner)

From *AM* (Domino Recording Co., 2013)

Sometimes a scale-based riff can also be a vocal melody. This is easier with the seven-note scales that lend themselves to tunes, namely the major and natural minor. A case in point is the Arctic Monkeys' "Do I Wanna Know?," the second single from their fifth album, which has a distinctive four-bar G Aeolian riff that has effective pauses between the phrases.

The riff is played over Gm, E♭, and Cm chords (I, VI, and IV for G natural minor), and these chords, along with the riff, are reworked at the end of the verse. The riff gains more presence as the track proceeds, partly in the traditional method of guitars doubling at the octave, but also because, as the melody, it becomes almost an anthemic chant, with vocals also doubling at the octave. Put bass guitar in the sonic picture too and the riff ends up covering a wide spectrum.

Europe

"War of Kings" (Tempest/Levén/Cobb)

From *War of Kings* (UDR, 2015)

Europe first came to prominence as something of a pop/metal crossover, with hits such as "The Final Countdown" and "Superstition." In later years, they have moved to a heavier style. This song, from their tenth album, is a good example of an economical heavy rock, reminiscent of Deep Purple; it keeps a strong grip on the priorities of a more commercial songwriting style for a rock audience.

The first riff uses the notes E, G, A, B♭, and C across two bars with two accents on the final beat—always a good thing to include. This is taken from E natural minor, with the flattened fifth added. The harmony makes the E minor key unambiguous.

The song has a number of effective arrangement details. After four riffs in the verse, high triads of D, Em, and F♯m are supported by a quasi-martial beat, the flanged guitar sound making it sound like Siouxsie and the Banshees. The chorus uses thirds and fifths as contrasted fills. Sound effects on the bridge lead to a guitar solo before the chorus returns. The E natural minor tonality is strong here, while the first strong chord in the chorus is delayed a couple of beats.

16 dorian

Like the Aeolian, the Dorian is another minor mode. The A Dorian scale is A B C D E F♯ G. The difference between it and A natural minor is that the sixth note is sharpened. This gives the Dorian a more "angular," tense quality:

A Dorian and

E Dorian

The sharpened sixth is not quite as "depressed" as the sixth found on the natural minor scale. One analogy might be that the Aeolian mode represents a group of emotions like regret, sadness, and melancholy, which are passive and introverted, whereas the Dorian makes them more active and extrovert. It's worth noticing that if the Dorian mode is played in fifths (likely in a rock riff), C♯ is introduced above the F♯, the sixth of the scale:

This C♯ temporarily undermines the sense of A Dorian as a minor mode in which the third note should be C. Conversely, if you harmonize the Aeolian mode in fifths, a Dorian note will appear as a fifth above the second note of the scale. A Aeolian is A B C D E F G. A fifth on B needs F♯. A riff with this effect can be heard in Guns N' Roses' "The Garden," where fifths are played on C♯, E, D♯, and B.

A Dorian and E Dorian (fifths)

The main exponent of the Dorian mode in rock has probably been Carlos Santana, as tracks like "Oye Como Va" show. Jimmy Page's guitar solo on the live version of Led Zeppelin's "No Quarter" has a strong Dorian flavor (as does his live solo on the *BBC Sessions* "Immigrant Song"). The riff in Wings' James Bond song "Live and Let Die" (later covered by Guns N' Roses) is constructed from a G Dorian scale in a1+a2 form.

Black Sabbath's "Sleeping Village" starts with one of those acoustic arpeggio minor add9 chords that Metallica are fond of, before a main riff on A pentatonic major comes in, followed by a Dorian A riff coming down A–G–F♯–D–E (reminiscent of a phrase in the theme to the '60s TV series *The Prisoner*). There's also a hint of the Dorian in the Sabs' "Looking for Today." The Smashing Pumpkins' "Quiet" has a Dorian flavor, with the E Dorian scale (E F♯ G A B C♯ D) harmonized in fifths, though the G♯ in C♯5 often cancels out the minor third (E–G) of the Dorian scale proper. Bon Jovi's "Homeward Bound Train" is in E Dorian.

The Who

"5:15" (Townshend)

From *Quadrophenia* (Track/MCA, 1973)

Today's puzzle: when is a Dorian riff not a Dorian riff? The riff in "5:15" (the tale of Jimmy the Mod's train ride to Brighton) illustrates how interpreting the scale a riff draws on is not always straightforward. "5:15" has a superb single-note riff that comes crashing in after the piano introduction. The first phrase has G–B♭–C; the second has a descending run of G–F–E–C–D. Put these together and it seems to be G Dorian (G A B♭ C D E F), from which only the note A is absent. However, the crucial determinant that influences how we hear this is the crashing G chords in the backing and the clear signaling of G major when the melody starts.

This riff is not heard as G Dorian because it is not supported by an unambiguous G minor. Instead, we hear the riff as G Mixolydian with a blues flattened third (B♭). The lesson is that for a modal riff to be heard as such, it must be supported by a harmony that won't undermine it.

Pink Floyd

"Shine On You Crazy Diamond" (Gilmour/Waters/Wright)

From *Wish You Were Here* (Columbia/Harvest, 1975)

The guitar phrase in "Shine On You Crazy Diamond" doesn't have the rhythmic drive typical of most riffs, but it is so well known, and such a perfect expression of the angular Dorian mode, that I had to include it.

This is the riff as color gesture. It consists of a four-note arpeggio, B♭–F–G–E, which implies a Gm7 chord. If the scale were G natural minor, the sixth note would be E♭; G Dorian has an E. Dave Gilmour's stroke of inspiration was to voice this riff in such a way that two of the guitar's open strings ring against each other (with the help of echo).

On the guitar, this idea is very key-specific. In a different key, it would not be so effective because the open strings would be missing. And, sure enough, when the rest of the band come in, they do so on a C chord, not C minor, as would be the case in G Aeolian—the Dorian chord IV is always major.

Thin Lizzy

"Don't Believe a Word" (Lynott)

From *Johnny the Fox* (Vertigo/Mercury, 1976)

Both melodically and chord-wise, modes tend not to occur in rock in a "pure" form where tracks stay absolutely within the mode. It's more usual to have the modes acting as a flavor. "Don't Believe a Word" opens with a Dorian riff in A, with the lower guitar moving down from A to G to F♯ while the upper moves A–G–A. The upper guitar then comes down in thirds with the lower, so the riff develops as it repeats.

Interestingly, the rest of the song features D minor chords, which contain F natural, so it isn't consistently Dorian. Brian Robertson's lead guitar solo in "Don't Believe a Word" is mostly A pentatonic minor, but it does have one striking chromatic phrase at 1:09–1:12, where an F♯ can be heard.

If you write an A Aeolian riff, try sharpening the F's and see if it sounds better. If you are writing a chordal riff, the Dorian offers some interesting possibilities. Chord IV in A natural minor would be D minor, but in the Dorian mode it could be D major, D7, or D9.

Def Leppard

"Pour Some Sugar on Me" (Clark/Collen/Elliott/Lange/Savage)

From *Hysteria* (Mercury/Bludgeon Riffola/Vertigo, 1987)

After the solo vocal intro, the first riff comes in on a C♯ Dorian idea over four bars structured a1+a2+a1+a3. The a1 phrase only uses C♯, B, and G♯, but the a2 steps sideways onto A♯—the raised sixth of the Dorian scale. Notice that these notes also belong to the C♯ Mixolydian, but the flattened third in the vocal melody pushes the song toward the minor at this point.

Halfway through the verse, at 0:33, a second riff enters, which is C♯ and A♯, this time with a definite major feel (compare it with the "Radancer" riff). This second riff supports the vocal for the rest of the verse.

The chorus itself is a I–IV–V riff in E. This E chord sounds lower than it actually is because of the use of C♯ as the tonal center for the verse. (Def Leppard are playing at concert pitch here, unlike many rock bands who regularly detune a semitone—see section 4 for more on tuning.)

Def Leppard

"Gods of War" (Clark/Collen/Elliott/Lange/Savage)

From *Hysteria* (Mercury/Bludgeon Riffola/Vertigo, 1987)

Like several other tracks on *Hysteria*, "Gods of War" makes clever use of C♯ as a tonal center. C♯ has never been a popular key for guitarists (the standard chords in C♯ major are barre chords, so there are no easy "open" chords), but it does have the effect of emphasizing the resonance of chords like E (a blues ♭III) and A (a ♭VI) and making them sound meatier than usual. This C♯ is all the more striking because the effects-heavy intro implies a D.

"Gods of War" has no less than three riffs of interest. The first is an angular ascending pattern that uses an octave leap from C♯, followed by a leap from G♯ to F♯ a seventh higher. It takes four forms: a1 ends on a B; a2 ends on E; a3 ends on A; a4 uses a different group of notes to finish. When this riff is partially played at the 4:00 mark, there is an effective touch when the last note of a1 is subject to tremolo-arm "gargling" as it feeds back.

Riff 2 is an E major riff with an almost folky repeated hammer-on/pull-off onto the open B string. On the second and fourth phrases, it ends on a D instead of D♯, implying a blues E.

The third riff comes at the end, under the sampled voices of UK prime minister Margaret Thatcher and US president Ronald Reagan. A distant relative of the coda riff on the Beatles' "I Want You (She's So Heavy)," it is a sequence of arpeggios starting on A minor. Interest is added by several of the chords being inversions and oddly accented. The riff is three bars of 4/4, though it might deceive some into thinking it was in a strange time signature.

Living Colour

"Cult of Personality" (Reid/Glover/Calhoun/Skillings)

From *Vivid* (Epic, 1988)

There was always more musical intelligence in Living Colour than in most comparable bands from the '80s—they had a way of throwing in the odd accent or beat here and there to make you take notice. *Vivid* is an effective splicing of heavy rock and funk—an approach that requires much technique and shows there's nothing like a touch of soul to make hard rock groove a little.

"Cult of Personality" starts with a fine G Dorian riff from guitarist Vernon Reid that serves as the verse, with answering fifths on either B♭5–F5 or B♭5–C5, and a startling overlaid G5add9 chord every now and again. The riff is subject to an excellent extension when it's turned into a longer scale figure. The bridge features similar inversions (as found in the album's brilliant riff song, "Desperate People"). Listen also for the Chuck Berry thirds in the solo as the track nears the four-minute mark.

Metallica

"The Day That Never Comes" (Hetfield/Hammett/Trujillo/Ulrich)

From *Death Magnetic* (Warner Bros., 2008)

This track is a near eight-minute epic with four distinct riffs. To begin, high arpeggiated Am chords lead to an Am–G–Em–C reminiscent of the instrumental "Classical Gas." The first chorus turns this progression into a riff by linking the chords with single notes from the scale of A Dorian minor (A B C D E F♯ G) and turning Em to E5 and the C chord to C/G.

On the middle section, a new riff appears based on a blues minor third, E–G over an E pedal. It has four phrases, the fourth sliding fifths from B5–B♭5. This riff is transposed up a tone to F♯ for a single time. The third riff is a very fast picking of E with a brief F note and a high E♭. This gives way to a twin-lead passage and the fourth riff near the end, in fifths, starting on a B5.

17 phrygian

The other mode that has an affinity with the natural minor is the Phrygian, which in A is A B♭ C D E F G. Notes 1, 3, and 5 make an A minor chord, as is the case with the Aeolian and Dorian's key triad, but the second note of the scale is lowered, so it is only a semitone away from the keynote. It shares this feature with the Locrian, with which it can be confused, especially if a song features Phrygian riffs plus riffs from the minor blues scale on the same keynote. Think of the Phrygian as the natural minor with a flattened second.

In flamenco music, the Phrygian is associated with a distinctly Spanish sound, but this evaporates in other genres—a cautionary tale for anyone who wants to overdetermine what any given scale might sound like in the abstract. Of all possible pitches, the Phrygian is best suited to E in standard tuning (E F G A B C D), because this enables the player to make full use of the open strings. The open strings and first-position note layout give the guitar a natural leaning toward E Phrygian.

A Phrygian and
E Phrygian

Judas Priest's "Metal Meltdown," the Linkin Park tracks "A Place for My Head" and "Papercut," and Limp Bizkit's "Stalemate" all suggest this mode. It's a popular mode in rap, too, as the synth riff in N.E.R.D.'s "Rock Star (Jason Nevins Remix Edit)" shows with its notes E–F–G.

As guitar tunings drop from standard to a tone or even two tones down, the flat second of the Phrygian sounds evermore lobotomized and sinister. A good example would be Machine Head's "Halo."

> **Siouxsie and the Banshees**
>
> **"Paradise Place"** (Ballion/Severin)
>
> From *Kaleidoscope* (Wonderland/Polydor, 1980)

As a rock band who never thought of themselves as such, Siouxsie and the Banshees predictably came up with riffs that were generally unorthodox. No blues pentatonics for them. The little-known "Paradise Place," from *Kaleidoscope* and the live double album *Nocturne*, achieved a far more intense performance onstage.

"Paradise Place" is in the style of so-called "raga-rock" (see the entry for R.E.M.'s "Time After Time" in section 3), but the Banshees give it a hard edge—there's nothing dreamy or laid-back about this. The riff makes powerful use of a drone on the top E string, with a single melody line moving from E to D to E to F, which could imply the E Phrygian mode (E F G A B C D). Underneath it, the bass guitar moves from E to C to A and down to E.

Another Banshees track, "Bring Me the Head of the Preacher Man" (from *Hyaena*), has a stunning flamenco-type E Phrygian riff that gets faster and faster as the song goes on. The implied chords are Em and F (the crucial change for the Phrygian), with the F often voiced as Fmaj7#11 (x33200), and further on there is a section moving from Bm to C (implying B Phrygian).

Deep Purple

"Perfect Strangers" (Blackmore/Gillan/Glover)

From *Perfect Strangers* (Polydor/Mercury, 1984)

It's not often that, 16 years into a career, a rock band comes up with a track worthy to sit beside the best material of their first five years, but that's what Deep Purple managed with "Perfect Strangers."

Led Zeppelin's 1975 "Kashmir" created a subgenre of epic, slow tempo, grandiloquent songs with riffs in odd meters and/or scales, and hints of Eastern promise. "Perfect Strangers" is one of the best. After an intro of dirty Hammond organ, riff 1 enters with the rhythm section: a tone-shift riff of C5–D5, F5–G5, with long gaps between them, which continues through much of the verse. When the music moves onto an A7 chord, with the notes A–G–E played individually, Blackmore adds some of his characteristic fourths.

The chorus moves through some conventional full chords (F, C, Dm, G, Dm, C), ending with a fine change from G to Gm. At this point, the song plunges to riff 2. This is based on the A Phrygian scale (A B♭ C D E F G). When this riff reappears after the second chorus, for the coda, it is transposed into E Phrygian.

By doing it this way around, Deep Purple maximize the power of the last riff, because it's using the lowest notes on both guitar and bass. At various points an open E string punctuates the scale, which is played roughly an octave higher. At the same time, 5/4 bars appear, and the riff itself is lengthened with an extra bar of 4/4. This asymmetry, combined with the Bonham-esque drumming, gives a powerful effect.

A Perfect Circle

"Judith" (Howerdel/Keenan/Freese)

From *Mer de Noms* (Virgin, 2000)

This song uses a detuned guitar with an excessively low C♯ moving to E5 (minor third) in the verse. The chorus opens up the dark chords; the sinuous opening riff is played in octaves on a Phrygian C♯, with a distinctive first semitone interval step, and then, after three phrases, a leap up to the seventh, B, and the sixth, A♯. Octaves give a cleaner effect compared to what it would have sounded with fifths.

After two plays, riff 1 gives way to riff 1b, which is not in octaves and drops by a fifth from B to E, nicely counterbalancing the leap in riff 1. The effect is vaguely Middle Eastern, a distant splinter of Led Zeppelin's "Kashmir" ambience, though here linked with satanic lyrics. The verse then drops the riff to a lower, simpler form (1c), though rhythmically it has an interesting off-kilter pattern. The time signature sounds like 6/4.

Mastodon

"Seabeast" (Mastodon)

From *Leviathan* (Relapse, 2004)

This heavy rock number qualifies for inclusion in several riff categories, one of which is the Phrygian riff. Dissonant arpeggios start the track on an Am–C change; both chords have a flattened fifth added to them. The riff for the verse is in fifths—a very odd sequence with strange timings and a prominent minor third. It is so convoluted that it doesn't gain much forward energy and has no spaces in it. There is a riff involving an octave drop of a D, which is a Phrygian D–E♭–D–C but harmonized with an F♯. A later riff in the song also has many flattened intervals, and fifths interspersed with single notes.

Alter Bridge

"Still Remain" (Kennedy/Marshall/Philips/Tremonti)

From *AB III* (Roadrunner Records, 2010)

This Alter Bridge song has something of the gravitas of the best Soundgarden tracks but also bears the mark of how the boundaries that shape rock riff composition have shifted in the decades since Seattle grunge. The riffs are defined by a memorable example of detuning: the whole guitar is down a semitone, with the jaw-dropping additional detuning of the sixth string down to a B♭! The riffs have a strong Phrygian flavor because of the minor tonality's flattened second and seventh. They are characteristic of the contemporary style in featuring fast sequences punctuated by a considerable drop in pitch to the low sixth string. One of the descending phrases spans an octave and a minor third. The initial riff is cleverly overlaid with a much higher clean triad arpeggio. The verse further startles with its chord changes, from B♭ to G♭ and D; the chorus uses F♯m–D–Bm, with a startling Dmaj7 at 2:15.

Another modern characteristic is the chromatic bridge riff, which enters at 3:15 and works the slack tension of the sixth string to wobble the pitch of the notes. This is a very different kind of string-bending to the traditional bending that goes on in solos.

18 lydian

The two remaining modes are far less frequently encountered. The Lydian mode is like the Mixolydian in only being one note different from the major scale. The Lydian in A is A B C♯ D♯ E F♯ G♯—a major scale with a sharpened fourth:

The Lydian mode was popular in speed metal and similar guitar styles. In the '80s and '90s, heavy rock bands used it in the bass register of the guitar. It has an unsettling effect because of the raised fourth—our old friend the tritone in a different guise, as an augmented fourth rather than a flattened fifth. In the true Lydian mode, you would expect to hear the raised fourth and the fifth. The Lydian mode lends itself to generating tritone riffs, but with major chords supporting them.

A Lydian and E Lydian

By subtly introducing the Lydian note into the harmony, there's an opportunity to use it in a more melodic way. The whole of the song doesn't have to be in this mode. A more flexible method for writing riffs on the Lydian mode is to keep the song in a major key and save the mode for the riff.

Harmonizing the seventh note of a major scale with chord IV of the same key results in a Lydian flavor without being in the Lydian mode per se. For example, the initial octave riff in Foo Fighters' "My Hero" puts the notes D♯, E, and F♯ above the root note A. The mode A Lydian does indeed have a D♯. But the next phrase plays the same D♯, E, and F♯ over an E root note. Since the key is E major, D♯ is merely the seventh note of the scale. For the song to be Lydian, there would have to be a D natural and an A♯. The same band's "How I Miss You" has a central figure with a Lydian quality: F♯ over D moving to G♯, instead of the G we would expect.

Led Zeppelin

"Dancing Days" (Page/Plant)

From *Houses of the Holy* (Atlantic, 1973)

"Dancing Days" is a fine deployment of the erotic possibilities of the tritone (G–C♯), here derived from G Lydian (G A B C♯ D E F♯). It opens with this single-bar riff (four bars in total) blazing in the middle register. Page accentuates the riff by bending the C♯ up to D twice, and then coming off onto B. Underneath, the accompaniment is playing a G–B♭ (blues ♭III) idea in between the upper bend to add to the tension. Unusually, the variation on the basic one-bar riff comes each third time in the form of overlaid, strident sixths on a separate guitar track.

Once the song enters the verse, Page innovates further by taking a standard-issue Keef/Stones rhythm riff and moving it from its initial C chord up a semitone to C♯—the C♯ a chord being foreign to G major. He adds another tritone idea over this C–C♯ change by altering the notes that are held—on the C chord, the notes F and A are added and taken away. Over the C♯ the upper note is sharpened, so we hear G instead of F♯—G is a tritone above C♯. There's also a noteworthy arrangement detail in the coda, where the main riff is pushed up an octave.

19 locrian

The Locrian riff is neither major nor minor but diminished. A Locrian is A B♭ C
D E♭ F G—like the natural minor with a flattened second and fifth:

The Locrian mode has a reputation for being dissonant and awkward to use.
There is a very good reason for this. Of all the scales so far, it is the first that lacks
a perfect fifth between the first note and fifth. All the other modes pitched on
A have E as their fifth note. This makes the Locrian mode distinctly unsettling.
Its chord I is a diminished triad (1–♭3–♭5), and there's a tritone between first
and fifth, so it's well-suited to expressing negative emotions, such as anger and
alienation.

A Locrian and
E Locrian

This mode became more significant in the '90s and early 2000s, as a trademark
for bands such as Linkin Park and Limp Bizkit. Its use indicates a rejection of the
harmony on which rock had been traditionally based. Twenty-first-century rock
has come a long way from blues and pentatonics. However, in practical terms,
few rock songs that use modes such as the Phrygian, Lydian, or Locrian maintain
a harmony rigorously fixed on them. What usually happens is that the modes
are harmonized in fifths, and the riffs are then played from those fifths. This has
particular consequences for the Locrian: if chord I is played as a power chord, it
fails the test of using the correct diminished fifth.

A power chord on the first scale degree of A Locrian should consist of the
notes AE♭, not AE. But you are more likely to hear AE (A5). This limits the
Locrian and has a tendency to make it sound like the Phrygian. System of a
Down's "Genocidal Humanoidz" (in drop C) is an example of this ambiguity.

Using regular fifths on the scale, while retaining the diminished fifth note
for single note passages, is certainly the simplest approach. A good example
would be a track like "Disasterpiece" by Slipknot, where the demonic ambience
is heightened by extreme detuning of the guitar. Their track "Everything Ends"

uses an A Locrian scale, with the fourth note sometimes flattened. The 1–♭2 movement is everywhere in their music.

The same ideas can be heard in Korn's "It's On" and "Dead Bodies Everywhere," and in Sepultura's "Roots Bloody Roots," which uses the deep sound of the BF♯BEG♯C♯ tuning—a good way to imitate the sound of a seven-string guitar. Megadeth's "Head Crusher" (2009) bucked the detuning trend by placing its verse riff of F♯ Locrian in standard tuning. Alter Bridge's "Last Rites," in drop C♯/D♭ tuning, is usefully described as Locrian, with an initial tritone riff pitting A5 against a D♯ bass note, a verse riff which brings in the flattened second of the scale, and a chorus riff that also features the tritone.

The Vines

"Get Free" (Nicholls)

From *Highly Evolved* (EMI/Capitol, 2002)

The Locrian mode is difficult to match with rock, but it can be more accommodating if you suggest it rather than attempting a pure Locrian riff. "Get Free" starts with a single-string riff with a bend of D–E♭ and back to C (this could be D Phrygian or Locrian). On the fourth run, two chords are added: C5 and G5. This riff also features in the verse, where it is played with less emphasis on the bend. The chorus uses the D–C note change with a bend on a low G5–A♭5–F5; the A♭ in D suggests the Locrian, if taken with the E♭ that occurred in the verse.

After the chorus, another 3+1 riff happens involving a single-note leap of D up to A–C–D–C (the Mixolydian). All these riffs are related musically. They show how much can develop from a single idea and suggest that you can mix modes on the same root note.

Metallica

"That Was Just Your Life" (Hetfield/Ulrich/Hammett/Trujillo)

From *Death Magnetic* (Warner Bros., 2008)

This track is from Metallica's ninth album, produced by Rick Rubin. *Death Magnetic* and its songs were nominated for five awards at the 51st Grammy Awards in 2009, and the album entered at the top spot on the *Billboard* chart, selling 490,000 copies in only days of release. Remarkably, it was Metallica's fifth consecutive studio album to go straight to the #1 position, making them the first band to achieve this.

The opening clean arpeggio in this track uses the notes E, B♭, and F, which suggests the Locrian mode on E. This initial idea recurs in slightly different rhythms and articulations—a reminder that a riff may have more than one means of presentation. Toward the end of the song, one of these variations appears in a harmonized form.

The notable feature of the opening minute of the track is the heavily accented chords with pauses between them, creating drama and anticipation. The faster scale riff that appears at 1:30 uses the Locrian mode, with a chromatic passing note of F♯ between G and F going down to the root E. This riff is a good example of 3+1 phrasing: one phrase three times answered by a different phrase on the fourth.

> **Deftones**
>
> **"Rocket Skates"** (Carpenter/Cunningham/Moreno/Delgado/Vega)
>
> From *Diamond Eyes* (Reprise, 2010)

This was the second single from Deftones' sixth album. It features a seven-string guitar riff that has characteristics of the modern heavy riff: deep pitch, rapid notes, and very short bends and pull-offs that smudge the pitch of notes on the lowest string, each followed by the open string itself. The higher notes interact with the repeated bass note in a manner that is distinctively post–hard rock. The upper notes shift about on the scale.

I've included this song in the Locrian mode section despite the fact that it lacks the flattened second degree of the pure Locrian because of the emphasis on the flattened fifth throughout. The riff strongly asserts the tritone between B and F. A further riff emphasizes the flattened fifth when it is reached via D5 and E5.

20 chromatic scales

A chromatic scale proper would consist of all 12 semitones. This in itself is not used for riffs, but adding a few off-scale notes to a riff can give it a chromatic quality. The *riff gallery* for this section groups together famous songs that have such riffs. Although they may be based on one of the scales or modes described previously, they include notes that are not in that scale or mode. Chromatic riffs tend to be characterized by stepwise movement. They lend themselves to creating longer riffs at faster tempos than pentatonics, because you are not moving so soon across the strings to get the next note. They also impart a jazzy quality to the riff, or otherwise blur the tonality.

Check out Free's "Over the Green Hills" for a speeded-up chromatic descending riff on E. Deep Purple's "Space Truckin'" has a chromatic riff starting on A, going up to E–E♭–D–C–B–B♭; and in Pink Floyd's "Money," B–D–D♭–C is the four-note riff leading to the guitar solo. Metallica's "The Thing That Should Not Be" has chromatic touches, as do the Stooges' "Not Right" (C5–B5–B♭5–A5), Stone Temple Pilots' "Heaven and Hot Rods," Soundgarden's "The Day I Tried to Live," Pearl Jam's "Spin the Black Circle," Pantera's "Mouth for War," and the chorus of T. Rex's "Jeepster" (C–B–B♭–A). Royal Blood's "Figure It Out" combines a four-note chromatic descent (D–C♯–C–B) on bass with pull-offs onto the open E string, so that the chromatic color is inflected by an extra rhythmic element.

Green Day's "Brain Stew" and "Hitchin' a Ride" both have riffs featuring descending chord sequences with chromatic shifts. Extreme's "Colour Me Blind" has a first riff with distinctive stepwise chromatic movement and a few leaps accentuated by squealing harmonics. The same band's "Peacemaker Die" and "Rest in Peace" show an approach to riff writing where the guitar is almost playing lead phrases.

AC/DC's recent "Demon Fire" has a two-bar, quickly descending riff in eighth notes based on the scale of E natural minor, with the major seventh (D♯) and the flattened fifth (B♭) inserted. The change of direction midway through this riff is very effective.

For a squelchy funk bass riff with a chromatic feel, check out the five-note riff (B–G–A♭–F–E♭) in Thundercat's "Them Changes."

Jimi Hendrix

"Love or Confusion" (Hendrix)

From *Are You Experienced* (Track/Reprise, 1967)

This example of a chromatic riff comes as the verse reaches the hook line. You can hear it start at 0:34 on the bass guitar, with the notes G–B♭–A–A♭ played four times, and then twice more with the guitar and a more urgent rhythm. As it occurs here, it is more of a fill than a riff. Still, it gives the idea of what could be done.

Hendrix's innovation was not only in guitar pyrotechnics, figurative or real. Much of this song is built on a G–F change, which Hendrix makes G5–Fsus2 to achieve, coupled with the bass line, a more subtle harmonic color. Listen out too for the fuzz guitar that holds G through much of the verse, the tremolo scoop into verse two and into the key change bridge, the octaves under the solo, and the majestic entrance to the last verse.

The Beatles

"Lady Madonna" (Lennon/McCartney)

Single A-side (Capitol/Parlophone, 1968)

"Lady Madonna" reprises the '50s-derived "Pretty Woman" riff. The first phrase is A–C–C♯ over an A chord, then D–F♯–A over a D chord. This happens twice. The third time, the D chord has D–D–E–E. Then the harmony changes to F and G chords, with the riff using those root notes to ascend to the A an octave above the A where it started. No one scale covers all these variations. The closest is A Mixolydian with a blues flattened third added, which leaves the F (♭VI) as the additional note.

The riff is first heard, in a slightly different form, in the left hand of the piano part, and then in the bass on the opposite side of the stereo image. At 0:44, two guitars start playing it, followed about ten seconds later by a sax. In the fullest statement, with all the instruments, the riff achieves an exhilarating stomp. One significant musical factor in its success is the fact that there is a phrase pitched against it that comes downward—either the right hand of the piano or the actual vocal melody. This is an example of contrary motion applied to a riff.

King Crimson

"21st Century Schizoid Man" (Fripp/McDonald/Lake/Giles/Sinfield)

From *In the Court of the Crimson King* (Island/Atlantic, 1969)

King Crimson were one of the quintessential progressive outfits, with a leaning toward jazz-rock improvisation apparent in "21st Century Schizoid Man." In Robert Fripp they had a strong-willed, intellectual guitarist with a European style that contrasted with the prevalent blues-rock of the time, and one who has pioneered different tunings on the electric.

This song startled its first listeners because of the viciously distorted vocal and accompanying discordant Cm7 chord. The verse is prefaced by a riff in C pentatonic minor, a single-note phrase, and a drop onto F5–F♯5 and G5. It's played in unison by guitars (with a harmonized line to thicken it) plus saxes and bass, achieving an epic effect.

Notice how, on the third time around, the fifth chords are replaced by higher single notes of F, F♯, and G. This riff acts as a kind of vocal-less chorus between the verses. After the second verse, the riff variation is repeated and gradually sped up. This leads to the introduction of riff 2, which takes the form of a phrase (a1) and its variation (a2), repeated. Riff 2 is also in C minor, but it uses chromatic semitone movement to go from C to E♭, E, and F and then from C downward, B–B♭–G. With each repetition of the whole eight-bar figure, the fourth phrase is changed, while the first three phrases stay the same. Some of the final phrases are fine examples of how to link up with the start of the riff an octave above where it was first heard.

Led Zeppelin

"Dazed and Confused" (Page, inspired by Jake Holmes)

From *Led Zeppelin* (Atlantic, 1969)

Page first used the riff (which originated as a song on Jake Holmes's 1967 album *The Above Ground Sound of Jake Holmes*) on the Yardbirds' version of this song "I'm Confused." This was Led Zeppelin's first attempt at an extended song structure, complete with shadowy bridge section.

The memorable riff starts with a leap of a tenth from E up to G, then a descent of G–F♯–F–E, and then D–C♯–C–B. Page magnifies the gothic menace by doubling it with a higher lead guitar two octaves above, and by incorporating various bent notes into the riff.

The riff functions both as an instrumental link and as the verse. A second one-bar riff on B enters to break it up, its notes being B–E–F#–A–B: the same 1–4–5–♭7 idea encountered in "Paperback Writer." The "Dazed" riff is the more effective because the notes do not simply ascend and descend.

Led Zeppelin made "Dazed and Confused" one of the centerpieces of their live sets, often stretching it out to more than 25 minutes, the tempo gradually dropping to a funereal pace quite different from the brisk walk of the studio cut.

Led Zeppelin

"Black Dog" (Page/Plant/Jones)

From *Untitled (Four Symbols)* (Atlantic, 1971)

"Black Dog" has three riffs. The first is a linear riff based on the A pentatonic minor scale, but with a chromatic G# and a hint of a C# on a bend. The chromatic quality grows when the riff is transposed down a fourth, and a variation is created that emphasizes the seventh (D#) on the E pentatonic minor. Although it sounds as though the music is now in a hideously complicated time signature, it is only a matter of shifted accents in 4/4. This riff was the responsibility of John Paul Jones (see the interview in section 5).

Riff 2 is based on an A5–C5 change with a contrasting A pentatonic major run. Riff 3 is a powerful tone-shift A5–G riff with accented G and D chords. This last riff is used for the guitar solo. The arrangement of "Black Dog," alternating solo voice with band passages, was influenced by Fleetwood Mac's "Oh Well." Compare it also with Jethro Tull's "A New Day Yesterday," where a similar riff idea to the first variation in "Black Dog" is put to very different effect.

Queen

"Stone Cold Crazy" (May/Mercury/Taylor/Deacon)

From *Sheer Heart Attack* (EMI/Elektra, 1974)

Coming in on an air-raid siren of feedback, "Stone Cold Crazy" qualifies as a chromatic riff for several reasons. Although the main element to the riff is a two-bar G5–B♭5 change, which sounds like G pentatonic minor, bars 3–4 bring in a semitone move that worms its way upward to D via B, C, and D♭. The riff is played four times, with an additional guitar overdubbed halfway through to give some notes an octave doubling. The fourth time, the riff ends with a different phrase that heads downward, G–F–D–B♭. This gives the riff the structure a1+a2 (x3)+a1+a3.

The verse is a solo vocal with only percussion accompaniment. The riff's second appearance is curtailed with another chromatic phrase (G–A–A♯–B) that leads to a guitar solo over a B minor chord (0:51), and a return to the first riff. At 1:20, a second solo is introduced, with another chromatic chord change from B♭ to B minor. The two tonal centers of G minor and B minor are distant from each other, which accounts for the song's strange, dislocated feel—an exotic world of riffery wrapped up in a little over two minutes.

The Cult

"Automatic Blues" (Astbury/Duffy)

From *Sonic Temple* (Beggars Banquet/Sire, 1989)

A neat way to create the feel of a chromatic riff from a pentatonic one is to put a passing note between the blues flattened third and the fourth of the scale. This note is the major third of the scale. The effect is reminiscent of scales used in bebop jazz, where a blues third is added to a major scale (E F♯ G G♯ A B C♯ D♯ E) or a pentatonic major (E F♯ G G♯ B C♯ E).

The riff in "Automatic Blues" consists of the notes E–G–G♯–A–G–E. The form is a1+a2+a3+a1, with each riff ending on a different high note. Fun as the riff is, what lifts it out of the ordinary is the timing and the arrangement. The song is an excellent example of the technique of alternating vocal and riff. This leaves the singer the chance to play around with the point where the vocals end, knowing the riff is going to enter on a certain offbeat. It's cleverly done here. Then, under the guitar solo, a second riff uses the notes D–C♯–A–G–E.

Radiohead

"Paranoid Android" (Yorke/Greenwood/Selway/O'Brien/Greenwood)

From *OK Computer* (Parlophone/Capitol, 1997)

Radiohead are not exactly a band associated with riffs. This makes the glimpse of riff heaven provided by "Paranoid Android" all the more startling. As a song, it not only has great guitar playing but also manages to pull off just about every other trick in the way of melody, dynamics, tempo, key, and time-signature changes. There's plenty to enjoy here from a guitar and songwriting viewpoint.

The song uses several keys, including Gm, Dm, and Am, shifting between them in an ambiguous way. The opening acoustic sequence cries out that it must be in some weird tuning, especially the opening chord change from a form of Cm to Gm—but it isn't. The chords move from this Gm to a first inversion Dmadd9 and then E7. The music sounds like it's going into A minor, but this only happens after the second verse.

The next section involves a skeletal heavy riff plucked from the depths of metal hell but played acoustically. Most rock bands would have made this riff a straight pentatonic one, but Radiohead introduce an A♭ note, implying a chromatic Am–A♭ chord change, followed by C–A♭6–B♭ chord sequence. When the heavy guitars come in, the riff's power is unleashed—but notice they don't overplay the headbanging, only repeating that heavy riff a handful of times. After the solo, the music enters its hymnlike third section: it starts on a Cm chord, changes key to Dm via an A7, and then finds its way to E7 and A before repeating. Notice the sense of dislocation when the music goes from A back to C minor. In 60 years of hit singles, this is the probably the only song to use this chord change.

The riff returns toward the end of the section, to introduce the second guitar break. Its power is all the stronger for the contrasting quiet of the middle section, making "Paranoid Android" an object lesson in dynamics.

chord-based riffs

Riffs can sometimes take the form of chords—groups of three or more notes that make up harmonies in music. This section examines different kinds of chord-based riff, and the various ways a riff can generate harmony.

21 pedal notes

After looking at intervals and scales as sources for writing riffs, a third group of possibilities lies with harmonic and chord-based ideas. A further step beyond using a pair of notes is to exploit one of the guitar's natural resources: the open string.

A "pedal" note is one that remains the same, usually low in pitch, while other notes or chords change above it. On the guitar, the favorite strings for a pedal note are the open E, A, and D strings, or their detuned equivalents (E♭, A♭, D♭); A♭ is the pedal note, for example, for the opening riff of System of a Down's "Lost in Hollywood."

For riffs, choose any of these and move a scale or even a sequence of intervals like thirds on the string(s) above it. For any other pitch, use a capo or leave the pedal note to the bass guitar.

Here are thirds using the A Mixolydian mode over an A string:

TRACK 8

Thirds over an
A pedal

The intro and chorus of Ozzy Osbourne's "Shot in the Dark" moves chords over a fifth-string pedal, as does the main riff of Led Zeppelin's "Ten Years Gone." The bridge section of Van Halen's "Jamie's Cryin'" puts thirds over a fifth-string pedal. The Who's "I Can See for Miles" has a sixth-string E pedal over which chords change (compare it with the Stooges' "Real Cool Time"). And the acoustic intro of their "Pinball Wizard" features chord changes over a fretted F♯ pedal, and is worth studying for how to combine a fretted pedal with a set of chords in that position.

The Cult's "Sweet Soul Sister" puts an A blues scale over an A pedal note, and their "She Sells Sanctuary" uses a D pedal. The Stooges' "I Wanna Be Your Dog" puts G5–F♯5–E5 over an open E string (these fifths imply the E natural minor scale). Queens of the Stone Age's "Better Living Through Chemistry" opens with an ambiguous scale that implies both major and minor keys played over an F pedal.

Smashing Pumpkins' "Cherub Rock" puts octaves over a pedal E, the octaves drawing on the E Mixolydian scale. Faith No More's "From Out of Nowhere" puts a C5–E♭5–F5 riff over a C pedal. Bon Jovi's "Roulette" has fifths over an E pedal, and "In and Out of Love" has as its second (verse) riff triads over an A pedal. Focus's "Harem Scarem" puts a blues-scale phrase over a frantic F pedal, with a clump of jazzy chords coming at the end of each riff. The pedal note is also moved up to C temporarily. "Out of My Hands" by the Darkness has a I–V–IV–V sequence in A over an A pedal.

On keyboards, it's easy to write a song in which chords in the right hand change over a static bass note. This songwriting technique creates a sense of drama. On guitar, a fretted pedal note like C or G will tie your hand to one place, so any riff will require notes reachable from that position.

A well-known riff-writing technique involves getting the bass player to provide a pedal note while guitars play a riff of single notes or intervals like fourths and fifths above. This features heavily on ZZ Top tracks. Genesis's hit "Turn It on Again" is a fine example of keyboard/guitar chords moving over a bass pedal note, complete with unexpected accents and dropped beats.

Fleetwood Mac

"The Green Manalishi (with the Two-Prong Crown)" (Green)

Single A-side (Reprise, 1970)

For a brief time in 1969–1970, Peter Green's Fleetwood Mac became something more than a competent English blues band. They created a musical world of their own—part blues, part late psychedelia, part pop—that was the best context imaginable for Green's poetic guitar skills. Green may have been a fine blues player—perhaps the subtlest of the English guitar heroes—but his best guitar work happened in contexts other than a 12-bar. The shuddering nightmare of "The Green Manalishi" is a case in point.

This song has two notable riffs: the first comes after the first line of the lyric and consists of I–♭III–IV chords. The coda riff is based on thirds moving down strings four and five over an E pedal.

The implied chords are Em–C, but the pedal stays in place on the guitars, although the bass moves to a C. Over this the guitars are stacked in an impressive arrangement, with spooky lead guitar in the background, like a lost stanza by Nostradamus.

The Sensational Alex Harvey Band

"The Faith Healer" (A. Harvey/H. McKenna)

From *Next* (Phonogram/Vertigo, 1973)

At a time when the UK music scene divided between chart pop and glam rock on one hand and prog rock on the other, the Alex Harvey Band carved out a niche for themselves that wasn't in either camp. Too hard and idiosyncratic for the charts but keeping clear of formal pretension, they became a popular live and recording act—by turns threatening and funny.

"Faith Healer" has a colorful arrangement, with exotic percussion, distinct from much of the rock of its era or any other. The first riff is a sequence of fourths derived from D pentatonic minor and played over the throbbing D pedal that has already been going for 47 seconds before the riff enters, then drops out, before re-entering at 1:13. The guitar does not carry the pedal, though a second guitar on the other side of the stereo image eventually enters with a D5 that supports it. The riff fits between the vocal lines.

At 3:06, a second riff comes in, also based on D pentatonic minor, in single notes, with an emphasized tone-shift element. Listen out for the exotic B♭–A–G–E♭ phrase over a G pedal that's repeated during the song's coda.

R.E.M.

"Green Grow the Rushes" (Berry/Buck/Mills/Stipe)

From *Fables of the Reconstruction* (IRS, 1985)

Here is a classic example of a riff based on a tonic pedal. The song is in D, and Peter Buck selects the open D string as a drone. He plays three one-bar rhythmically similar phrases, descending string three from the 14th fret A. The scale he uses is D Mixolydian—D major with a lowered seventh (D E F♯ G A B C). This mode is favored for its dreamy quality when used in this style.

Playing a D pedal on the guitar gives a lighter feel than an A or E pedal. Two other memorable pedal-note R.E.M. songs are "7 Chinese Brothers" (over D) and "Be Mine" (over E and A).

Radiohead

"Bodysnatchers" (Radiohead)

From *In Rainbows* (Xurbia Xendless, 2008)

This is an example of a Mixolydian melody riff moving over an open bottom string. Some of the time this is played in octaves. The guitar sound is unconventional, as is the accent pattern of the rhythm section. The riff has four phrases, and it includes moments that answer it.

After a couple of minutes, the arrangement abruptly changes to a more ambient sound with sustained single notes on the guitar. The harmony at this point is implied since there are no obvious chords. The key is D, so the open string six is probably detuned. The riff starts with an F♯ (the major third) over the D pedal note.

On the first verse, Thom Yorke sings part of the riff's phrase. This is distantly related to the kind of riffs that crop up in Jimi Hendrix's later recordings (1969–1970), though if they were his they would have been more rock-funk arrangements.

> **Nazareth**
>
> **"Lifeboat"** (L. Agnew/P. Agnew/D. McCafferty/J. Murrison)
>
> From *Big Dogz* (Edel Entertainment, 2011)

Formed in Scotland at the end of 1968, Nazareth enjoyed some success with hard rock albums and singles in the 1970s, some of which were produced by Deep Purple's Roger Glover. Despite many lineup changes, the band were still releasing new material as recently as the 2010s.

The riff of "Lifeboat" is an example of a pedal-E riff with a variety of third, fourth, and fifth intervals played over it on the fifth and fourth strings. The adjacent minor and major third (EG and EG♯) gives an element of harmonic surprise that a straight pentatonic wouldn't have. The aspect that lifts this riff to "above average" is the timing. Each time the riff goes back to the start, it appears to come in unexpectedly, owing to the placement of accents.

22 drone notes

We can define a "drone" note as one that is either in the middle of what you're playing or above it. Have a look at this example:

TRACK 9

Fifths with a
G drone note

In first position, there's an Fsus2; then, at fret three, G5 with the G doubled; at fret six, a B♭6/Gm7; and at fret eight, the same shape creates a C5 with the G doubled again. The open G acts as a drone. How you play the riff and how long the G rings affects how the riff sounds.

That example was based on the interval of a fifth combined with an open string. You can also use scales with drones, as with pedal notes. Play the right scale for the key or the progression up and down one string (instead of across the fretboard) and hit an open string above it. The result is a bigger sound, and one that not only might make a riff but reinforces the harmony. This is a significant factor in a power trio, and a good technique for lead guitar, as the Edge demonstrates on the guitar solo in U2's "Sunday Bloody Sunday."

The simplest application of the drone is to treat the open string as the root note of a major or minor chord. So, for a high riff over an E chord (major or minor) in the overall harmony, the top open E is available as a drone. The open B works for B major or B minor, and the open G string for G major or minor. The fretting hand then chooses the riff notes from the right scale up and down the adjacent string. Since the top three strings make an E minor chord and the second, third, and fourth make an open G, if you're playing in either of these keys you could have two drone notes vibrating, rather than one.

Open strings can also function as the third or fifth of the chord. E is the third of C major (C–E–G) and C♯ minor (C♯–E–G♯); B is the third of G major and G♯ minor; and G is the third of E♭ major and E minor. E is the fifth of A major/minor; B is the fifth of E major/minor; and G is the fifth of C major/minor.

Treating E, B, or G as the sixth or seventh of a chord provides even stranger effects. If you compose a riff using the open string as something other than a root note for the given chord, this may not work if the bars given to the riff involve chord changes. Songs like R.E.M.'s "Time After Time" and the Velvet Underground's "Venus in Furs" give an idea of the possible texture achievable with drone notes.

Chord progressions with a common note running through them can also create a drone effect, as can be heard on Marshall Crenshaw's "Cynical Girl," where the top E string is heard through many of the chords (in A major).

Led Zeppelin

"When the Levee Breaks" (Page/Plant/Jones/Bonham/Minnie)

From *Untitled (Four Symbols)* (Atlantic, 1971)

The main riff of "Levee" is based on a blues flattened third idea combined with fifths. What brings it alive is the open tuning on an electric 12-string, combined with dropping the tape speed, which gives the riff a droning quality that fits the overall hypnotic effect. The top two strings sound for much of the track. There is a secondary riff that immediately precedes the verse, with heavily accented fifths using the flattened seventh and the flattened third—a quintessential, dynamic Zep moment.

In lesser hands, such simple musical elements would probably have been nowhere near as engaging, and it's a matter of historical record that Led Zeppelin themselves struggled to make the song work until they found the drum sound. But the band won through with skillful arrangement, not masses of overdubs—in fact, by not adding other ideas, the intensity never drops. The result is Zep's greatest take on the blues. You only have to compare it with Kansas Joe McCoy and Memphis Minnie's 1929 song of the same title to realize the breadth of the band's imagination and power—particularly Bonham's amazing, much-sampled drum part, and the production skills of Jimmy Page and Glyn Johns. The magic of "When the Levee Breaks" was not repeatable onstage—the song never became a fixture of their live act.

R.E.M.

"Time After Time (AnnElise)" (Berry/Buck/Mills/Stipe)
From *Reckoning* (IRS, 1984)

In a very different vein to Led Zeppelin, this track from R.E.M.'s second album shows how drone notes gave rise to the term "raga-rock"—coined to describe songs that imitate the droning strings of an Indian sitar. This style originated in the '60s with songs such as the Rolling Stones' "Paint It, Black," the Kinks' "See My Friends," the Yardbirds' "Heart Full of Soul," the Byrds' "Eight Miles High," and the Velvet Underground's "Venus in Furs."

The "Indian" effect is emphasized by the opening percussion (congas) and the rapid arpeggio rolls on the guitars that punctuate the first minute, on what sounds like a suspended second chord. The top E string is sounded throughout the verse in 16ths, sometimes panned back and forth. Notice how, when the song hits the two-minute mark, the drone note temporarily disappears into the background.

"Time After Time" is a good example of the hypnotic effect of a drone note—being static, it suggests the music is merely looping around.

23 arpeggios

There's one last approach to discuss before reaching riffs made from full chords. When the notes of a chord are played one after the other in a rising or falling pattern, you have an arpeggio. If an arpeggio is brief enough and catchy enough, and has enough rhythmic emphasis, then it can qualify as a riff.

Arpeggios imply a chord (handy in a power trio) but have clarity because the notes are offered to the listener one by one. Favored arpeggios on the guitar are those that either start with an open string, or feature one or more open strings, which makes fingering easier. Arpeggio riffs also tend to have more impact played on the lower strings, which give them force and body, compared to more decorative higher-pitched arpeggios.

Here's an example of an arpeggio that might be considered a riff:

An arpeggio can be made from any chord, and it doesn't have to be a simple major or minor. The dominant 7 and 9 chords, for example, have been popular in rock. But the more notes there are in the chord the longer it takes to play through the arpeggiated riff.

TRACK 10
Arpeggio riff

Arpeggio riffs are effective with the bass either doubling an octave lower or harmonized. Another arrangement idea is to have the bass play only the root notes of the arpeggio and accent them to emphasize the chord changes. This is how the arpeggio riff in the middle of Cream's "Badge" works.

Arpeggios often occur in intros, as in Paul Weller's "Sunflower," where notes on string three descend D–C♯–C–B while the top two strings remain on E and B; Type O Negative's "My Girlfriend's Girlfriend"; the intro and verse of the Strokes' "Is This It"; the intro of the Stone Roses' "Made of Stone"; and Radiohead's "My Iron Lung."

The Doors' famous "Light My Fire" has a long bridge/solo section carried by an A minor/B minor arpeggio bass riff. The intro to Guns N' Roses' "Sweet Child O' Mine" has one of the most famous guitar arpeggios—this figure, played high at the 12th fret, spans an octave and a fourth, starts with an octave leap (D–D), and takes the form a1+a2+a3+a1, in which the bass notes cycle through D–E–G and then D again. Living Colour's "I Want to Know" uses an arpeggio riff to link the chorus to the verse. Weezer's "Pork and Beans" has an unusual arpeggio riff based on an F#maj7 chord, the notes of the riff being F#–A#–E#–D#.

Rainbow's "Jealous Lover" has a fine arpeggio riff on F#—it climbs up first, then comes down onto the bottom E before reascending. It's another good example of a riff exploiting the possibilities of F# on the guitar as a key center. During the verse, Blackmore uses the same dramatic arpeggiated power chords (root, fifth, octave) that he used in "Smoke on the Water."

The Byrds' "Turn! Turn! Turn!" is an example of an arpeggio riff that depends on three separate instrumental parts. The arpeggios occur on an electric 12-string, in a fingerpicking style, but the descending fifths in the bass, and the accentuated Bm–A chord change at the end of each two-bar phrase, are essential to the effect. Soundgarden's "Black Hole Sun" also depends on arpeggios for its accompaniment, though these don't function as riffs. It is at 2:53–3:22 that a true riff enters the song: a potent chromatic riff using two short phrases: C–B–A–C and then a lower G–F#–F.

Focus's "Hamburger Concerto" is punctuated throughout by an arpeggio riff in drop D with a blues flat third played through a Leslie speaker effect. Another Focus track, "Carnival Fugue," has a delightfully playful riff in its second half that involves playing up an F7 chord, and dropping an octave from G to G to land on a C. Arpeggio riffs also work well on bass, as in the intro to the Jam's "Eton Rifles," where Bruce Foxton plays an Am7 chord (A–C–G–E).

Roy Orbison

"Oh, Pretty Woman" (Orbison/Dees)

Single A-side (Monument/London, 1964)

Coupled with driving, four-to-the-bar drums, this song has one of the most famous early guitar riffs. In "Oh, Pretty Woman," the riff is pulled in to stoke anticipation; heard for the first time, it consists only of five notes, ending on an unresolved D—the flattened seventh of an E7 chord (the song is in A major).

This is played twice on an acoustic 12-string. Only then do we hear the riff in its full form, extended to eight notes and reaching as far as F♯ before its downturn. These notes—E, G♯, B, D, and F♯—constitute a dominant ninth arpeggio.

In this second form, halfway between a scale and an arpeggio, it's played four times, with added instruments such as electric guitar and bass, to lead into the verse. After the second verse, it is slightly shortened as the song moves into the bridge.

At the end, expectation is generated by the riff's shortened form twice, followed by no less than nine repetitions of the riff's second form. This ties in with the lyric's discovery that the woman the narrator thought was not interested turns out to be interested in him after all. The creative tip here is to write a riff, then make a shortened version to delay the full thing.

The Beatles

"Day Tripper" (Lennon/McCartney)

Single A-side (Parlophone/Capitol, 1965)

The riff for "Day Tripper" is a development of the riff from "Oh, Pretty Woman." The connection is made more apparent because of the song's frequent one-chord crescendo technique.

Like "Oh, Pretty Woman," the notes imply an E dominant ninth chord (E–G♯–B–D–F♯) with the inclusion of a G (blues ♭III) as an additional second note. The last few notes jump around unpredictably, in contrast to a riff that simply goes straight up and then down. During the verse, the riff is transposed onto A. Notice that the riff is doubled by bass guitar on the intro.

"Day Tripper" was recorded a few days after "Drive My Car," a track that features a similar riff.

Van Halen

"Ain't Talkin' 'Bout Love" (E. Van Halen/A. Van Halen/Anthony/Roth)

From *Van Halen* (Warner Bros., 1978)

This well-known arpeggio riff (based on the chords Am, G, and C) cranks in on the left, with the notes racketing about in the reverb on the right. Van Halen's legendary "brown sound" guitar tone is a mixture of echo/distortion and phasing on a customized Strat with a Gibson humbucker pickup at the bridge through a Marshall Super Lead 100-watt amp. Few bands or producers would have been able to resist doubling the guitar riff on the right, but it sounds amazingly full as it is.

The riff is heard four times before mutating into a more chordal form, where the Am–G5 chords are fully voiced with a descending C–B in single notes. Eddie interjects lead fills toward the end of each second bar in the riff's second form; a third variation is used for the verse.

This riff carries virtually the whole song, since the only other chords come in on the coda. At 1:52, the riff is heard quietly and with a cleaner tone. Van Halen's guitar provides the track almost with a second "voice."

> **U2**
>
> **"Sunday Bloody Sunday"** (Bono/Edge/Mullen/Clayton)
> From *War* (Island, 1983)

As described in section 1, with his smart use of an echo unit, the Edge is able to make simple phrases sound interesting; and by playing against the echo pattern, new rhythms and harmonies are generated. "Sunday Bloody Sunday" takes a standard rock progression of VI–I–IV in a major key (here D) and plays arpeggios over those chords (B–D–F♯, A–D–F♯, G–D–E), so that the chords B minor, D, and G6 are implied. Allied with the martial drum rhythm and Bono's impassioned, anti-violence lyric, the effect is powerful, as heard on both *War* and the live album *Under a Blood Red Sky*.

The riff takes a second form at the start of the verse, where the Edge plays the progression as chords. The later U2 song "A Sort of Homecoming" revisits those arpeggios to present them in a more lyrical way.

Two other early U2 songs are also worth a mention. "I Threw a Brick Through a Window" has a two-phrase riff in which the first phrase implies E7sus4 (E–E–A–E–D) and the second A/E (E–E–A–E–C♯). "Rejoice" uses a G♯m triad up at the eleventh position.

Bryan Adams

"Run to You" (Adams/Vallance)

From *Reckless* (A&M, 1985)

The songs of Canadian rocker Bryan Adams tend not to be built around riffs in a hard rock manner, but "Run to You" is an exception. The riff is unusual because it has thirds on the bass strings—generally, the lower the pitch of thirds, the muddier they sound. Adams plays here with a capo at the second fret, so the actual pitch starts on F#m, but for ease of reference I will describe the riff as if it were in E minor.

The first bar uses E–B–D, which ascends to a G–B–D triad and then A–C#–D. The D string remains open throughout. The chords implied are Em7, G, and A. On the A, the fretted C# and open D clash, lending piquancy to the riff. The guitar tone is necessarily free of distortion for this riff, with some chorus and delay. Urgency is imparted by the quarter-note sidestick from the drummer. Notice that this riff is carried on through much of the verse.

The Seahorses

"Love Is the Law" (Squire)

From *Do It Yourself* (Geffen, 1997)

Ex–Stone Roses guitarist John Squire turned out to be the lost talent of British Guitar Herodom (he now paints), but this single from his short-lived Seahorses period did contribute to the list of memorable '90s guitar riffs. The riff (which you need to use a capo to play) is an arpeggio-type figure on an open A chord—the sustained A string helps support the higher notes. It's a distant relative of the Smiths' "What Difference Does It Make," though the string bend in the last bar of each riff is definitely not from Johnny Marr.

For considerable stretches of the song, not much use is made of the riff, though it is heard with a different guitar in the center of the mix at 3:10, now transposed down from A to E. For another John Squire arpeggio riff, try "Waterfall," from the Stone Roses' debut album.

24 major chords

As I pointed out in the introduction, just as with arpeggios and scales, there is also a fine line between riffs made of chords and chord progressions. For example, is the Spin Doctors' "Two Princes" a four-chord riff or a progression? I think we can usefully talk about chord changes taking on the function of a riff when the changes are sufficiently short, repeated often, and are rhythmic enough. But these definitions can't be rigid. Chord riffs have the attraction that they create a full sound. It's possible to generate a riff from the rhythmic way in which a single chord is played, as happens on many James Brown tracks, like "Sex Machine," where the guitar basically plays a ninth; or the Red Hot Chili Peppers' "Get Up and Jump," "Backwoods," and "Behind the Sun"; or Stone Temple Pilots' "No Way Out."

Another way of generating riffs is to take a chord and move it a semitone step back or forth, or to lift a finger or two fingers off the chord to alter notes within it, as Peter Buck does in R.E.M.'s "Departure." Since a major key has three major chords in it—namely I, IV, and V (E, A, and B in E major)—these are the three most likely candidates for a riff—or at least they would be, were it not also for rock's flattened seventh chord and fondness for the Mixolydian mode and its harmony. There are probably two or three Mixolydian I–♭VII–IV riffs for every major key I–IV–V. It is also possible to make up chord riffs by turning chords II, III, and VI into major chords and combining one of them with the main three (more than that and you may blur the key).

Bachman Turner Overdrive's "You Ain't Seen Nothing Yet" and Arrow's "New York Groove" are I–V–IV riff songs. Sheryl Crow's "Soak Up the Sun" starts as a I–V–IV riff. Marshall Crenshaw's "Mary Anne" plays a poignant variation on this, with a I–V–II/II–V–I chordal riff in C major. Pulp's "This Is Hardcore" would not be described as a riff song, but listen to the opening, where a Gmaj7 on brass sounds several times over a heavy, slow drumbeat—that has the focus and power of a riff.

A chordal riff can mix major and minor chords. The verse of Marillion's "Kayleigh" is carried by a chord pattern of Bm–A–F♯m–G (VI–V–III–IV), played with sufficient rhythmic distinction to constitute a riff. In Gorillaz's "Feel Good Inc.," the opening piano arpeggio on the chords of B–C♯m–G♯m–E (I–II–VI–IV) could be thought of as a riff. Coldplay's "Viva La Vida" has a four-chord sequence of D♭–E♭7sus4–A♭–Fm7, which is played by strings with a sharply defined rhythm that could be classed as a riff.

The Troggs

"Wild Thing" (Chip Taylor)

From *From Nowhere . . .* (Wild Thing/Fontana, 1966)

Perhaps the definitive use of a I–IV–V–IV chord riff, "Wild Thing" is now better known through Jimi Hendrix's version (as on his Monterey Festival 1967 set). It has always appealed to young players because the chords (A, D, and E) are easy to change. The riff is also effective because these chords use the three lowest open strings for their root notes.

Its effectiveness is enhanced by the stomping drum rhythm and an eccentric arrangement in which the verse leaves the vocal almost unsupported. The only chord change in the verse is to lift the A chord on and off. Instead of a guitar break, the Troggs chose an ocarina break (not exactly in tune, either!) to add a bizarre element of rustic delinquency. It's like rock 'n' roll played by the local village idiots, but sometimes dumb is the new clever.

From the same innocent era, the verse of the Monkees' "A Little Bit Me, a Little Bit You" has the same chords, but I leave it to you to decide whether that is a riff or a progression. Likewise, Wayne Fontana and the Mindbenders' "Game of Love" (1965) has a I–IV–V–IV verse, but it is more a progression than a riff.

The Who

"Baba O'Reilly" (Townshend)

From *Who's Next* (Track/Decca, 1971)

Few bands have put the rock guitar riff to such sublime use as the Who did on the milestone *Who's Next*, which fuses the energy and drama of rock with significant lyric themes. The album was also innovative in its inclusion of synths, and the Who never enjoyed better production.

As a rock guitarist, Pete Townshend was always in a different area to everyone else. As he has readily admitted, he was never a quick or fluent lead player: his gift was for rhythm and punctuating a song with gargantuan chords.

"Baba O'Reilly" is a fine instance of a titanic Who riff. The key, F major, is unusual on the guitar (on some footage Townshend, has a capo at the first fret, allowing him to use key-of-E shapes), and the entry of the guitar riff is delayed. The sequencer synth starts with an arpeggio based on F major, then a piano strikes the I–V–IV chords, and then the drums enter. These instruments carry the song through the first verse, whereupon Townshend finally crashes in on guitar with the F–C–B♭ chord riff. There is a fabulous live version on the soundtrack to the film *The Kids Are Alright*—the last time the Who played it with Keith Moon.

David Bowie

"Queen Bitch" (Bowie)

From *Hunky Dory* (RCA, 1971)

Hunky Dory was David Bowie's transitional album from the singer/songwriter mode of his earlier music toward the more commercial and theatrical rock of *Ziggy Stardust* and *Aladdin Sane*. "Queen Bitch" opens with a strummed acoustic 12-string moving C–G–F (I–V–IV). One might be unsure as to whether this constitutes a riff, but when Mick Ronson's electric guitar blasts in, first on the right and then also on the left, there's no doubt. It's an exhilarating moment.

Since the tempo makes the changes fast, many guitarists who want to play "Queen Bitch" have a problem moving their fingers that quickly. The solution is not to fully barre the F and the G but play them with a partial first-finger barre on the top two strings only and a thumb on string six (with full barres, the thumb frequently has to change position on the back of the neck, which takes marginally more time). Also, the third finger never leaves string five, so it becomes the guide that holds everything together.

Insofar as the riff has a variation, it's the fact that the second C–G–F has the C just before the bar line, in a typical rock "anticipation." Throughout the verse, the riff comes in at the end of each lyric line—a neat way of dovetailing a riff into a verse without drawing attention away from the words.

Nirvana

"Smells Like Teen Spirit" (Cobain/Nirvana)

From *Nevermind* (Geffen, 1991)

The most influential rock song of the '90s, "Smells Like Teen Spirit" is also memorable for its clever arrangement and powerful dynamics, of which Nirvana had an intuitive and determined grasp. The verses are sinister and quiet, the choruses raucous and loud. The verse is the same chord sequence as the chorus, but on the verse only the bass is playing the root notes, in eighths, so the chords are implied, not stated.

"Teen Spirit" is like the key-striding progression F–Bb–G–C, but Cobain's inspired twist was to dislocate it by forcing the second two chords a minor third away from the first two: F–Bb–Ab–Db. There's a further fragment of similarly dislocated harmony at the end of the chorus: F–Gb–Bb–Ab.

This track also foregrounds the idea of inserting a unison string bend into a riff to give the impression of another voice (something Nirvana also do in the chorus of "Heart-Shaped Box"). This is a very different use for the unison bend compared to its common use in lead solos.

25 mixolydian chords

Of all the modes outside the major scale, the Mixolydian deserves a section to itself because of the many rock songs that have riffs drawn from its harmony. Remember that the only difference between a major scale and the Mixolydian mode is the flattened seventh note. E major is E F# G# A B C# D#, while E Mixolydian is E F# G# A B C# D. This D natural makes available two different chords to what would be expected in E major: chord VII becomes D instead of D diminished, and chord V becomes B minor instead of B.

The latter is unusual because turning chord V of any major key into its equivalent minor undermines the key. Pure Mixolydian harmony on a given pitch has the same seven chords as the major key a fifth below. The chords of C Mixolydian are the same seven as F major, though their functions are different. These two chords lead to the two basic Mixolydian chord riffs: I–bVII–IV (in A this is A–G–D), and I–IV–Vm (A–D–E minor).

Green Day's "American Idiot" is another garage-punk chordal riff based on A–D–G (I–IV–bVII), where it is the defined rhythm that makes it a riff on the intro and during the verse, whereas the chorus chords simply act as accompaniment.

The Raconteurs' "Salute Your Solution" is I–bVII–IV–V (E–D–A–B). On "Steady, as She Goes," the riff is at first implied by the bass and consists of four root notes: B–F#–A–E, which become guitar chords in the progression I–V–bVII–IV, where I is sometimes B5 and sometimes Bm.

Black Rebel Motorcycle Club's "Love Burns" ends with an acoustic coda with an E–D–A Mixolydian riff in 5/4. The first riff of AC/DC's "Back in Black" is based on an E–D–A sequence; an E pentatonic minor run, like the riff of "Shakin' All Over"; the E–D–A sequence again; and then a clever "tripping-over" chromatic phrase, where the accents are shifted away from the normal rock beat.

One AC/DC trademark is that the A chord has C♯ on the bass guitar the first time, making it a first inversion. Many of their songs take familiar rock pentatonic chord riffs and give them a harmonic twist by using either inversions or pedal notes in the bass. The idea can be extended with the addition of the flattened third blues chord, as in Lenny Kravitz's "Fly Away," which uses A, C, G, and D (I, ♭III, ♭VII, and IV).

A variation on the I–♭VII–IV riff would be I–V–♭VII–IV, as heard on the Offspring's "She's Got Issues" (as E5–B5–D5–A5); or ♭VII–IV–I–IV–I, as on U2's "Desire" (also in E). For the intro and chorus of "Living After Midnight," Judas Priest put this in an E–D–A–B sequence (I–♭VII–IV–V).

The Kingsmen
"Louie Louie" (R Berry)
Single A-side (Jerden/Wand, 1963)

This song was groundbreaking because of its sheer primitiveness—some have called it the first garage-rock record. In the early '60s, it was a staple of bar bands; by the end of the decade, it had generated something in the region of 300 cover versions.

This riff belongs in the Mixolydian camp because it has the minor form of chord V—one of the chords that Mixolydian harmony offers. The song is in A, and the chords are A, D, and Em—this is the Mixolydian version of the I–IV–V major-key riff. This single two-bar riff carries the entire song, with only the occasional change of accent to add variety.

Eric Clapton's "She's Waiting" uses a similar Mixolydian riff with the minor version of chord V.

Rolling Stones

"Not Fade Away" (Petty/Hardin)

Single A-side (Decca/London, 1964)

The Stones' third single, a cover of a song originally recorded by Buddy Holly, has a chord riff that popularized a rhythm known as the Bo Diddley beat, named after the '50s US rocker with the box-shaped guitars and sheriff's hat. The main chord change is E to A, with the A chord only struck for a moment. During the verse, this change is transposed to A to D. The three chords suggest a blues-derived E Mixolydian harmony.

"Not Fade Away" is a good example of how the guitar's three most popular chords can be used when E, rather than A, is taken as the key chord. (For A–D–E when A is the key chord, see "Wild Thing.") The other possibility—with D as chord I, E as a major form of the normally minor chord II, and A as chord V— isn't heard so often. On this Stones track, exotic percussion like maracas also helps things along.

Another Stones song based on the E–D–A change is "The Last Time": here, over the strummed acoustic chords, the electric part borrows a classic blues lick, as heard on Howlin' Wolf's "Smokestack Lightning." It consists of a slide on string three from A to B (frets 2–4), implying an E7 chord. During the second half of the riff, a C♯ is thrown in when the underlying chord is A. Notice this riff is not transposed onto either A or D during the chorus. "The Last Time" can be thought of as a distant relative of David Bowie's "Rebel Rebel."

The Who

"I Can't Explain" (Townshend)

Single A-side (Brunswick/Decca, 1965)

The Who's debut single ignited a career of memorable chordal rifferama. With Townshend's orientation to rhythm guitar, it's no surprise that many of the Who's best riffs are chordal. "I Can't Explain" uses a I–♭VII–IV–I sequence, and this Mixolydian riff is in fact the definitive Who chord change, occurring repeatedly in their songs. In this instance, it is in E major, moving E–D–A and back to E. There is a variation of I–♭VII–V–I (E–D–B–E) in the middle and at the end of a verse.

The guitar sound is distinctive, its organ-like tone resulting from being played on an electric 12-string. The late John Entwistle once told Roy Carr that it was written as an answer to the Kinks' "You Really Got Me," though lurking behind both records is "Louie Louie."

Notice the strong contrast created by the bridge section ("I think it's love"), which is a pop I–VI–IV–V (E–C#m–A–B) progression in E major. (A ♭VII–IV–I riff occurs in another Shel Talmy production, the Creation's "Making Time" from 1966, which sounds Who-like.)

Them

"Gloria" (Berns)

From *Them* (Decca/Parrot, 1965)

"Gloria" is well known not only for the spelling-out-letters lyric (always a great ruse, to see if the singer can find a way of fitting the word in the available space), but also for its single-minded chord riff. Like "Louie Louie," almost the entire song is carried on the E–D–A change (I–♭VII–IV), which is bashed out with garage-band fervor.

This is the same as the verse of "I Can't Explain," but with a different rhythm. The exception is the guitar break where the chords are played E–D–A–D on triads around the 12th fret. The concentration on a single riff throughout an entire song marks a development (and simplification) in the rockier side of earlier '60s pop music.

Cream

"Tales of Brave Ulysses" (Sharp/Clapton)

From *Disraeli Gears* (Atco/Reaction, 1967)

Here's an example of a Mixolydian riff with extra harmonic development. From the same album that features "Sunshine of Your Love" comes Cream's evocation of the Homeric legend of Ulysses. Used almost throughout the whole song, the riff consists of the chords D–Cadd9–G/B–B♭ (or Gm/B♭). It's built on a descending bass line using the progression D–C–B–B♭. The first three chords are the I–♭VII–IV riff.

These chord shapes characterize many guitar-based songs because they are easy to play, though not necessarily as riffs (see the Beatles' "Dear Prudence"). Cream liked the progression sufficiently to write another song with a variation on it, "White Room," where Jack Bruce adds a clever bass touch by putting an F under the Cadd9 chord every other time. In both songs, additional sonic color is added by Clapton's wah-wah pedal. (There is a ferocious live version of "Tales" on *Live Cream Volume II*.)

Part of this descending riff idea occurs in Blind Faith's "Can't Find My Way Home," the Stone Roses' "Tears," Dokken's "Little Girl," and Neil Young's "The Needle and the Damage Done." It also occurs as A5–G–D/F♯–F in the intro to the White Stripes' "Dead Leaves and the Dirty Ground." The D–C–G/B Mixolydian chord progression features on many rock songs, including Bad Company's "Feel Like Making Love" and Radiohead's "The Bends." A variation starting on Dm is the arpeggio riff to Siouxsie and the Banshees' "Spellbound."

Led Zeppelin

"Communication Breakdown" (Page/Jones/Bonham)

From *Led Zeppelin* (Atlantic, 1969)

Nothing could be further from the turgid clichés of Zeppelin-inspired heavy metal than this, a taut 2:26 that seems closer to a band like the MC5 but is played with rampaging energy and impeccable musicianship. It's a sonic storm punctuated by a mad Page solo that careers off the splash of white noise from Bonham's cymbals.

The riff is two bars of the I–♭VII–IV change, this time going E–D–A–D. A fast string of eighths on the bottom E is dramatically interrupted by the D and A chords played around the fifth fret, probably on a Telecaster. Led Zeppelin returned to this riff on "In the Evening," also in E.

The Who

"Won't Get Fooled Again" (Townshend)

From *Who's Next* (Track/Decca, 1971)

"Won't Get Fooled Again" is the Who's definitive expression of the I–♭VII–IV riff, this time in A, using A, G, and D—A being one of the most resonant guitar keys in which this riff might be played. All the band's musical prowess is captured on the recording: Entwistle's ever-nimble, restless bass, Moon's surging, unpredictable drums, Daltrey's bark 'n' scream vocal, and Townshend's windmill guitar-blitz, for which the term "power chord" must surely have been invented.

Townshend was drawn to this chord combination again and again. It features in a host of Who songs, including "5:15" (verse, G–F–C), "The Seeker" (intro and chorus), "Round and Round" (link), "Naked Eye" (verse), and much of *Quadrophenia*. A song like "Drowned" from that double album is a variation on the theme, going I–IV–♭VII–IV.

In the bridge of "Won't Get Fooled Again," it is transposed up to B–A–E (for the "I know that the hypnotized never lie" part). Compare that with the Bm–A–E change in the loud bridge section of "Behind Blue Eyes," which is the other type of Mixolydian riff.

Thin Lizzy

"The Rocker" (Lynott/Bell/Downey)

From *Vagabonds of the Western World* (Decca/London, 1973)

For sheer dumbness, the macho lyric of "The Rocker" takes some beating—but what a guitar riff! The song is based in A, and the Mixolydian ♭VII chord (G) is heard throughout. Original Lizzy guitarist Eric Bell plays block chord shapes on a Strat at the fifth and third frets (A, G, C, and D are all heard), but he doesn't hit all the strings and adds hammer-ons within the A chord.

The riff serves as the chorus, where its effect partly depends on what the bass is doing—an A minor line using the notes A, B, C, and G. Putting a minor scale–based bass line under a major chord is a good way to make tension in a progression or riff (as heard in "Ball of Confusion"). Midway through the song (1:56), the riff appears as a link with heavy phasing.

The creative lesson of "The Rocker" is to use block chord shapes for a riff but only play a few notes within them. To hear how fine the studio version is, compare it with the one on the twin-guitar later Thin Lizzy's celebrated live album *Live and Dangerous* (1978).

The Hives

"Hate to Say I Told You So" (Fitzsimmons)

From *Veni Vidi Vicious* (Burning Red Records, 2000)

In essence, this is a nice '60s punk riff that, for all the sweeping synth part, sounds halfway between the Rolling Stones and the Kinks. It consists of D–C–F–B♭ (I–♭VII–♭VI–♭III), so it's a chordal riff played by moving a single shape around. Listen for the way the chords are accented in the second verse.

After the second chorus, the bass plays the root notes on its own, this serving for the third verse. It's heard twice with one guitar and then is doubled by a guitar on the left and right.

26 minor chords

It's rare in rock to find a riff made entirely of minor chords. The very fact that rock uses so many fifths instead of full chords demonstrates its unease with the overt emotion of the minor chord. So, for this category, I've allowed chord-based riffs that include a prominent minor chord.

The commonest rock riff led by a minor chord is either I–VII–VI from the natural minor scale (Am–G–F in A minor), or the same with a major or minor chord V (E or Em in A minor) tacked on. The former is the progression that (with different guitar voicings) drives Blue Öyster Cult's "Don't Fear the Reaper," Patti Smith's "Because the Night," Dire Straits' "Sultans of Swing," and the solo and final verse of Led Zep's "Stairway to Heaven," among many. Other popular chord riffs that include a minor chord are I–V–VI–IV (G–D–Em–C), as heard on Rainbow's "Since You've Been Gone"; and I–IV–VI–V (G–C–Em–D), the chorus of Boston's "More Than a Feeling." Greta Van Fleet's "Black Smoke Rising" has a riff that uses VI–V–III–IV (Em–D–Bm–C) in G major, and their "Age of Machine" makes extensive use of an arpeggio on a Dm chord. The White Stripes' "I Think I Smell a Rat" almost manages to sustain a whole song on a rhythmic use of an Am chord (listen for the A and E natural minor lead phrases).

Queens of the Stone Age's "Auto Pilot" makes a riff out of a Bm–D–A/C♯ progression that runs through the intro and much of the verses. Deep Purple's "Demon's Eye" features a minor arpeggio on Gm. Focus's "Anonymous" on their first album, *In and Out of Focus*, features a chordal riff in G minor: Gm–F–Gm–B♭–C, which they liked so much they reprised it for the track "Anonymous II." Santana's "Soul Sacrifice" has a similar riff. Siouxsie and the Banshees' "Overground" is a very powerful chordal riff in D minor, hammering out the turnaround of A/C♯–Dm–B♭–C.

The Beatles

"Come Together" (Lennon/McCartney)

From *Abbey Road* (Apple, 1969)

This spooky riff from the twilight of the Beatles' career is a blend of bass and guitar parts. The basic chord is Dm7; the bass guitar plays a Dm arpeggio that jumps D–G–A through the next octave to a high F, then slides back down from the fifth, A. The guitar overlays a Dm7 figure (D–G–A–C), so the C coincides with the bass's F. (The guitar riff is like a slowed-down version of the riff from "Paperback Writer.") The combined effect of these parts as a riff in "Come Together" gives the song an unusual texture.

Focus

"Hocus Pocus" (Akkerman/Leer)

From *Moving Waves*, (Sire/Blue Horizon, 1971)

In the early heyday of '70s rock guitar, Jan Akkerman stood out. Like many fusionists, he sometimes played too many notes, and he could be cool, cerebral, and apparently easily bored. But there is much to admire about the best of his recorded work with Focus between 1970–1976. Here was a rock guitarist who didn't play obvious blues licks, was phenomenally fast (few people had seen anything like it at the time), and had a funky sense of rhythm.

The inventive "Hocus Pocus" riff is based on Am, though it uses both minor and major chords. It comprises two four-bar phrases, each with a slightly different ending. These are then repeated (giving 16 bars altogether), and an extra phrase is fitted on the end, consisting of Am–C–D, D–F–G, E7♯9. The initial riff is a clear tone shift from G to A over an open A string, subject to considerable multitracking, which doubles the riff at higher pitches.

This was a send-up of heavy rock—part of the musical joke is that a heavy band would never write a riff with these chords, and so many of them. As for the three lead breaks in "Hocus Pocus," well, they're something else. The band tried to repeat the trick in the later "Harem Scarem," but it doesn't match "Hocus Pocus."

The Police

"Driven to Tears" (Sting)

From *Zenyatta Mondatta* (A&M, 1980)

Songs like "Roxanne" might have been entertaining enough, but when the Police turned their considerable musical talents to more serious concerns, they went up a gear. "Driven to Tears" demonstrates that protest songs can be musically inventive as they make their lyrical point (in this case, poverty and the media). Cast in the key of A minor, the main riff is a four-note phrase using the notes A, E, and G over an Am7 backing. During the verse, this is transposed up a tone to fit over Bm7. The chorus uses Dm7 and Em7 chords, with the occasional additional note. The song's urgency comes from the rhythm section—Sting's eighth-note bass line through the verse, and Copeland's ever-inventive drumming. After the second chorus, the riff is transposed down a minor third to F#, and then down a further tone to E for Summers's brilliant angular guitar solo.

Siouxsie and the Banshees

"Candyman" (Ballion/Clarke/Severin)

From *Tinderbox* (Geffen/Wonderland/Polydor, 1986)

The Banshees had just acquired yet another guitarist, John Valentine Carruthers, when they made *Tinderbox*, one of their rockiest albums. "Candyman" was its fierce opener, a sordid tale of child abuse related in the band's usual melodramatic and excoriating manner (the Banshees always believed it was better to curse the darkness than light it with a candle).

This song's inclusion here in the minor-chord riff section is because of the highly inventive verse, which is pitched unusually on Gm with a suspended fourth arpeggio. As the bass descends on a four-note sequence, the rapidly picked guitar chord ascends two frets. Toward the end of the song, the riff is transposed onto Cm in first position—also an unusual fingering. The song contains two other fast arpeggio passages, which from a guitar angle make it worth learning.

27 suspended chords

There are two types of suspended chord: the suspended fourth and the suspended second. When it comes to riff writing, both types are handy since they add drama to music. In both cases, the third of the chord—the note that determines whether it is major or minor—is removed, leaving a bare fifth. But in a fifth there are only two notes left, whereas in a suspended chord there are three notes—the third is replaced by either the fourth or the second of the scale. Few riffs are made entirely of suspended chords—they almost always form a part.

The suspended fourth

A C major chord is CEG; the notes of C minor are CEbG. The only note that distinguishes them is the one in the middle, the third. In a suspended fourth, that middle note rises to F. It sounds tense because it wants to fall back (resolve) to either E or Eb. Here are examples for the chords of C and A.

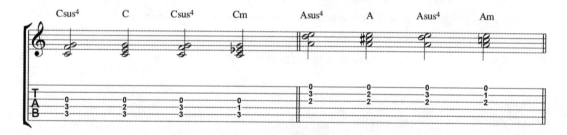

Suspended fourths

Suspended fourth chords are common in pop, rock, and folk. They often feature in transitions from one song section to another. For a concentrated dose of suspended fourths, try the Who's "Pinball Wizard," Family's "Burlesque," Bruce Springsteen's "Two Hearts," the Rolling Stones' "Rock and a Hard Place," and the Police's "Spirits in the Material World."

Manic Street Preachers' "You Stole the Sun from My Heart" uses an arpeggiated sus4maj7 (an unusual effect), and "Tsunami" has a sus4 arpeggio, played high on what sounds like a Coral sitar guitar to give an oriental sound. The verse of Def Leppard's "Animal" uses a sus4 chord on C, and Simple Minds' "Waterfront" is largely driven by a repeatedly detonated 7sus4 chord.

The suspended second

Not quite as dramatic as the suspended fourth, the suspended second can have an empty, spacey sound. Here, the third of the chord falls to the second note of the scale. So, A major (AC♯E) becomes Asus2 (ABE); C (CEG) becomes Csus2 (CDG), as below:

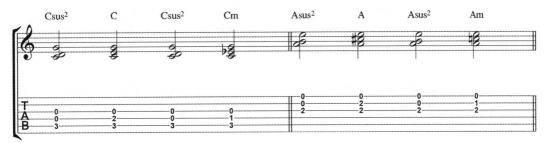

It still sounds tense and unresolved because the second note wants to rise to E or E♭. Suspended seconds are found in pop, rock, and folk, often combined with suspended fourths. The popularity of some of these chords is connected with how easy they are to play. With Asus2 and Dsus2, you only have to lift a finger off a string; Esus4, Dsus4, and Asus4 only need a finger added. The sound of a suspended second chord alters depending on how low or high the second is: the Csus2 (x3301x) has it low within the chord, Dsus2 (xx0230) has it as the highest note.

Suspended seconds

The suspended second chord is closely related to the add9 chord, but the add9 also has the third of the chord, so nothing is suspended. So, while Csus2 is CDG, Cadd9 is CEGD. There is also a form of add9 that doesn't have a third, which consists of two fifths on top of one another: CG and GD (or CGD). This could be termed a sus2 in a full voicing, or "5add9" if there are only three notes, as spread out in the second and fourth chords here:

Fifth/add ninth chords

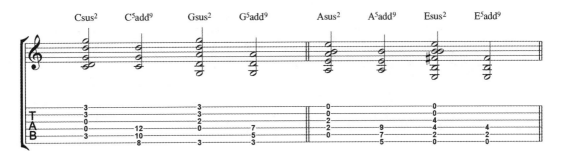

The G5add9 (357xxx) is the shape Andy Summers uses for the riff of the verse of the Police's "Message in a Bottle" (in that case, two frets higher on A). This type of chord is also heard in E on the chorus of Linkin Park's "Papercut." I'm sure there's more to be made from this riff, it just needs a fresh angle. (Incidentally, "Message" features some prodigious harmonizing of that musical idea.)

The sus2, sus4, and add9 chords are inseparable from the style of rock nicknamed "jangle"—the folk-rock of bands like the Byrds, who based their music on the bright, ringing tone of the electric 12-string in songs like "I'll Feel a Whole Lot Better" and "All I Really Want to Do." Elements of this sound are present in the Smiths and R.E.M., in the Pretenders' "Brass in Pocket," in the Bluetones' "Slight Return" and many other indie bands of the '90s, and in a "high-octane" version in Bruce Springsteen's "The Ties That Bind." In this genre, riffs tend to be played without distortion and constructed around effective chord changes with open strings and unconventional voicings. Suspended chords are okay for heavy rock, too: Smashing Pumpkins' "Soma" has a haunting intro that shows what can be done with chord voicings that have many open strings.

The suspended fourth and more

When the suspended fourth is combined with other notes in a chord, a classic rock riff idea is created. Barre your first finger across the top four strings at the second fret. This makes an A6 chord. Ignore string one and just work with strings two, three, and four, which form the major triad of A. As it's an A, add the open string five to the chord. Now, put your second finger on the third fret of the second string. You're playing AEAD (x0223x), which is Asus4. Next, use your third finger to hold down fret four on string four. Now you're playing AF♯AD (x0423x), which is either a second inversion D major or Asus4/add 6, depending on musical context:

TRACK 11

Sus4/6 and sus 6/9 in A

Hit the chord with the two fingers off (just holding the barre A chord), then put them both on, then take them off again. It's a sound you'll recognize from songs by the Rolling Stones such as "Start Me Up," the Dandy Warhol's "Bohemian Like You," Free's "All Right Now," Thin Lizzy's "Rosalie," Be Bop Deluxe's "Maid in Heaven," Bad Company's "Can't Get Enough," David Bowie's "John, I'm Only Dancing" and "The Jean Genie," Sheryl Crow's "If It Makes You Happy," ZZ Top's "Jesus Just Left Chicago," Queen's "Hammer to Fall," Bruce Springsteen's "Crush on You," Manic Street Preachers' "Slash and Burn," Elton John's "Saturday Night's All Right for Fighting" and "The Bitch Is Back," and the middle section of the Eagles' "Life in the Fast Lane." With the right amount of distortion, this chord gives a pleasing, meaty sound. Try the barre at the 14th fret and do the same figure for a very Brian May sound (as on "We Will Rock You").

This riff can also be found in acoustic music, as in the intro to John Mayer's "Queen of California," where a capo at fret four turns the key of B into the user-friendly G major. This use of the figure is laid into a Mixolydian I–♭VII–IV harmony, all in the space of two bars.

Another related riff involves putting the third finger on string three instead of string four, with the second finger doing its stuff on string two (x0243x). But what if we need to play this on a chord other than A? Well, forget about string five; take the triad on strings two, three, and four, and move it up to wherever you need it. Follow the note on string three, because that's the root. For example, to play this figure on D (as below) go to fret seven.

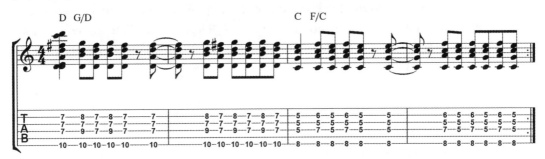

With only three strings, the sound is not as full as the example on A. If you can stretch with your little finger to string six, the right root note is three frets ahead of wherever you are. So, for D at fret seven, the little finger holds down the D at fret ten on the bottom E string (10x777x). The little finger also mutes string five.

TRACK 12

Sus4/6 and sus 4/9 in C

This is an awkward shape to play at the best of times, let alone in full rock 'n' roll mode, duck-walking across a stage with a Fender Tele just above your knees or hoisted vertically on your chest. That's why Keith Richards is almost always in an open G tuning when playing this riff. With a triad on strings four, three, and two, strings one and five are redundant. But tune them both down a tone and—hey presto!—you can now barre across five strings, hit all of them, add the two notes and take them off, and get a fuller sound (see "Altered tunings in rock" in section 4). This should not be confused with the Doobie Brothers riff, which is a minor seventh chord shape in standard tuning with fingers two and three going on and coming off. This minor seventh idea was also used by Andy Summers on Police tracks like "The Bed's Too Big Without You."

The Searchers

"Needles and Pins" (Bono/Nitzsche)

From *Meet the Searchers* (Kapp, 1964)

The year 1964 was when pop music discovered the 12-string, and it would remain a dominant guitar sound until late 1966 and the mainstreaming of distortion. "Needles and Pins" (or "Needles and Pins-zer," as they sing) is a British example of the "jangle" guitar style. The opening riff is an A chord played on an electric 12-string: by lifting a finger off string two, an Asus2 chord is created; by putting it back and then putting the fourth finger on the third fret on string two (playing a D), the Asus4 chord is produced. This type of suspended chord riff can also be heard on "To Be Someone" by the Jam, "Happy Xmas (War Is Over)" by John Lennon and Yoko Ono, "I Need You" by the Beatles, and "So Sad About Us" by the Who).

The Beatles

"I Feel Fine" (Lennon/McCartney)

Single A-side (Parlophone/Capitol, 1964)

"I Feel Fine" is renowned in rock guitar history for the blast of feedback with which it commences before moving onto a memorable riff with two components. The first few notes use the root note (with an octave leap), the flattened seventh, and the fifth; the second piece is the 4–3–2–3 movement, implying the momentary tension of a suspended fourth chord. All of this is generated on the guitar by holding a single barre chord and deftly picking while lifting fingers on and off. The riff is played first on D up at the tenth fret, then on C, and then at G (the key chord) at the third fret.

The riff is not doubled on the bass but supported by roots and fifths. The riff does receive support from a second guitar, which is shadowing the chord changes. Listen to the riff carefully to hear not only the contrasted tone of the guitars playing it, but also that it isn't strictly a one-note-at-a-time riff at all. Other adjacent strings within the chord are also hit and allowed to ring.

> **The Beatles**
>
> **"Ticket to Ride"** (Lennon/McCartney)
>
> From *Help!*, (Capitol/Parlophone, 1965)

George Harrison's acquisition of a Rickenbacker 12-string early in 1964 popularized its sound in pop music and changed the sound of the Beatles, as "Ticket to Ride" demonstrates. The electric 12-string's chiming drone is heard on the opening bar, which is played on the top three strings, moving from A to Asus2. (Unusually, the lead guitar part here is played by McCartney.) The droning sound of such a figure marks the advent of the psychedelic pop of the mid-'60s with its static harmony, repetition, and emphasized higher frequencies.

The 12-string dominates throughout bars 1–6 of the verse and then returns after the chorus. The guitar is balanced by bass and second guitar playing an A drone at different octaves. What is noticeable about the track as a whole is how much of it lacks full chords.

John Lennon later (and confusingly) called "Ticket to Ride" one of the earliest heavy metal records, presumably because of its static riff and heavy drums.

> **Free**
>
> **"All Right Now"** (Fraser/Rodgers)
>
> From *Fire and Water* (Island/A&M, 1970)

Due to its use in TV commercials, "All Right Now" has outshone the rest of Free's output—which is a pity, given the quality of songs like "Be My Friend," "Mr. Big," "Little Bit of Love," and "My Brother Jake." Free's blues-rock was particularly effective at a slower tempo, with Andy Fraser's wide-spanning melodic bass and Paul Rodger's blues-inflected vocals.

Thanks to a brave arrangement decision, the verse riff of "All Right Now" has no bass to support it—the bass only enters at the chorus. The main guitar riff is difficult to emulate, partly because its character depends on the combination of two guitars playing similar but not identical parts. The basic idea is an A chord with a Stones-like double "suspension" (the notes D and F♯ coming on), an idea that can also be thought of as a second-inversion D major or Asus4/6. (The Stones element is interesting, since *Rolling Stone* magazine's reviewer said "All Right Now" reminded him of "Honky Tonk Women.")

After a suitably sexy gap, the A is followed by a G5 and another D before a return to A. Paul Kossoff liked to beef up the A chord by doubling the open A string at the fifth fret on string six. The underlying chord change is A–G–D–A (the Mixolydian chordal idea), as is the chorus, which simply finds another way of "voicing" it.

T. Rex

"Cadillac" (Bolan)

Single B-side (EMI/Reprise, 1972)

Marc Bolan's approach to electric guitar rhythm playing was shaped by the three years (1968–1970) he spent in Tyrannosaurus Rex where he mostly played acoustic guitar to the accompaniment only of bongos. Unconsciously or otherwise, when he started writing riffs on electric, the bongo-influenced strumming patterns remained, as did whole chords. For a rock guitarist, he always made little use of fifths.

"Cadillac" is a two-bar riff made out of a D–Dsus4 change. The rhythm is syncopated in an almost Motown fashion. The only variation on the riff happens as Bolan goes into the guitar breaks, where he takes out a couple of offbeat strikes of the D chord to make a little space. For contrast, the verses end with a I–VI–IV–V sequence in C (C–Am–F–G) that he knew from doo-wop records—as also happens in "I Can't Explain."

David Bowie

"The Jean Genie" (Bowie)

From *Aladdin Sane* (RCA, 1973)

By a strange coincidence, glamsters the Sweet released "Blockbuster" at about the same time as David Bowie released "The Jean Genie," and both used the same Esus4 blues riff. The riff itself is the ultimate rock 'n' roll chord of E major played with dirty distortion, the bottom E driving the beat and the A and G chords making a fleeting decoration on the fourth beat. But listen carefully to the bass, which hits an A on that fourth beat while the second guitar hits an A chord. Like "Satisfaction," the sound of the riff is not self-contained but depends on the other instruments (in contrast to a riff like "Rebel Rebel," which circles between D and E, with open strings bleeding into one another, supported by the bass). Notice also the E/B (sus4/6) to B and D/A (Dsus4/6) to A on the chorus, and the Dsus4 to D at the 12th fret.

Bruce Springsteen

"Born to Run" (Bruce Springsteen)

From *Born to Run* (CBS/Columbia, 1975)

After two fine albums that drew misplaced comparisons with Bob Dylan and Van Morrison, Bruce Springsteen had by 1975 earned a 24-carat reputation as a live act, but he had not yet made a commercial breakthrough in record sales. It finally came in 1975, with "Born to Run," on which, flying in the face of the rock trends of the mid-'70s, he reached back in musical time to the late '50s and early '60s.

Over the initial E–A–B chord changes, Springsteen lays a riff that evokes the spirit of Duane Eddy: a low-string E major–derived figure that avoids the root note E over the E chord, opting instead to jump a minor seventh from B up to an A that functions as a fleeting Esus4.

Suspended fourth chords can also be heard through the song's bridge section. On the album, an Esus4 riff is also critical to "She's the One," and another suspended fourth change dominates "Night." For a very different arpeggio approach to an E7sus4 chord, listen to the Smiths' "The Headmaster Ritual."

28 triads

The next two subsections look at other ways of writing chordal riffs. First, instead of full chord shapes, why not experiment with triads? It only takes three notes to make a harmonically complete major or minor chord. Full guitar chords double or treble these notes to project more sound, but such doubling or trebling doesn't add anything harmonically.

The advantage of triads is that there are more of them on the fretboard, and they are easy to play and move around. They can facilitate chord progressions in which each note moves only a short distance to the nearest next note in the succeeding chord.

Have a look at this example:

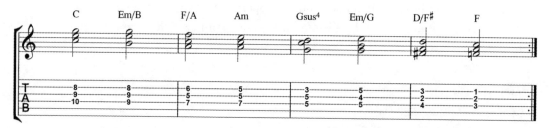

TRACK 13

Close-voiced triads

With common barre and open-string chord shapes, it's often difficult to preserve such close movements (known as "voice-leading") within a chord progression. Triads make this straightforward, and that can create riffs with a unique sound. Triads also "sit" well over pedal notes, whether on guitar or another instrument.

You can hear triads (including suspended chords) on the verse of Van Halen's "Dance the Night Away," and on the Who's "Substitute" and throughout their instrumental "Sparks," mostly over a D pedal. Angus Young puts triads over the main chords on the intro to AC/DC's "For Those About to Rock."

Suspended second and suspended fourth chords work well in riffs because of their extra tension. Queens of the Stone Age's "No One Knows" creates its opening riff simply out of a Csus4–Cm change, and Gary Clarke Jr.'s "Bright Lights" makes a similar opening statement with an accented Am–Asus4 change.

ZZ Top's "A Fool for Your Stockings" makes excellent use of major triads that are turned into minor seventh chords by the right bass notes, in a slow 12/8. Their track "Beer Drinkers and Hell Raisers" puts minor triads over eighth-note bass lines in a verse structure derived from a 12-bar. Ozzy Osbourne's "Crazy Train" has E, D, and A triads over an A pedal, similar to the Tom Robinson Band's "2–4–6–8 Motorway." Pearl Jam's "Not for You" puts second inversion E, F, and G triads over an E pedal.

Argent

"Hold Your Head Up" (Argent/White)

From *All Together Now* (Epic, 1972)

Having played in the '60s group the Zombies (of "She's Not There" fame), keyboard player Rod Argent formed Argent in 1970 with Russ Ballard on guitar—he of the shades and silver Fender Strat with holes in the body. "Hold Your Head Up" is a great example of a chord riff based on triads on the top three strings while the bass plays a D pedal. The guitar chords are Dsus4–D–C–Csus2–Dsus4–D–G–Cmaj7–Am. The pedal note in the bass adds to the harmonic richness. The steady slow rhythm and sustain allows the chords' sonorities to be enjoyed.

Dire Straits

"Sultans of Swing" (Knopfler)

From *Dire Straits* (Vertigo/Warner Bros., 1978)

An unlikely guitar hero, Mark Knopfler found his own voice as a guitarist by backtracking—looking past the flash excess of mid-'70s Marshall/Les Paul riffery to a less distorted Fender "twang" in which silvery bends seemed to have been corralled in from country rock and reframed. His sound was also influenced by a penchant for the Strat's so-called "out of phase" pickup positions (two and four), and the fact that he didn't use a pick. The sound of thumb and fingers pulling at the strings makes a big difference.

This technique also influenced his compositional approach because, when pulling three strings at a time, triads make perfect sense, rather than full chords. Part of what makes the "Sultans" riff so memorable are the triads, most of which are second inversions (using strings four, three, and two), and the way Knopfler slides them around. The riff is heard at the end of most of the verses and implies a Dm–B♭–C progression.

This sequence is a rock staple (the chorus is the same sequence as "Layla"), but Knopfler found a new way to present it. He reuses similar triads in "Lady Writer."

All About Eve

"Tuesday's Child" (Bricheno/Cousin/Price/Regan)

From *Scarlet and Other Stories* (Mercury/Phonogram, 1989)

As well as having one of the best British female voices of the '80s in Julianne Regan, the Eves had a guitarist, Tim Bricheno, with a flair for constructing riffs that have energy without going down the usual bare fifths route. A track like "Flowers in Our Hair" makes no bones about the D–F♯m chords of the riff. Consequently, as a live act, the Eves could bang heads with an inimitable velvet elegance. Sadly, a mix of business pressure and band relationships caused them to implode.

"Tuesday's Child" has all the virtues of the Eves' melodic rock. The verses are carried by twin-lead guitar fills and Bricheno's trademark filigree arpeggios. The triad riff comes in the chorus, with a fierce guitar part that has a standard A5 riff followed alternately by G and F and Em and F triads. During the guitar break, these arpeggiated triads occur again, but with a couple of A pentatonic minor phrases crammed between them.

29 inverted chords

A second resource for riffs is the inverted chord, where the order of notes in a chord is changed. First and second inversions can be spotted in printed guitar music by the presence of a "slash" (/), provided the two letters are either a third or a fifth apart. A "slash" chord is one with apparently two letter names, like C/E or C/G—the note on the left is the original root note, and the note after the slash is the new lowest pitched note resulting from the inversion.

Slash chords fall into three categories: inversions of simple major and minors, chords with a passing bass note, and complex (extended) chords. For riff purposes, we'll simply consider inversions.

Understanding inversions is easy. Changing the order of the notes in a major or minor chord makes a difference to the musical effect. In a simple major or minor chord, there are three notes—for instance, C major is C, E, and G. If C is at the bottom, it's a root-position chord. Most guitar chords tend to be root position. But if the middle note (known as the third—here it's an E) is lowest, the chord is a "first inversion." If the top note (the fifth) is lowest—here it's a G—it's a "second inversion."

The number of possible inversions is always one less than the number of notes in a chord. So, with a simple triad, the first and second inversions exhaust the mathematical possibilities.

Here are inversions for C and G:

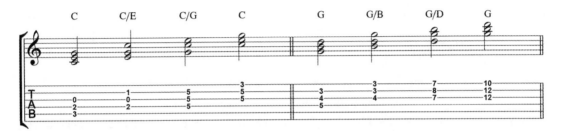

Compared to the root chord, a first inversion has a "mobile" quality—it sounds like it wants to move. The bass note wants to either rise or fall a step. For this reason, the most frequent use of first-inversion chords is in descending chord progressions, linking the root chords, such as C–G/B–Am–G–D/F♯–Em–D–A/C♯–Bm (which would have the descending bass line C–B–A–G–F♯–E–D–C♯–B). You can also invert minor chords: if C minor is CE♭G, we make it a first inversion by putting E♭ as the lowest note, or a second inversion by making G the lowest note.

Inversions of C and G

Second-inversion chords don't sound as mobile as first inversions, but they can also feature in descending or ascending progressions. Try this one: C–G/B–Am–C/G–B/F♯–Em. The second inversion has a dreamier, less focused effect. Surprisingly, it occurs in some of Nirvana's grungier numbers. Minor chords can have a second inversion too, but they're rare.

A chord progression with no root chords in it at all would sound unstable, since it is not really anchored, but a few inversions inserted between root chords can make for more interesting music. There are combined second- and first-inversion chords in the intro to Jimi Hendrix's "The Wind Cries Mary." There are inversions in songs by the Stereophonics ("Have a Nice Day"), Muse, and Dire Straits, and in the choruses of Keane's "Spiralling" and McFly's "Lies." The riff in Queen's "Tie Your Mother Down" ends with the chords G–D/F♯–C–G/B, one on each beat. There are plenty in AC/DC's catalogue, too: "You Shook Me All Night Long" wouldn't be the same without the G/B chord in the chorus, and nor would

"Highway to Hell" without the D/F♯ chord in the Mixolydian riff of A–G–D/F♯.

A complete major or minor scale can be harmonized with just inversions of chords I, IV, and V:

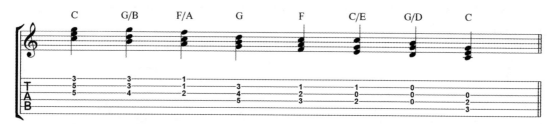

C major scale harmonized with intervals

Imagine a descending bass line: C–B–A–G–F–E–D–C. Using as many root major and minor chords as possible, it would normally be harmonized like this: C–G/B–Am–G–F–Em–Dm–C. The first inversion G/B takes care of chord VII, which is the awkward diminished triad. Using inversions, you can limit yourself to a three-chord trick and still keep the same bass line: C–G/B–F/A–G–F–C/E–G/D–C. That has only the chords of C major, F major, and G major. Play the chords in a sufficiently rhythmic way and you'll have a great riff.

The most popular inversion shapes on guitar are the easy ones: G/B, D/F♯, and A/C♯. The result is that only songs in certain keys on the guitar tend to employ inversions. If you play in a band and want to explore inversions, ask your bass player to change his or her note. That's an easier way of doing it than changing the guitar chord. Say you've got a song based around a G–C–D progression; for variety, invert it by getting the bass to play B under G, E under C, and F♯ under D. That has a different sound from the root version.

Living Colour

"Desperate People" (Reid/Glover/Calhoun/Skillings)

From *Vivid* (Epic, 1988)

"Desperate People" shows off not only Living Colour's musicianship but also their excellent grasp of song construction. It starts with feedback imitating a siren, and then plunges into a musical whirlwind of 16th notes at a tempo of about 175bpm! It's in this intro section that inverted chords are used. The sequence goes E/B–B–G/B–D/A–A (twice) and then an ascending sequence of B–G♯/B♯–F♯/C♯–C♯. This means the bass is moving up in semitones (half steps).

The musical effect of these inversions is twofold. It gives the music an up-in-the-air quality that creates anticipation of the moment it will crash to earth (which it does at 0:55, with the main riff at a tempo of approximately 103bpm). Second, it lends extra color to the harmony. The band exploit the intro's inversions further by recycling them during the bridge at the slower tempo. Listen out for the shifting ways in which these bridge chords are accented.

30 unusual chords

We've been looking at chord-based riffs that fit within the frame of a major, minor, or Mixolydian harmony. Another way of experimenting when writing riffs is to throw in the odd unusual chord. So, what makes a chord count as "unusual"?

Imagine music in the key of E major. The expected chords would be E, F#m, G#m, A, B, and C#m. (Chord VII in a major key is always a diminished triad—here D#dim—so in a rock riff the inclusion of that would sound unusual.) If the music has a hard rock/blues edge, the chords G and D are likely to occur. Since minor chords are not so common in a blues-based hard rock song, even a chord like C#m—technically in key—might strike the ear as something out of the ordinary. Any other chords will probably sound unusual, to a degree. Inserting one or two in a standard chord sequence is a good way to make an out-of-the-ordinary riff.

Radiohead's "Just" (from *The Bends*, 1995) is a good example of a song with adventurous harmony, though none of the elements really constitute a riff. Written in the key of C major, its verse pattern starts with a sequence of C–Eb–D–F (I–bIII–II^–IV), where a flat degree chord is next to a "reverse polarity" chord—a D that should be D minor. The verse also includes an Am–Ab chord change, and a chromatic descent to the chorus from A minor through Ab–G–F#–F. The chorus has the unusual chord change of C–F#–F. Such changes could easily be translated into a more rhythmic riff idiom.

A further refinement is either to add a note to a simple triad where it wouldn't be expected—turning a major chord into a sixth or a minor chord into a ninth, for example—or to use the "wrong" form of a more complex chord. Let's take sevenths as an example. In the key of E, building the correct sevenths by taking the additional note only from the scale of E major gives this: Emaj7–F#m7–G#m7–Amaj7–B7–C#m7.

Playing an unexpected type of seventh (such as Bmaj7 instead of B7, thus introducing a note not in the key) creates an unusual chord. Turning minor chords into majors or moving them up or down a semitone will have similar results. But such chords must be used sparingly in a riff, otherwise they blur the fundamental sense of key—after all, if there was no "normal," how would you know what was strange?

Here is an example of a riff with unusual chords in it:

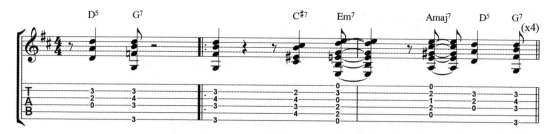

TRACK 14

Unusual chord riff

The key is D major. The first change is from D5 to G7, which gives a hard, bluesy start. (Chord IV would normally be Gmaj7, but G7 isn't so far out in a rock song.) Then the riff moves to C♯7 (instead of the usual rock ♭VII, which would be C), Em7 (chord II in D), and Amaj7 (instead of the "correct" A7). Two of the five chords (D and Em7) are in key, two are "off-key" by a single note (G7, Amaj7), and one is wholly off-key (C♯7).

> **Weezer**
>
> **"Undone—The Sweater Song"** (Cuomo)
>
> From *Weezer* (aka *The Blue Album*, DGC, 1994)

Weezer formed in 1992, and this song shows something of the influence of Nirvana on bands at that time. The chorus is a I–IV–V–IV progression, which is straightforward enough (with an occasional ♭III chord toward the end). What is arresting is the opening sequence. The song is played in detuned standard. The shapes involve G7–C7–D7–C7. This arpeggio riff is G–E–B♭–B, C–E–B♭–B, D–F♯–C–B, C–E–B♭–B, using an open string and a collision of sevenths. This makes for an unusual dissonant arpeggio. The underlying chord movement is familiar, but the additional dissonant note isn't. See also the G♯ chord with an open B string in the verse of "Say It Ain't So (Version 3)."

Black Rebel Motorcycle Club

"Red Eyes and Tears" (BRMC)

From *Black Rebel Motorcycle Club* (Virgin America, 2001)

Along with the Hives, San Francisco three-piece Black Rebel Motorcycle Club enjoyed some success playing a guitar rock loosely based on the Stooges and the MC5—with elements of Television and the Velvet Underground. It reached an audience who didn't like nu-metal and wanted a new take on some traditional rock virtues—like short songs and hooks.

"Red Eyes and Tears" is a fine example of a rock song given an exciting slant by the inclusion of an unusual chord riff. The verse features a C♯ octave riff, which indicates the altered tuning for the guitar (C5 = CGCGGC). The unusual chords enter at 0:58 and 1:50, and at 2:14 during the guitar break. The riff consists of major thirds on the guitar—EG♯ sliding down to D♯G (or F double-sharp), and then to a phrase that implies C♯m. The bass line moves to B and A♯, and then back to C♯. The net result is a sense of an E–D♯–C♯m progression, which is unusual because D♯ isn't usually found in C♯ minor. It's a dark, sleazy riff that gives the song a haunted quality reminiscent of the Smiths' "How Soon Is Now?," though coming from a West Coast band it isn't surprising that "Red Eyes and Tears" also includes guitar phrases out of the '60s "raga-rock" book. Other unusual chord progressions occur in BRMC's "Love Burns," with the E5-implied C♯m–C5 over an E pedal during the verse, and "As Sure as the Sun."

At the Drive-In

"One Armed Scissor" (At the Drive-In)

From *Relationship of Command* (Fearless Records, 2004)

"One Armed Scissor" shows how contemporary rock bands combine riff ideas from a variety of sources. It enters with a frantic stabbing Em7 chord out of the Hendrix of "Foxy Lady," then it unexpectedly subsides into an unusual "floating" verse that has an Amadd9 chord. An overdub on the left of the stereo image has a chord that includes a dissonant G♯ note.

The chordal riff for the chorus is the sequence Em7–D–F–C (I–VII–♭II–VI), which, with its vocal phrase of "get away," recalls Nirvana. Notice the punchy gaps between the chords.

The second verse has different guitar ideas and arrangement to the first verse, with an implied sequence of Am–G–D/F#–Em. The arrangement changes quite frequently. The bridge has another sequence of Em–G–D–C (I–III–VI–VII). It's a track that shows how rhythms have become more asymmetrical in recent decades.

Alice in Chains

"Check My Brain" (Cantrell/Duvall/Kinney/Inez)

From *Black Gives Way to Blue* (Virgin/EMI, 2009)

Alice in Chains emerged in the early '90s Seattle grunge scene, along with bands like Nirvana, Soundgarden, and Pearl Jam. Taken from the band's fourth album, this track made the *Billboard* top 100 and won a Grammy nomination. It begins with a striking update of the semitone riff idea that Eddie Cochran played in the rock 'n' roll era. On a detuned guitar by a semitone, a first-fret E on the sixth string is bent a semitone to F and then released back, with a G♭ (♭2) completing the figure. It is a modern way of using the sound of a bend—quite different from how bends were played in blues-rock days.

The chorus comes as something of a surprise, having a more conventional I–♭VII–IV–♭III–IV–V sequence. The bridge provides an unusual chromatic chord progression: D♭–G–G♭–F, which in F is ♭VI–II^–♭II–I.

techniques for playing riffs

Having surveyed 30 types of riff, let's proceed to musical approaches and guitar techniques to inspire new riffs of your own, and maybe to develop the riffs you already have.

Repetition and development

Possibly the greatest trap for writers of riffs is not realizing the potential of the riffs they create. Rock music should be exciting, so don't bore your listener. Repetition is essential, but always estimate where the line is between hearing a riff too many times and hearing it too few. Err on the side of too few repetitions. It's always good to leave people wanting more. If the listener hears your song and thinks, *That's a great riff, that song was over too soon*, chances are they will listen again—exactly what you want.

A new riff takes shape in a specific key, with a given rhythmic feel, at a certain speed. Once these are decided upon, write your riff down and/or record it. Then, with its initial form captured, mess around with it. Most bands don't do enough of such exploration. Do it too early and the original inspiration might get blurred or lost. But once the riff is captured as audio, you are free to realize its potential. The original is always there to go back to if nothing better comes up.

Don't think of a riff as a finished entity with the first version preserved. Think of it instead as maybe only showing one of its faces to you. Walk around it and have a look at its other sides. How is this "walking round" done? Remember the RHM formula: rhythm-harmony-melody. Your riff has a rhythmic facet, a harmonic facet, and a melodic facet. So why not try consciously altering them?

Tempo

Try changing the rhythm of some of the notes. Shorten some, lengthen others. First, check the tempo. If the riff is intended for a medium- or high-tempo song, speed it up gradually and see how fast it will go before losing its character (or your fingers fall off). What you're looking for is not the fastest tempo at which the riff could be played, but the fastest tempo at which the riff can be played without losing its identity. You can test this notion of a riff losing its identity: take any famous riff cited in this book and play it faster or slower than the original—there's always a point where it doesn't sound as good, or where the riff loses something. The change in tempo eventually robs the riff of its character. To test the tempo of a slow riff, make it slower. At a certain point it becomes ineffective because there isn't enough forward momentum. An audience will get bored—and so might the band.

This principle of what happens when the tempo of a riff is changed was impressed on me years ago, when I heard a bootleg of Led Zeppelin's 1979 Knebworth performance. Either the show was recorded on a slow-running tape deck, or the vinyl pressing was cut at the wrong speed, but the consequence was that the songs were faster than they should have been, and the pitch was a whole semitone sharp. The fast songs sounded silly and lost their power, but the slower numbers sometimes gained: "Kashmir" became even more relentless, and "Ten Years Gone" was simply spectacular when played with more drive. Jeff Buckley's amusing send-up of "Kashmir" (on *Live À L'Olympia*) shows what happens when the increase is too great. He pretends to copy a 33-rpm vinyl album turning at 45 rpm. The "Kashmir" riff instantly loses its grandeur.

Many songwriters record a song, as a demo or even for release, only to find later that the song now sounds too slow. There is a natural reason why demos often turn out too slow: they are generally recorded when the composer is effectively still getting to grips with the song. As a result, it's not surprising this should affect the tempo by keeping it below what it could be.

One further type of rhythmic variation involves shifting the accent on a riff. More complicated would be repeating a riff in a different time signature altogether, or rewriting an idea that initially arrived as a 4/4 riff in 5/4. (We'll look at alternate time signatures in a few pages' time.)

Reharmonizing

The next way of developing a riff would be to change the chords that go with it. Try turning major chords into their relative minors, and vice versa. The relative minor is always three semitones below the major chord (C to Am, D to Bm, F to Dm, and so on). If the riff has only fifths or fourths, which are tonally neutral, you could put major chords behind some of its appearances and minor chords in another part of the song.

Otherwise, with a simple unison riff where guitar and bass are playing the same notes several octaves apart, change the bass note to imply different chords, or even inversions of the same chords. First inversions will imply major and minor chords without actually playing them, and they are also useful to delay a root note unison riff, because the inversions will sound less "grounded" than when the guitar and bass play the same notes at different octaves.

A good example of reharmonizing is Garbage's hit "Androgyny." Leaving aside the A pentatonic minor phrase that punctuates the verse and intro, the main riff comes at the chorus—an E pentatonic minor phrase with an octave leap from the bottom E to the E at fret seven on string five. As such, it's a distant relative of riffs like "Black Night" and "How Many More Times." But it's what Garbage do with this riff that is interesting. The predictable approach would have been to transpose the riff onto the same root note of each chord in turn. Instead, in the first bar of the chorus, the E pentatonic minor riff is played against an E minor harmony, so it fits. But through the rest of the chorus the riff stays the same while we hear it against the chords of G, C, and F. This causes tension and makes the riff sound different, even though it hasn't gone anywhere. Type O Negative's "My Girlfriend's Girlfriend" uses a similar technique.

Transposing a riff

Another way of changing the harmony is to transpose a riff into a different key or onto a different root note. The term "transposition" implies that the shape of the riff stays the same—none of its internal musical relationships change. You simply raise or lower it in pitch. The structural importance of this is that it shifts the music away from the key pitch, so a return to the riff is possible, the riff having been refreshed. One of the striking things about Tool's epic 15-minute "7empest" is how much of the track clings to the keynote. Although there are changes in texture, this creates a curiously static feeling.

There are three main ways of using transposition. The first is to follow the structure of the song. One time-honored way of developing a riff is to repeat it during a verse and move it up with the expected chord changes; another is to transpose it several times at the bridge, or for the guitar solo. Think of Blind Faith's "Presence of the Lord," which starts as a pentatonic minor riff on A, then is transposed to D and E. Hendrix does this in the middle section of "In from the Storm," where an A blues-scale riff is transposed onto B and then C. Transposition comes into its own toward the end of a song where it can breathe new life into a riff that's been heard many times, by re-pitching it.

A riff can be transposed by any interval. Within a 12-bar progression where the riff replaces overt strummed chords, the transposition is likely to be first onto the note a fourth higher, then a fifth higher. The first type of transposition was developed in rock in the '60s during the British blues boom, when many songs were 12-bar sequences with the expected chord changes.

In bands with a single guitarist and no keyboard player, the guitar part could be a riff rather than the actual whole chord. So, for a 12-bar in G, that could mean a riff on G played four times; then at bar 5, when the music changes to a C chord, this riff would be transposed up a fourth to the note C; and in bar 9, when the music reaches a D chord, the riff would transpose up a fifth from G to D. In this manner, the 12-bar could be played without chords but with a single one-bar riff occurring in three different positions, as in this example:

TRACK 15

Transposed riff

Often in such an arrangement, the guitar plays the riff with the bass doubling an octave or two lower. This kind of transposition is easy on the guitar; if the initial riff is played on the lower three strings only, it moves up or down the neck or across so the root is on string five and retains the same pattern. The Jeff Beck/ Rod Stewart track "Rock My Plimsole" is a good example, as are Cream's "Strange Brew," Free's "Worry," Taste's "Same Old Story," and Rory Gallagher's "Messin' with the Kid" (in E Mixolydian, with the riff crammed into eight bars). Bass lines can also be transposed, as in James Brown's "Papa's Got a Brand New Bag."

The second type of transposition doesn't depend on supporting a preordained musical structure like a 12-bar. It involves transposing a riff wherever you like, depending on which section of the song you're in. Probably the most popular shift for a riff is to go up a tone. One heavy rock formula has a riff shifted up a tone after the second chorus for a guitar solo. Another favorite shift is the minor third, because of its relationship to the pentatonic minor scale (which has a minor third between the first two notes—i.e., A–C). In fact, you could transpose a riff on the basis of the pentatonic scale, so the first riff on A is shifted in turn onto C, D, E, and G, these being distributed through the song. For a more unsettling transposition, move up or down a semitone, or even a tritone.

Free's "Moonshine" has a single-note A pentatonic minor riff transposed to D in the verse. The bridge of KISS's "Detroit Rock City" has a C pentatonic minor riff that's then shifted up a tone. Jimi Hendrix's "Izabella" has a verse riff transposed up a minor third, and "Beginnings" has even more instances. In Led Zeppelin's "Heartbreaker," the main riff first appears on the note A, is then heard on B, and then returns to A. After the second chorus, when the riff comes in again it appears on C, then D, and finally on E; one two-bar riff has appeared at five pitches.

One point about working with the guitar is that if the original riff uses open strings, these will be lost after most transpositions. Chord-based riffs or riffs with inversions, and pedal/drone-note riffs, are susceptible in this regard. It may not be possible to find another open string to do the job of the one in the initial riff—in which case either cheat (in the recording process) by using a capo, or retune the guitar to overdub the transposed version of the riff. Or (more sensibly, given live performance, etc.) take the transposition challenge as an opportunity to write a variation. In other words, "compose out" the problem of the un-transposable open string—as shown in the example that follows.

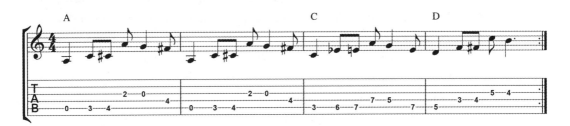

The third transposition method involves deciding that an initial riff idea is not in the most effective key—whether for the singer's voice range or for the guitar. So, what keys suit the guitar? Is there such a thing as a riff-friendly key?

In hard rock and heavy metal, the number of keys is more limited, since

TRACK 16

Transposed riff
with variations

it requires keys that are low in pitch with regard to open strings. This means preeminently E and A. F♯ and B are also hard rock favorites, as in both keys the open string a tone below the keynote (E below F♯, A below B) is the flattened seventh of the scale, as is common in rock. To increase the "heaviosity" of their riffs, many bands resort to detuning (which we'll come to in a moment).

We could extend this and say that there are keys in which the guitar simply sounds better. With some instruments, the question of which key to play in is not vital. There might be a minor inconvenience of fingering, but not a substantial difference to the sound (on the piano, for instance). The guitar, though, is key-sensitive. So, what are the main factors that determine whether a key gets used on the guitar?

First, will the key allow open strings as notes on the major scale or natural minor? The majority of keys allow at least one open string, but it's more effective to have several. The more notes a key has that are open strings, the more likely there will be resonant open-string shapes. The six open strings, EADGBE, are present in the keys of C, G, and D and their respective minors Am, Em, and Bm. If we allow ourselves a Mixolydian A (A B C♯ D E F♯ G: a major scale with a lowered seventh), all the open strings are "in key."

Notice that these keys are on the "sharp" side of C major. The guitar has a natural bias toward sharp keys and away from flat keys. For example, write a riff in F major, the first flat key, and the guitar "loses" one of its open strings, B, which becomes B♭. This didn't deter Franz Ferdinand from using the flat key of C minor on "Jacqueline" and other songs.

In some keys, important notes of the desired scale will be open strings. The Yardbirds' "Stroll On" depends on the chords G and A, with the bass note dropping to the open E string. This would not work as well in any other key.

In rock music, major-key harmony is often replaced by a hybrid based on the pentatonic minor for that note. The formula is as follows. First, take a pentatonic minor scale and build major chords on each note. So, if A pentatonic minor is A C D E G and we think of it as a "cut down" version of the A minor scale, the chords that arise on that scale are Am, C, Dm, Em, and G. For a hard rock song, it would be more promising to make up a sequence using the major chords A, C, D, E, and G. You can also throw in an F chord for good measure.

This approach is heard on *White Blood Cells* by the White Stripes. The album has three songs centered on A, five on G, two on Em, one on Am, two on D, one on B, and one on E. In each, chords occur that don't strictly belong in the major key on these notes but are constructed on these pentatonic minors.

Another way to think of this is to take a major key and map out its seven primary chords. In E major, these are E, F#m, G#m, A, B, C#m, and D#dim. Throw away the diminished chord (because this is rock 'n' roll, not jazz) and the three minor chords (because minor chords are for wimps, apparently). That leaves chords I, IV, and V—E, A, and B—the good old "three-chord trick."

Next, take notes three, six, and seven of the scale (G#, C#, and D#), lower them all a semitone to G, C, and D, and turn them into major chords. The result is a scheme of six major chords to play with for songwriting. Now, to evolve into the White Stripes, dump the bass player and get a strong color scheme . . .

Riff-friendly keys

The following table shows the classic rock Mixolydian chord riff of I–♭VII–IV in a variety of keys. They are all the same chord change, merely at a different pitch, but that change of pitch has considerable implications for the guitar, because the voicing of the chord—how many open strings it has, its lowest bass note, and so on—is critical to how it sounds.

I	♭VII	IV	
C#	B	F#	
F#	E	B	
B	A	E	"Broad Daylight," Free
E	D	A	"Communication Breakdown," Led Zeppelin
A	G	D	"Won't Get Fooled Again," the Who
D	C	G	"Freebird," Lynyrd Skynyrd
G	F	C	"Queen Bitch," David Bowie
C	B♭	F	
F	E♭	B♭	
B♭	A♭	E♭	
E♭	D♭	A♭	
A♭	G♭	D♭	
D♭	C♭	G♭	
G♭	F♭	C♭	
C♭	B♭♭	F♭	

Chord shapes

The second factor in whether a key is "guitar-friendly" concerns chord shapes. The more open-string chords a key allows, the easier it is to play, and the more sound comes from the instrument—especially on an acoustic. This is one of the reasons for the appeal of open tunings, which increase the amount of open-string "ring." C major's primary chords for songs are C, Dm, Em, F, G, and Am, and Bdim, the latter usually replaced by a B♭. Among the first six, there's only one barre chord: F. It would be easy to substitute for that by playing an Fmaj7, which is why in tutor books beginners are often taught to play Fmaj7 before F.

Now compare the chords of C with those of E major, which are E, F♯m, G♯m, A, B, and C♯m. There are four barre chords. Using the hard rock formula outlined above would lead to E, G, A, B, C, D—much easier. Or how about a key like B♭? The main chords for songs are B♭, Cm, Dm, E♭, F, and Gm. All except Dm are barre chords—and this is a key with only two flats! So, it's clear that changing key in a "flatward" direction introduces barre chords.

This is why, when you are transcribing a song that appears to be in E♭, you should always ask the following:

- Has the artist detuned a semitone, so the shapes, patterns, and open strings are those in E, though the guitar is actually pitched lower by a half step? Detuning is common among rock bands.
- Are they using capos at the first fret (where E♭ is a D shape), or the third fret (where E♭ is a C shape)?
- If the song is by a singer/songwriter, suspect the presence of a capo. Ringing open strings, descending bass lines on the lower strings, and easy inversions (G/B and D/F♯) are a giveaway that there's a capo in use.

So, the guitar-friendly keys are pretty much F, C, G, D, A, and E, and a capo puts a difficult flat or sharp key into the guise of one of those. One final point concerns riffs that start with an open A string. With a 12-bar, three-chord format, if you put the song in A, each of the three riffs (A, D, and E) should be transposable and still commence from an open string.

To see how choice of key can alter a riff, take Jimi Hendrix's "Freedom," from the album *First Rays of the New Rising Sun*. The opening riff is C♯ pentatonic minor. What is unusual about this riff is the fact that because the key is C♯, the open bottom E becomes the flattened third of the scale. So, Hendrix drops a sixth from the root note C♯ on string five to the bottom E and then climbs up. This has the effect of making the E seem lower than it is (a technique known to bass players).

The effect is more pronounced if the drop is to the major third of a chord, which in this key would be E♯. Each time Hendrix comes back up to C♯, he hits a C♯m7 (possibly C♯7♯9) chord on that note. I recommend the version of "Freedom" recorded at the Isle of Wight Festival in 1970, which is full of brilliant guitar ideas—an example of how Hendrix's compositions became more soul-influenced and sophisticated toward the end of his life.

Detuning for riffs

The simplest detuning is when the entire tuning of the guitar is lowered by one semitone to E♭A♭D♭G♭B♭E♭. The chords and scale patterns of standard tuning remain the same; they are one semitone lower in pitch. Some players in the '80s and '90s took this further by detuning by a tone (DGCFAD), or even a tone and a half (C♯F♯BEG♯C♯). This greatly increases the "sludge" factor of riffs and will make you feel neck-deep in cold mud—which for a death metal band may be the desired effect.

Drop D tuning can be applied to any of these, giving drop D♭/C♯, drop C, etc. These all share the property of creating a power chord (fifth) on the lowest three strings that can be held with a single finger barre.

Detuning by this amount has interesting effects on a set of light-gauge "9" strings, because they go slack. This is fine for bending, but not so good for intonation, and they won't take kindly to being hit hard. Most players who detune compensate by shifting up a gauge in strings for every semitone they lower them. A "10" set for E♭ standard tuning gives standard string tension and more tone. Experiment and find a combination that feels comfortable. Using a slacker tension can yield results with riffs that incorporate sleazy quarter/semitone bends on the lowest strings.

Tony Iommi was a heavy metal pioneer of detuning. On Black Sabbath's third album, *Master of Reality*, he succumbed to the evil lure of D♭ major by detuning down a tone and a half on "Children of the Grave," "Into the Void," and "Lord of This World," and he took the same approach for the later "Supernaut," "Cornucopia," "Snowblind," "Sabbath Bloody Sabbath," "A National Acrobat," and "Killing Yourself to Live" (though the key center there is G♭). The lower tuning (and light-gauge strings) also relieved some of the discomfort Iommi experienced because of his damaged fretting hand.

Black Sabbath's use of detuning was to be highly influential on such subgenres as grunge, "sludge metal," and nu-metal. Tracks that feature detuning include Linkin Park's "One Step Closer," Limp Bizkit's "Pollution" and "Rollin'," the Offspring's "Americana," Dokken's "Sunless Days," and Korn's "All in the Family."

Another possibility for players who want their riffs to sound heavier is to get a seven-, eight- or nine-string guitar. On a seven-string, the additional string is a B a fourth below the standard bottom E; on an eight-string, there is an F♯ or E below that at the same pitch as the lowest string on a bass guitar! A nine-string guitar is often tuned C♯F♯BEADGBE. Korn tracks like "Twist" and "Swallow" feature seven-string guitars tuned down a semitone; on songs such as "Porno Creep" and "No Place to Hide," they are tuned down a tone. The usual shapes for fifths, fourths, and so on remain intact, and for something really insane you could always put the seven-string into its equivalent of drop D with the low B down a tone to A, which provides a bowel-shocking low fifth on the bottom two strings.

Mike Mushok of Staind has used BEADGB, which is standard tuning with a low B but no top string (like the lowest six strings of a seven-string guitar). Drop D on this would be BDADGB. He has also used variations such as ADADGB, and AEADGB, and AEBDGB. (For examples of how bassists can get into five-string riffola and more, see the interview with John Paul Jones in section 5.)

Aside from this detuning malarkey, the illusion of a detuned riff can be created by playing fourths on strings five and six where fifths might have been expected. This shape, which has become more widely used, is 5577xx for D/A. Back in 1967, Jimi Hendrix played this shape in two positions in the verse of "Spanish Castle Magic." The effect is startling: it sounds as though he's fallen off the bottom of the Strat. More recently, this shape has been extended to 555710x (GDGDG) in any of the drop D tunings.

Altered tunings in rock

New riffs can evolve if detuning goes one step further. Instead of just detuning each string by the same amount and ending up in a lower version of standard tuning, move into a new tuning. Altered tunings can yield different types of riff— maybe with an unusual chord or run of notes. Although mainly explored by instrumentalists and singer/songwriters, there's no reason why rock guitarists can't use altered tunings for their own heavier purposes, as bands like Sonic Youth have demonstrated.

Altered tunings came into rock music from two main sources. One was the blues, because blues slide players often played in open A or open E. Rock guitarists tried these open tunings for slide, got to grips with Elmore James's classic blues riff "Dust My Broom" (a slide to a 12th-fret Em7 chord), and thought they could write other music in these tunings.

The other source was the '60s acoustic guitar style known as "folk baroque," pioneered by players such as Davy Graham, Bert Jansch, John Renbourn, and Martin Carthy. They were interested in open tunings that enabled a fingerstyle guitarist to play a melody, a bass line, and a harmony in the middle—all at once.

From the rock perspective, it was highly significant that Jimmy Page chose to put his adaptation of Jansch's "Blackwaterside" (as described below) on the first Led Zeppelin album as "Black Mountainside." Page went on to record many other tunings, and, as Led Zeppelin's fame grew through the '70s, more players were influenced by his example.

Open tunings

Altered tunings can be divided into two main groups: those that make a simple major or minor chord, and those that don't. The former we can term "open tunings." When it comes to rock riffs, the most significant open tuning is open G (DGDGBD). This tuning was adopted by Keith Richards in the late '60s and is a cornerstone of the Rolling Stones sound. Open G is heard on Stones classics like "Brown Sugar," "Tumbling Dice," and "Start Me Up," and on Black Crowes tunes such as "Hard to Handle" and "Hotel Illness."

The popular way to use this open tuning for riffs is to add additional suspended fourth, sixth, and ninth notes to the major chord that results from a barre at any fret. The open tuning allows these on/off chord figures more effectively than standard tuning. Ronnie Wood has written similar riffs with both the Faces and the Stones in open E (EBEG♯BE).

With any open major tuning, frets three, five, seven, ten, and twelve are the crucial positions. These frets represent major chords on a pentatonic minor scale. In open G tuning, fret three is B♭, fret five is C, fret seven is D, fret ten is F, and fret 12 is G (the octave above the open-string chord). The notes G–B♭–C–D–F make a G pentatonic minor scale, and these represent the root notes of chords I, ♭III, IV, V, and ♭VII in G.

This is the obvious way to work in open G tuning, in the key of G. An oblique approach would be to write a riff in the key of A in open G. Fret two is now A, fret five is C, fret seven is D, fret nine is E, and fret 12 is G, which gives the notes of A pentatonic minor. In this key, the open-string chord becomes the flattened seventh (♭VII) blues chord in A.

A third approach is to write a riff in the key of C in open G tuning. Now the open strings and 12th fret are G (chord V), fret three is B♭ (♭VII), C is at fret five (I), E♭ is at eight (♭III), and F is at ten (IV). Other keys are obtained by using a capo. Billy Corgan tuned one of his guitars to EGDGBE (giving an open Em7 tuning) for Smashing Pumpkins' "Sweet Sweet."

Non-open tunings

An altered tuning that doesn't form an open major or minor chord is DADGAD. This tuning originated with acoustic folk-blues guitar pioneer Davy Graham. Inspired by the music of Morocco, the story goes, Graham worked out the tuning to imitate the drones and pedals he heard in North African music. It was poetic/musical justice that the tuning's greatest moment in rock consequently came in Led Zeppelin's epic "Kashmir." Jimmy Page also used it on "Midnight Moonlight" from the Firm's first album, and on the instrumental "White Summer."

One of the appeals of DADGAD for the rock guitarist is that the three lowest-pitched strings, DAD, make a perfect fifth plus an octave that can be played with a single first-finger barre.

Drop D

Something of the effect of altered tunings can be had by the simpler method of a single string alteration. The most popular is drop D. The name is misleading because it isn't a D that's being dropped, it's the bottom E string, which has gone down a tone to D, but it's a good first step into altered tuning. Retune either by comparing the open fourth D string until the sixth string is in tune an octave lower, or tune down until the seventh fret of string six is in tune with the open A string.

Remember that for every semitone you tune down, the notes on a string move up a fret. Straightaway, you'll find drop D alters the guitar's standard tuning bias from E toward D. You can bend notes on this detuned bottom string easily because of the decrease in tension. Smashing Pumpkins' "Hummer" and "Jellybelly," Bon Jovi's "Let It Rock," Led Zeppelin's "Moby Dick," and Guns N' Roses' "The Garden" are examples of drop D.

Velvet Revolver's "Slither" lives up to its title courtesy of a drop D riff using the D blues scale (D F G Ab A C) with the addition of the major third (F#). The repeated F–F# and Ab–A changes in the riff give it a snakelike quality. Listen for how the riff is doubled in various ways as the song progresses, notably at several octaves up on the second chorus and the outro. Alice Cooper's "Gimme" is an example of how the tuning makes it very easy to play progressions such as fifth chords on the degrees 4–b4–3–1 and 5–b5–4–3 (using the natural minor scale as reference) and to alternate V→bVI in fifths, as the song does at the end of the chorus. "Gimme" is also an example of combining a semitone lower tuning with the principle of drop D, to create what is now called drop C# (C#G#C#F#A#D#).

An intriguing variation on drop D is "double drop D," where the top and bottom E strings are both tuned down to D. This gives DADGBD—only one string away from open G. Neil Young uses DADGBD to great effect in "Cinnamon Girl" (see below).

Recent bands have experimented with taking the sixth string even further down, opening up a bigger interval with the fifth string. Drop D tuning means there is a fifth between the lowest two strings. In Alter Bridge's "Still Remain," the gap widens to a minor seventh (Bb to Ab). This extreme detuning will mean the sixth string is almost certain to be the keynote.

When playing altered and open tunings with overdrive/fuzz, you will find that, because of the increased resonance, sustain, and enhanced overtones, you may want to back off the distortion. This is especially true for chords more complicated than fifths, and also with riffs that take advantage of one of the benefits in altered tuning: playing notes on adjacent strings only a tone or semitone apart. This is tricky in standard tuning, but in altered tunings it's possible to get harp-like clusters. There's no reason why you can't use these in a riff, but they sound better if the guitar is clean(ish).

When writing riffs in altered tunings, write them down in some way—chord boxes will do. It can be frustrating, years later, to try to relearn a riff written in an altered tuning—even if you know it—to find you can't remember the shapes nor work them out from an audio source. Chances are, if you write a couple of riffs in altered tunings, you will get to like the tunings; you'll soon find you've invented several tunings and it's too much to remember without notes.

For more details about tunings and an altered-tuning chord dictionary, see my book *How to Write Songs in Altered Guitar Tunings*.

Bert Jansch

"Blackwaterside" (trad arr. Jansch)

From *Jack Orion* (Transatlantic, 1966)

Riffs don't only occur in electric guitar music. "Folk baroque" is the label given to a complex style of acoustic guitar that flourished in the mid-'60s and influenced a generation of players. It was initiated by Davy Graham, who wrote "Anji," an attractive solo piece on a descending Am–G–F–E sequence that might also be considered a riff, and a version of the traditional tune "She Moved Through the Fair." Associated with Graham were John Renbourn and Bert Jansch, and the latter's album *Jack Orion* was a big influence on the young Jimmy Page.

The essence of folk baroque is that it's a self-contained fingerstyle for steel-string acoustic. A typical Jansch or Renbourn instrumental has a melody with a bass line and supporting harmony. The bass line is often an alternating octave played with the thumb. The other fingers play higher notes in a syncopated rhythm against this. A single piece may contain marked breaks in this rhythm, where the player strikes all the strings by a flick of the finger. It's a style that encourages thinking in other than standard chord shapes. Instead, each string is almost a separate instrument; the fingerpicking unites them.

"Blackwaterside" was played in drop D (DADGBE), with a capo probably at the second fret. It features the archetypal British folk guitar riff, being to the genre what "Whole Lotta Love" or "Smoke on the Water" is to heavy rock. Jansch's riff consists of an accented hammer-on/pull-off figure that he hits in between some of the lyrics. He develops it by adding extra pull-offs from time to time. The effect is hypnotic.

Jansch played variations of the same riff on "The First Time Ever I Saw Your Face" and "The Gardener," and it was also the model for Jimmy Page's instrumental "Black Mountainside."

The Move

"Brontosaurus" (Wood)

From *Looking On* (Capitol/Fly, 1970)

This was one of the last Move singles before writer and multi-instrumentalist Roy Wood formed ELO and then swiftly moved on to his glam-era band Wizzard. "Brontosaurus" is a good example of what can be done by detuning the E string to D. The riff is a slow climb up a D blues scale, three times; each time, the bass supplies a different root note, with a descending phrase at the end to give balance and wind the whole thing up to repeat. This is a very early example of using the slack tension of a dropped sixth string to create "smudgy" pitch bends, several decades in advance of the technique becoming *de rigueur* in '90s nu-metal.

The main guitar riff is multitracked and partly doubled on one side by a synth. The last bar of the riff is heard frequently in the chorus at the end of various lines. At about 2:35, the music goes into a thrilling double time and a new pentatonic major riff enters, changing on each chord. Notice the hint of piano the last time the slow riff is played, like a much slowed-down "Lady Madonna."

Neil Young

"Cinnamon Girl" (Young)

From *Everybody Knows This Is Nowhere* (Reprise, 1970)

This track has a surprising and haunting erotic charge, caused in no small measure by the tuning. "Cinnamon Girl" is a wonderful example of "double drop D" tuning (DADGBD), recorded early in Neil Young's long, eventful career (and on his first outing with Crazy Horse). It sounds like a heavy rock band rehearsing in a barn somewhere in Arizona. The main riff is two bars long and has two phrases: the first is a C–D chord change, followed by a descending run that goes down a D Mixolydian scale to a flattened third (F) and then to the note G. The second bar repeats this, but the run stops on that low bluesy flattened third.

Listen for the frequent omission of percussion on the last offbeat of the 4/4 bar during the riff. Though it's possible in standard tuning, this riff would lack the low D and a couple of other notes.

The DADGBD tuning comes into its own on the verse, where it creates a resonant D5 (with a unison D on the top two strings), a beautiful Amadd4, a

Cadd9, and a G, before culminating in a quick ascending phrase that moves in fifths up a D pentatonic minor scale (F–G–A–C–D).

The Faces

"Stay with Me" (Wood/Stewart)

From *A Nod's as Good as a Wink . . . to a Blind Horse* (Warner Bros., 1971)

Ron Wood remains one of the less appreciated rock rhythm guitarists—something not helped by the fact of sharing rhythm duties in the Rolling Stones with one Keith Richards. Much of Wood's rhythm work is driven by fuzzy pungent dyads—pairs of notes or even threesomes, where a note is hammered on or pulled off to create tension. Wood has always had an astonishing tone, unlike anyone else's, courtesy of a custom-made, Les Paul–shaped, metallic-fronted Zemaitis with a fuzz box built in. Nothing captures this tone better than the opening seconds of "Too Bad," where Wood, in standard tuning, constructs a riff from a C–F chord change by hammering-on various notes and using the blues flattened third in both instances—or "Miss Judy's Farm," or "Stay with Me." It is a real workout for your little finger.

"Stay with Me" uses open-E tuning (the electric version of open D, favored on acoustic because the strings aren't tuned up) and the block on/off chords you would expect. What lifts it far above other examples of boozy, goodtime rock is the contrast in tempos and keys. It starts fast and frenetic in E, puts its verses and choruses in a half-time A major, and then reprises the intro for the wild coda.

Form and length of riffs

An important aspect of the craft of composing good riffs is to understand their form. By form, I don't mean specific musical elements like melody, harmony, or rhythm. Rather, it refers to how many times bits of the riff are repeated, how many bars a riff takes to play, and so on.

The simplest riff form is a single phrase lasting one bar. But riffs also last two, three, and four bars. Three is less common, because if repeated it gives a six-bar phrase, which goes against the tendency in rock to group in multiples of four. However, a three-bar riff repeated four times gives 12 bars. Riffs longer than four bars are harder to articulate as a single unit—though of course this depends on factors like the tempo and how many notes the riff has.

Let's call our example one-bar riff "a1." A typical approach would be to repeat it in multiples of four, with the arrangement changing around it:

a1 a1 a1 a1

To add interest, change the bass guitar's part underneath with a pedal effect, or make the bass note imply a different harmony.

Imagine a one-bar riff on the notes A, C, and G. With a bass A underneath it, it would probably sound like A pentatonic minor, but the bass could enter with an F or a C and give it a different harmonic color.

The next variation on this riff form is to change the fourth bar. This gives us a 3+1 pattern: three riffs the same, and then one with a slight variation ("a2"):

a1 a1 a1 a2

If there are eight bars to play with, instead of repeating this idea we could make the repeat end with a third variation, so the eight bars would look like this:

a1 a1 a1 a2
a1 a1 a1 a3

If there were 16 bars, another option would be to repeat the eight-bar form but add a fourth variation on the last time:

a1 a1 a1 a2
a1 a1 a1 a3
a1 a1 a1 a2
a1 a1 a1 a4

This is the limit of what can be done with the "a" riff without something else happening, since in the 16-bar example the riff has occurred in its original form 12 times. The trick with getting a2, a3, and a4 to fit is to make sure they work harmonically. You don't want a2 and a3 to sound more decisive and finished than a4, since a4 is the last in the whole block. So, if this riff is based on the chord of A major, it is more effective if the a2 and a3 variations end on a note that implies a D or E chord, or perhaps the ♭III C chord or the ♭VII G chord.

Another angle is to take the original "a" riff and make a four-bar phrase, placing its variations one after another:

a1   a2   a3   a4

Whether the listener hears this as four riffs or a single one with four parts would depend on how similar the individual bars were.

Another popular variant on this is to make the riff in bars 2 and 4 an answer to the original riff:

a1   a2   a1   a3

A slightly less common riff form is where there's a single variation in bar 3:

a1   a1   a3   a1

So far, the assumption has been that the riff is a one-bar phrase. But riffs can also be two bars long, in which case some of the forms above can be applied to a two-bar riff. Just treat "a" as two bars instead of one.

There are many more variations to the form of riffs, but these basic patterns of repetition, answer, and variation are the most relevant. They can be expanded by combining them with the principles of rhythm, harmony, and melody.

How riffs are used in songs

As with a lead guitar solo, how impressive a riff is can depend also on the musical context in which it's placed. This is connected to the genre of music to which it belongs.

In most styles of hard rock and metal, the riff is at least as important as anything else in the song, including the chorus, which in traditional songs is supposed to be the "hook"—the most memorable part. In heavy rock, the riff can be found as the intro and then kept going during the verse with the vocalist singing over it.

Writing a song along these lines, where almost every part is accompanied by riffs and not chord progressions, you either need to write several riffs, or variations on the initial riff, for the various sections. There may also be a necessity to alter the riff's presentation in terms of arrangement or dynamics.

One method is to play the riff at full volume during the intro and chorus, but for the verse pull the guitars out of the mix and have the bass play the riff instead (as on Nirvana's "Smells Like Teen Spirit"). Another approach is to simplify the riff for the verse and keep its full form for the chorus or links. Otherwise, use the riff for the intro and as a link between the chorus and the verse. The same riff can then support the guitar solo, or lead the way out of the solo, or occur again in the coda (the final section of a song). This is a more mainstream way of writing a rock song, where the vocal sections of verse and chorus are supported by chords.

A "busy" riff can take attention away from the vocal line. It can also be difficult to create a melody over a riff—because a riff not only sets up competing melodic shapes and rhythms but also doesn't offer the same harmonic support to the vocal melody as chords. To fit a melody over a riff, strive to match the melody rhythm with the riff's rhythm, and choose notes that harmonize with the riff. If the riff has lots of gaps in it, the melody may work in those gaps.

In a song that comprises a riff, or riffs, plus chord sequences, there are great possibilities for strong musical contrasts through mixing harmony. Pentatonic minor or blues scale–based sections can contrast with major key sections, as on the Levellers' "Hope Street." The pentatonic minor or blues-scale riff could contrast with a chord progression in a major or minor key. Robert Plant's "Tie Dye the Highway" has a fierce A pentatonic minor riff using the notes A, C, and G, but this contrasts with the more poignant Em–C chord change, the Em intensified by being voiced as a ninth. This song's arrangement also gains power from the fact that a drum machine provides the beat for about two thirds of its duration, before real drums increase the energy level.

Riffs and rock music are almost synonymous, so it's easy to think that a riff has to be loud. This isn't the case. Riffs can be as effective in quieter material where they can be equally hypnotic. Take Tracy Chapman's hit "Fast Car" (1988). During the verses and links, a two-bar riff based on the progression IV–I–VI–V (D–A–F♯m–E) is played on an acoustic guitar with a sparse backing. The repetitions of this riff express the lyric's theme of feeling trapped in a certain life situation. On the choruses, the lyric talks about escape, so the riff is abandoned, and full chords break out. This is a good example of how a riff can express a lyric and a song's dynamics.

Rhythm and time signatures

The most popular time signature in rock is 4/4. The symmetry of this time signature has a universal appeal: the "magic" number four is also present in rock in other structural details, such as the length of phrases, how many times something is repeated, how many chords there are in a phrase, etc., so the majority of the riffs are in 4/4. Every now and again, however, you might want something different, or a riff may suggest another time signature. The expressive effect of an odd time signature or unpredictable accents is vividly demonstrated by the desolate piano chord riff in Radiohead's "Pyramid Song," where there is none of the self-regarding cleverness of jazz or prog's use of such a technique.

Here's a quick guide to other possible time signatures for riffs.

Simple time

Simple time signatures are those in which the beat can be divided by an even number. For instance, 3/4 (three quarter-notes, or crotchets, in a bar) is a time signature associated with the waltz. Single 3/4 bars can be used in many ways in a song that is primarily 4/4. Imagine a four-bar intro in 4/4—16 beats in total. Substitute a 3/4 bar for bar 4 and you have a touch of asymmetry. Now there are only 15 beats. This means the next section (presumably a verse) arrives one beat before the listener expects it.

Such a huge proportion of rock music during the past 50 years has been in 4/4, and dominated by fours of everything, that as listeners we unconsciously expect things to happen in fours. Breaking with this is a nice way of introducing the unexpected. Think of it like this:

symmetry = beauty

asymmetry = drama

Another possibility would be to alternate 4/4 and 3/4 bars. This again creates an element of surprise, because either the two-bar riff would be one beat short, or bar 1 repeated would lose a beat, or bar 3 would arrive a beat before the listener expects it.

In 2/4 time, bars tend to be too short for a riff to get going, but they can be used effectively at transition points between song sections, to cut a phrase or riff by two beats or lengthen by two, or to make the listener wait another two beats before the next section. You can imply a six-beat bar by linking bars of 4/4 and 2/4—sort of 4/4 with a bit more room, so you can fit in an extra couple of notes or words. This offers intriguing possibilities for adding pauses to a riff, or shifting the accents of either a riff or a melody if they are written as though the bars were all 4/4. What happens is that the start of a phrase won't always line up with the first beat of a bar, and since the first beat has a stronger emphasis than the other beats, that emphasis falls in different places. But because six is an even number, every so often they will line up:

4+2 beats	1	2	3	4	5	6	1	2	3	4	5	6	1	2	3	4	5	6	1	2	3	4	5	6
riff	G				C				D				Em				G				C			

This, incidentally, is different to 6/4 time, which is discussed under compound signatures below.

There has been the occasional chart hit in 5/4 time, most famously Dave Brubeck's 1959 cool-jazz classic "Take Five." The asymmetry of 5/4 is useful for giving relief from the steady beat of 4/4. Use it in a bridge section, for example, or under a guitar solo, or just for the intro, and then drop into 4/4 for the verses and choruses. Peter Buck of R.E.M. once said, "We count measures. It's a dumb trick, but if you're doing repetitions of four measures, repeat them three times instead of four—or five. The ear is going to hear if you're working in fours, but if you do three, to the ear things are changing faster. Or sometimes you'll add two beats to a bar." The same principle applies to beats and employing odd time signatures.

If you're intrigued by the whole business of odd time signatures, listen to Brubeck's albums *Time Out* and *Time Further Out*. Although it's jazz, not rock, you might pick up some ideas for use in a rock song. Jazz-rock, fusion, and progressive rock also feature odd time signatures. Jethro Tull's "Living in the Past," in 5/4, is a good example of the last genre; Led Zeppelin's "Four Sticks" makes use of 5/4, and "Achilles Last Stand" has some bars of 5/4.

For a witty use of an unusual time signature applied to a standard rock 'n' roll shuffle, there's the intro of "Going for the One" by Yes. Pink Floyd's "Money" uses a B pentatonic minor riff in 7/4. Led Zeppelin's "The Ocean" has bars of 7/8, which are like a bar of 4/4 with the last quaver offbeat missing (very good for emphasizing the first notes of a riff). One staggering example of the use of strange time signatures is Jethro Tull's "No Lullaby," which uses 4/4, 5/8, 2/4, 7/8, 3/4, and 6/8, and has a complex riff that starts as E pentatonic minor and ends chromatically. Kansas's "Carry on My Wayward Son" has a change from simple to compound time. Tool's "Schism" is renowned for its constantly shifting time signature.

Anything longer than 7/4 (the larger the first number, the more beats in a bar) would probably not be heard as such by the listener. It would take great skill on the part of the composer, and the musicians playing it, to write a riff in, say, 8/4 (or 8/8), because the listener would probably hear it as two bars of 4/4. Similarly, a 9/4 bar would be heard as 4/4 + 5/4. Even 7/4 has to be handled with care to stop it breaking into 4/4 + 3/4. Time signatures with more than four beats have an inherent tendency to "sag" in the middle, which is more pronounced at slower tempos.

You might wonder what the difference is between a 4/4 + 3/4 combination and a single bar of 7/4. This is where the understanding of the emphasized first beat is crucial. In 7/4, the strong beat only occurs once, and six beats must pass for it to be felt again. With alternating bars of shorter number of beats like 4/4 and 3/4, a strong beat is heard twice as frequently. To ensure your 7/4 bar is heard as such, emphasize the first beat (loud chord, cymbal crash), and let the vulnerable beats in the middle of the bar go slightly underemphasized.

Compound time signatures

Compound time signatures are those in which each beat is divisible by three. The commonest are those in which a quaver (eighth note) forms the basic unit of the bar. In rock, the most popular is undoubtedly 12/8, which has four dotted-crotchet/quarter-note beats to a bar (just like 4/4), with each of them splitting into three quavers. The same rhythmic effect can be achieved by playing constant triplets on the beat in 4/4. The 12/8 time signature is for blues shuffles and similarly "swung" songs. After 12/8 comes 6/8, which has two (dotted crotchet) beats—use it instead of 12/8 to get the feel of only two beats in each bar.

This, incidentally, is how to distinguish 6/8 from 3/4. At the right tempo, it's easy to confuse the two, since a slow 6/8 would count as one-two-three, one-two-three—which might be mistaken for two bars of 3/4. In fact, the difference would be that in 6/8 only the first "one" is stressed, whereas in 3/4 each of the "ones" in successive bars is stressed because both fall at the start of a bar.

To introduce a little asymmetry into 12/8 or 6/8 sections, add a bar of 3/8 (equivalent to one extra beat). For a rarer effect, try 9/8, with its three groups of three. There is plenty of scope for creating a whole song based on units of three instead of the four: Jimi Hendrix wrote "Manic Depression" in 9/8, as discussed below.

Other rhythm effects

You can spice up the rhythmic effect of your riffs even without resorting to odd or changed time signatures. Stay in good old 4/4 and try one of the following:

- Insert an accent during one repetition of a riff where there wasn't one before.
- Reverse one of the rhythmic components of the riff. If there's a dotted-quaver or semiquaver combination on one beat, reverse the time values (i.e., put the 16th note first).
- Try augmentation and diminution: the former increases the time values of the riff; the latter decreases them. It works best if done uniformly, otherwise the riff changes shape too much. Of the two, diminution is probably more useful in rock.
- Toward the end of a track, decrease the time values of a riff by 50 percent. This would reduce a four-bar riff to only two bars. To the listener, it would seem as though the speed of the music has increased, though it would be at the same tempo. This is closely related to the approach of half and double time, which is effective if the switch is from 4/4 at one speed to a matching 12/8 at another.
- Some bands adapt rhythms from outside rock. Led Zeppelin's "How Many More Times," Jeff Beck's "Beck's Bolero," and Deep Purple's "Child in Time" have the rhythm known as bolero, after the orchestral piece by Maurice Ravel. Jimi Hendrix even put a foxtrot rhythm (!) into "House Burning Down."
- One of the best compositional friends is silence. Listen to Robert Plant's "Messin' with the Mekon" for the startling use of silence to add power to a ♭II–II–I riff.
- Change what the rhythm section is doing. The Police used a G Mixolydian riff on the chorus of "Invisible Sun," but they made it special by setting it without a standard rock drum rhythm. Listen for the heavily accented fourth beat of the second bar of the riff.

Syncopation

Another vital technique for making rock riffs rhythmically interesting is syncopation. This means working in some way against the beat by placing accented notes on offbeats, and sometimes letting them stretch across beats and bar lines. A drum part will bring the beats through; the guitar and bass can play against them.

One thing that made classic rock bands of the late '60s and early '70s sound as good as they did was the fact that their bassists were often influenced by the syncopated bass heard on soul records. What syncopation provides straightaway is that magical ingredient: the groove.

Bands often fill bar after bar with nothing but straight eighths in the bass, but it sounds much better to have some syncopation. One way is to have a one-bar riff that repeats not from the first beat of the second bar but from the last offbeat of the first bar (tied across to the next bar). This creates a distinctive "pulling" effect. The appearance of triplets in a riff in 4/4 will give "bounce" to it. Although eighth-note triplets are common, you can have quarter-note triplets, where three quarter-notes are played across two beats, giving six notes in all (the technical term is "hemiola"). This results in a curious sense of the bar being stretched, with the music floating across it. It is a signature of Latin American–inspired music, so there are examples in the recordings of a band like Santana, such as "Se a Cabo."

Led Zeppelin were well known for adding unusual rhythmic effects to their riffs. People often think this indicates the presence of an uncommon time signature, but it isn't always the case. Exiting the guitar solo in "Over the Hills and Far Away" there is a climbing figure played by guitar and bass over a steady drumbeat. The notes are grouped in threes. This means the beginning of each group of three notes is accented against different beats within 4/4: the accents fall on beat 1 of bar 1, beat 4 of bar 1, beat 2 of bar 2, beat 1 of bar 3, and so on.

Led Zeppelin repeated this idea of three against 4/4 in the verse of "Misty Mountain Hop," with its chromatic triad riff. For more riffs developed by shifting rhythmic accents, listen to Metallica's "The Thing That Should Not Be," Bon Jovi's "Bad Medicine," and Jethro Tull's "Aqualung."

Another combination of riff and time signature is to take the riff and fit it into a new time without any change in the rhythm or the number of notes. If you fit a 4/4 riff into 3/4, you lose whatever note was on the last beat. If you put a 4/4 riff into 7/8, you will lose that last eighth note or chop an eighth note's duration from the last quarter note. Alternatively, fit a 4/4 riff into 5/4 and your riff has gained a beat's rest. What happens with that rest is up to you: it could be a drum fill, a moment of silence, a new bass note, or room for a chord.

Spaces and drum boxes

Thinking about time signatures should not blind us to one obvious factor that affects how a riff sounds: the musical rest. Many great riffs depend on a rest or two to punctuate them, and such rests allow the rhythm section to come through all the more forcefully.

Writing great riffs also means being aware of what the bass and drums are doing. The two basic choices when it comes to writing with a rhythm section are to dovetail your notes between drum strikes or play at the same time as them. Two bits of the kit to be especially conscious of are the kick (bass) drum and the snare. You can work a riff off either, or leave a gap where one or the other comes through. A fine example of this is the pentatonic minor riff on the chorus of Deep Purple's "Strange Kind of Woman" (in 12/8), where the riff is punctuated by cymbal crashes. Another Purple track, "Space Truckin'," has an interesting rhythmic relation between the drums and the riff.

Rhythmically, the best guitar riffs are often doubled by the bass, and their rhythm patterns coincide with what the drums are doing. The vintage idea is to leave a gap where the snare drum is hit and play around that. That's why some of the best riffs come from improvising against a drum machine, drum loop, or drummer. Hearing a rhythm is the best way to spark a riff that has punch. For this reason, one of the best aids for writing riffs is a drum pattern of some kind. Some guitar effects units and amps are now equipped with basic drum loops or grooves, and there are many software options and sample libraries.

It's amazing what a difference the presence of a drum loop makes to writing and playing rhythmically. Without rhythmic accompaniment, you are more likely to attempt to generate excitement in the riff by concentrating on the harmonic or melodic elements. You'll try to make it memorable by choosing notes in an interesting shape or by working in unusual harmonies. There's nothing wrong with this, but since rock music is primarily about rhythm—and this is especially true of riffs—it's better to at least combine such aspirations with a strong rhythm. The simplest ideas take off with a drumbeat. Even a metronome providing the steady click of the tempo is better than nothing. At the very least, tap your foot and make the riff dance against the rhythm of that tap—the end result will be more rhythmic. Any harmonic or melodic twists included will come across better if welded to a great rhythm.

The final point about timing and rhythms in riffs is to do with speed. Some riffs sound better at slower or faster speeds. An increase or decrease of tempo on a drum machine, drum loop, or metronome will automatically change the nature of the riff you write, because certain speeds suggest riffs with a particular character—sometimes because they are like things you've already heard.

Jimi Hendrix

"Manic Depression" (Hendrix)

From *Are You Experienced* (Track/Reprise, 1967)

"Manic Depression" is possibly rock's most innovative use of 9/8 time (three beats, each split in three). The riff is a simple arpeggio on A and G, returning to A via D. Hendrix plays four before the verse, and each lasts a bar. After each of the first two lines of lyric in a verse, the riff comes back.

Hendrix makes plentiful use of unison bends to fill the spaces, singing in falsetto with them at the start of the solo. Some of these bends are wonderfully vocal, like the two "moans" at 3:00, before the whole thing collapses in a welter of bleeping guitar feedback.

Jimi Hendrix

"I Don't Live Today" (Hendrix)

From *Are You Experienced* (Track/Reprise, 1967)

This song is in 4/4, but it shows what can be done if you borrow a rhythm pattern from elsewhere. For the intro, Hendrix uses a heavily accented eighth-note rhythm, which is distinctly Native American, giving the feel of 8/8—a time signature where every beat is equally stressed. He also makes hay with a high B7 chord before the fierce descending single-note riff on B pentatonic minor.

"I Don't Live Today" features feedback at 0:35, and octaves in the rhythm guitar during the guitar solo before the second chorus at 1:52. There's some great tremolo work at 0:41 and 2:08, where Hendrix seems to bang the back of the guitar as the pitch drops slowly until 2:22, giving his patented "alien spaceship parking" effect. The frenetic coda has more feedback in the center, with the solo off to the left. This fades out at 2:51 into a terrifying wail.

Deep Purple

"Black Night" (Lord/Blackmore/Gillan/Glover/Paice)

From *Deep Purple in Rock* (Harvest/Warner Bros., 1970)

What makes "Black Night" successful is the combination of 12/8 time and the E pentatonic minor riff played around the fifth fret position. It's unusual for heavy rock riffs to occur in 12/8, but it gives this riff real bounce. It consists of an initial phrase, a variation, and then two contrasted approaches to the tonic E—one from below, one from above, so they answer each other.

The first two bars have a single phrase that ends in bar 3 with a tone shift from D to E, the keynote approached from the flattened seventh. The fourth bar approaches the keynote E from G (the flattened third)—a good example of how these two flat notes of the pentatonic minor can be juxtaposed. The riff has a lovely rhythmic contrast because bars 1 and 2 are flowing, whereas bars 3 and 4 have long rests in the guitar part.

Notice also that the guitar solo is supported by the D–E tone shift, and the organ solo by a G–A tone shift—an example of transposition. Toward the end of the verse, a longer variation of this riff is developed with the vocal melody in unison.

Soundgarden

"Fell on Black Days" (Cornell)

From *Superunknown* (A&M, 1994)

It's notoriously tricky to write good melodies over heavy riffs, yet "Fell on Black Days" by the Seattle grunge band Soundgarden manages exactly this. Listen for the major seventh chord at the end of each verse, just before the chorus. Major sevenths are rarely heard in heavy rock because they are often deemed too "sweet." But when their emotive appeal is successfully linked up to the power of heavy rock, the effect is tremendous. (Foo Fighters' "Everlong" also contains instances of playing major sevenths where they would not be expected.)

Listen also for the bass going down to the really low register from the first "how would I know?" The extreme wah-wah break and the singer's shift up to a higher range for "I sure don't mind a change" is another highlight, as is the guitar harmony line toward the end of the song. The six-beats-in-a-bar time signature also makes a pleasing change from rock's standard 4/4. Though Soundgarden's music has a line of ancestry that goes back to Black Sabbath, the slow burning, introverted feel of "Fell on Black Days" is reminiscent of a heavier Free.

Arranging and recording guitar riffs

Let's imagine you've written a song with a good riff: now it's time to record and arrange it. How should you set it out? This depends on many factors that cannot be anticipated without knowing the intended effect of the song, but here are some suggestions.

Some guitar-effects devices can enable you to construct a riff out of the simplest musical material. Perhaps the best example of this in rock is the wah-wah pedal. Even on a single chord, the EQ changes and the rhythm it creates can be highly effective. Much of Isaac Hayes's "Theme from Shaft" has as its foundation an almost continuous G octave on the guitar, played through a wah. Korn's "Pretty" uses a single chord for the riff but changes the EQ to make it work. All About Eve's album *Ultraviolet* contains a great track, "Freeze," with echoed wah-wah.

As anyone who's ever messed about with delay knows, echo units transform your playing. As soon as you venture beyond shorter, reverb-type delays, all the habitual scales and licks sound messy and cluttered, and distorted notes aren't too brilliant, either. Echo units make you want to hear only one or two notes at a time; they set you thinking straightaway about that magic word, texture. You sense potential harmonies and chords you've never heard before. Random clashes of notes as you change chord produce startling musical phrases. Echo units make space itself a positive quality to work with, not an absence to be fought. This is strongly felt in a Big Country song like "Chance," and in some of U2's lesser-known tracks, like "Heartlands" and "Walk to the Water."

What's more, in a three-piece with a singer, delay provides a fuller concert sound. So it was with the Edge. U2's music up to *The Joshua Tree* was characterized by his growing awareness of guitar textures using delay. The 1983 live recordings released as *Under a Blood Red Sky* gave a good indication of how full this could be. On a song like "11 O'clock Tick Tock," the guitar part is almost a countermelody to the vocal, at the same time sketching the harmony. The Edge's parts are often typified by open strings ("I Will Follow" and "Gloria"), including solos ("Sunday Bloody Sunday"), moving up and down a string while hitting the adjacent one. "Pride (In the Name of Love)" has this too, along with effective harmonics and chords that hang while the bass part changes. Songs like "Where the Streets Have No Name" and "I Still Haven't Found What I'm Looking For" are classics of rhythmic playing with a delay, where the simple opening phrase is transformed by the notes bouncing back from the echo.

Multitracking a riff

The chance to multitrack raises the question of how many guitars should play a riff. In a power trio or a group with one guitar, or on four-track demos, the options will initially be limited. The easiest way to generate the illusion of two guitars playing a riff is to use a stereo delay, along with a little EQ to differentiate the channels. For example, the direct guitar signal might go to the left; the signal that goes to the right might have a short delay on it. This gives the illusion of two guitars. How short the delay needs to be depends on the tempo. Too long a delay will make it sound as though the virtual guitarist on the right is half-asleep and not keeping up.

A variation on this is to add distortion only after the guitar signal has split. Live, this would mean using two amps, one set to overdrive and the other not; or keeping both amps clean but putting an overdrive pedal after the delay, so one side is distorted. You don't have to have the delay itself switched on to have the signal split.

Some players prefer to double-track a riff in real time by recording it twice. Unless you are a very precise player who can duplicate every nuance of expression in the first pass, enough small differences of timing and volume creep in to make the two sound close but not exact, thus thickening the riff. You can, of course, deliberately play a bit more loosely to give a riff more "feel." It depends on the style you're going for.

If you're double-tracking a riff at the same pitch, distinguish the tone of the guitars from each other. This can be done with:

- different amps and settings
- different effect pedals
- varying amounts of EQ and reverb at the mixing stage

- different pickups on the same guitar
- different models of guitar: double-coil pickup versus a single-coil or a mini-humbucker—the traditional Gibson/Fender contrast. One guitar could be clean, one distorted. Or how about one with slight overdrive and the other with '60s fuzz? There are many permutations.

Bloc Party's "Helicopter" opens with a fast B natural minor scale riff played on two guitars. What's interesting about the arrangement of this riff is that the two parts are not identical but feature slightly different notes at a couple of points. Further mileage is found during the verse by having the bass guitar play a B–D–E progression, these root notes each coloring the riff in their own way.

Different instruments

Another option is to multitrack a riff with other instruments. In funk, a riff might be doubled on a synth. In rock 'n' roll, it might be doubled by saxes. Good results can also be had by doubling the riff on strings, especially cello (think of the texture of the Beach Boys' "Good Vibrations").

For an earthy, funky effect, why not bring the riff in first on acoustic guitars—two six-strings, say, or even a six and a 12—and then hammer it home with the electrics later? Electric 12-string gives an unusual tone to a riff, especially with a little overdrive, since it is an instrument that is more often heard with a clean tone, in styles of rock that are more chordal than riff-based. If an electric 12-string doubles an overdriven six-string playing the same riff, the 12-string can be mixed a little quieter, so its higher octave strings add a feeling of overtones to the original. For an example of this, have a listen to Led Zeppelin's "Living Loving Maid" from *Led Zeppelin II*.

Another consideration is what the bass might be doing. Think carefully about when the bass enters, and if it's going to double a riff one or two octaves below. On the basis that a rock number shouldn't blow all its ammunition in the first minute, you may want the bass to double the guitar riff only an octave down at first, and save the lower octave for later on in the song.

Another possibility, noted earlier in the pedal/drone part of section 3, is to have the bass play a repeating pedal note (usually the keynote) under the first repetitions of the riff and then go into a unison effect. Let the bass play the riff first, then bring the guitars in on top.

Once a riff is double- or triple-tracked at the same pitch, the law of diminishing returns comes into action. An extravagant number of guitars multitracking a riff doesn't necessarily make it sound bigger. Eight guitars are not eight times louder or fuller than one. The more distortion is used, the more this is the case (surprising, but true).

After recording two or three tracks of the riff at one pitch, consider doubling the riff at a different pitch—say, an octave or so apart. What can be done with octave doubling depends on where the riff is pitched in the first place. If the riff is down in first position, in the lowest octave on the guitar, there are two positions above where it could be played and doubled. Previous suggestions about mixing different guitar tones on such parts applies here as well.

If the riff is in fifths that change rapidly, they may be too quick for one guitarist to play cleanly. In this case, fast fifths can be played by two guitarists, each taking a single note, as on KISS's "Detroit Rock City."

For more ideas on recording, see my book *Arranging Songs*.

Harmonizing a riff

A further refinement of this idea of doubling at a different pitch is to harmonize the riff. This doesn't mean you have to harmonize the whole riff, or the whole riff every time. Sometimes, it's enough to add musical color by putting a few notes at a suitable interval above part of the riff—say, in the last bar. These touches of musical color can be effective without disrupting the riff itself. They have a less drastic effect, for example, than transposing the riff to another note.

The most popular interval for harmonizing a riff would be:

- a major or minor third
- an octave plus a third (a compound third or a tenth)
- a major or minor sixth
- an octave plus a sixth (a compound sixth or a thirteenth).

Fourths, fifths, and octaves give a typically "hollow" sound. Thirds and sixths bring in the major/minor coloring and can imply chords. With careful thought, it's possible to construct a riff that consists of a bass line, a guitar riff, and a harmonizing part in thirds or sixths, with only three notes at any given moment, which would imply whole chords.

Feel free to vary the interval; you don't have to harmonize in the same way all the way through. Choosing thirds but ending on a fourth or fifth can imply a particular chord on which you might want to end. When you've selected the right octave for the harmony, consider also where the vocal line is pitched.

Some of the riffs in Black Sabbath's "Supernaut," "A National Acrobat," and "Electric Funeral" are harmonized. Ram Jam's "Black Betty" (1977) shows how effective a harmonized riff sounds (this one is in thirds, with a strong major key feel) when it occurs several minutes into a track that has had several riffs on the B pentatonic minor and B blues scales.

If a riff is chord-based, the obvious doubling trick is to have another guitar play in a different position on the neck. There is also the use of fifths to toughen up and support a chord riff. Fifths will match a chord regardless of whether it's major or minor.

Riffs and the band

The riffs you compose are influenced not only by playing style and other creative pressures, but also by the type of band to which you belong. In a power trio or a quartet with a vocalist, there's only one chordal instrument to establish harmony—namely, the guitar. To generate a bigger sound, you may incline to riffs with at least two notes sounding at any one time, rather than single-note riffs. Chord-based riffs will be attractive.

If there's a second guitar in the band, harmonized riffs are an option, and any single-note riffs can be doubled. If there's a keyboard player, try single-note riffs that have more "cut," because the keyboards can fill in much of the harmony. Part of the musical discipline in working with a keyboard player in a band playing riff-based rock is to get them to limit the number of notes they play for the sake of the riff. Look to a band like Deep Purple for arrangement examples.

a masterclass with john paul jones

With album sales second only to the Beatles, Led Zeppelin have long been regarded by fans and critics alike as definitive exponents of heavy rock. John Paul Jones not only played bass at the core of rock's great riff machine, he also composed some of those riffs. Led Zeppelin's nine studio albums contain 81 tracks; Jones has a writing credit on 32 of them.

Jones came to Led Zeppelin with several years' experience in the music business. As a child, he'd toured in variety theatre with his parents, absorbing eclectic musical ideas; by the age of 17, he was touring with Jet Harris and Tony Meehan (ex-Shadows). Before long, he had made a name for himself as a session bassist (for the likes of Dusty Springfield, Lulu, and Tom Jones) and as an arranger, scoring the strings on the Rolling Stones' "She's a Rainbow" and arranging Donovan's "Mellow Yellow" and "Sunshine Superman," and Jeff Beck's "Hi Ho Silver Lining."

Eventually, Jones found session work was stifling his creativity, but the diversity of music he'd encountered was significant for the development of Led Zeppelin. After 12 years (1968–1980) in the world's premier heavy rock band, he returned to the studio. Alongside the Diamanda Galas album *This Sporting Life* and the soundtrack to *Scream for Help*, he's composed music for early music group Red Bird and synthesizer music for Eno's record label Opal, and produced bands like the Mission, R.E.M., and the Butthole Surfers.

Jones has continued writing heavy riffs, including for multi-string bass—as can be heard on his solo albums *Zooma* (1999) and *The Thunderthief* (2002). If anyone doubts how important Jones was to Led Zeppelin, these albums underline his contribution. He was also responsible for changing the musical vocabulary of the rock riff with scales other than pentatonics—his fondness for the minor second interval mirroring the interest among nu-metal bands in scales and modes like the Phrygian and Locrian.

In 2007, Jones publicly reclaimed his place as one of the world's greatest rock bassists at Led Zeppelin's London O2 Arena gig, and since then he has recorded and toured an album with Dave Grohl and Josh Homme as Them Crooked Vultures. So, who better to provide a unique insight into the world of the riff?

Jones is quoted here from conversations with the author; insights into the riffs on *Them Crooked Vultures* follow the interview.

On influential riffs

I loved the classic "Lucille" riff. Little Richard's original was too fast to register for me as a riff—what I mostly heard was the pounding piano part. The first time I really thought of it as a riff and went crazy was when I heard the Everly Brothers' version on the B-side of "Cathy's Clown." Not only does it contain that riff pre-"Pretty Woman" (which had a slight difference—I didn't like that as much because the ninth softens it too much) but it also contains the thing that got me playing steel guitar, the solo, which I worked out and got off as a lap steel part. Some of the early riffs came from boogie-woogie piano, translated onto the guitar.

The other one from that time, the reverse of that riff, was "Shakin' All Over," which went downward. Then there was [Duane Eddy's] "Peter Gunn" theme, the ancestor of "Grind" [from *Zooma*]. Again, not the original version from the film, which is much softer and uses a major third on its penultimate note. Duane Eddy flattens it—he changed the riff, made it more economic and harder. That to me was the riff of all riffs.

I was very affected by Duane Eddy in the old days—that whole low-melody thing, as with Jet Harris.

I had a pop upbringing as far as my session days were concerned. You could hear what was going to work and what wasn't, how the music took you through the bridge and into the hook or chorus…the formula for why it works. You could almost lay the songs on top of one another.

It's like a book, or film, or theater—it always has these stages of development, tension, release. If you're aware of this, you can do it on a micro or macro level. You have to tell a little story.

On the influence of bass riffs from Motown records

I had to play a lot of it in sessions when Motown was the fashion. They knew they could give me a chord chart and I could improvise a reasonably authentic Motown or Stax-sounding bass line, and they didn't have to worry. So I used to be playing those wonderful James Jamerson lines and remaking them as I went.

[M.G.'s and Stax bassist] Duck Dunn wasn't a riff player, but I got my soul stylings from him, and from the Phil Upchurch combo, and later from Willie Weeks. There was more riffing in jazz: with a riff, you don't have to worry about knowing a chord progression.

On Zeppelin riffs

You can always tell my riffs from Page's because mine have got lots of notes and are linear. His are chunkier and chordier: I like the riff in "The Ocean," and "Kashmir" is a great one. I was coming at it from another angle. "In the Light," during the verse—that's a riff of mine. I leave the seventh ringing. Page doesn't do riffs like that. In fact, anything with chromatic movement would be mine.

When Page starts soloing [in concert] and goes up high, there's a big gap, and you have the problem of filling it. We filled it with eight-string bass. Page complained bitterly when the eight-string first appeared. He said [in a grumpy voice], "I'm not playing to that." Then he realized how much sound it made and how it gave him a much better base to solo over—then he liked it.

When Page came out with the first riff of "Achilles" [Em–F♯m], he said, "What are we going to do with the rest of it?" I said, "The eight-string bass." It fitted perfectly.

Both Page and I had a high degree of discipline in routining, and making sure things were right—being able to turn your hand to anything, and to know authentically how it should be done. Every piece of music I listen to, every piece of music I play, influences the next thing I do.

A lot of the problem with the bands who imitated us was that they all listened to the same sort of music. In Zep, we had areas where our tastes would cross, but not that many. We were into completely different things a lot of the time.

On solo riffs

I often write my stuff away from instruments and then I work it out on them. Sometimes patterns will suggest a riff, but then I'll go away, walk around, and think of how it starts, what it's going to be from then, how I would like to hear it if it were the next track of an album. Otherwise, I just end up playing, and then I forget I'm writing something. I do that for arrangements as well—literally while walking.

When I write riffs in my head, I can often hear the drums as well. So, what I'll usually do is come back and write a drum part on the machine and practice it, and I'll often fine-tune it—move a beat here or there, so the riff works best. If there's anything wrong with the riff, I fix it.

The most common scale I use is [in E, coming down] E D C♯ B A♯ G♯ G F. It's not a straight mode, though it's like the Lydian. It's all through *Zooma* and *The Thunderthief*. It's based on tritones as well. In jazz, it's the scale that links all 13th chords and augmented ninth chords, which are the reverse of each other. It's the universal scale over the lot—the one that links all keys. I learned it a very long time ago, in the '60s.

You've got the minor second in "Angry Angry," from A to B♭, and in "Tidal" from *Zooma*. A lot of the riffs really work the minor second. I like the tensions— it's a riff of two halves: you can superimpose one half on top of the other if you need to. You can play so many different major scales over it, which all fit in: in E, you could play an E major scale or an F♯ major scale; a D♭5 would probably fit on it as well. There are just so many things it links together—so many tension spots.

It's half a blues scale, because it has the flattened seventh, but it also has the major third. There's also a slight whole-tone feel about it as you move between them. It's got a lot going for it as a scale, it's very flexible—you can accentuate different aspects of it.

On "B Fingers" (clearly a riff from the man who dreamed up "Black Dog," complete with trademark tricky bit)

There's an added beat to make a 5/4 bar, but it's not like, *Oh, I think I'll do a tricky 5/4 here.* That extra beat was crying out to be there, and it felt very natural. It must be governed by the music. There was a tendency for some of those [progressive '70s] bands to be "spot the beat."

You've got to be able to feel those things. In Mediterranean music, they always have things like 9/4: Greek, Arab, and Indian music always has those naturally— and they dance to it, so it must feel natural.

All my weird timings are melody led—and if it happens to be a beat longer, then the time signature has to change to fit it in. It's like the cross-rhythm in the riff of [Led Zeppelin's] "Nobody's Fault But Mine"—I just started playing it like that. That was me saying, "What shall we do with this, chaps?"

On "Grind"

I like the shifts from the stark fifths to the minor—that juxtaposition. It starts as a good-time rock 'n' roll track, almost Stones-y in a strange, swaggering sort of way. Then it turns into a snake-like riff on the bottom of the 12-string bass. In fact, that's the only one where I use the low B-string almost exclusively. To be honest, it's a big sub–Duane Eddy riff, which I've wanted to do since I was 14.

As for the texture of riff 1, it's because I've always liked the 12-string guitar—the way you can do those passing notes, the classic Byrds arpeggio sequences. Multi-string basses allow me to do that. They're very guitar-y instruments—I can play them like a 12-string guitar. The octave strings bring out the melody lines; if you did that on a four, five, or six-string bass, it would all get lost in low harmonics.

On "Freedom Song"

The riff to "Freedom Song" was me picking up the ukulele and playing a little African thing. I tuned it differently to a straight ukulele. That's the first take—it has a mistake in it, but why make it perfect? It had such a great feeling about it.

I've found that playing while watching meter levels is a brilliant idea, because I find the half of my brain that usually interferes with my playing is involved in checking levels. So, you just get on with it.

On "Leafy Meadows"

I didn't want it bluesy. I'd done a lot of blues-based riffs before on *Zooma*. I thought, well, riffs don't have to be bluesy all the time. So, it was intentional that I went for the major third. The second half is slightly more bluesy, but it's all based around the major third or the minor second.

The time signature change in the second riff came because it just needed a little tag on the end of a phrase. It's almost a Zeppelin thing. They're all in 5/4, with a bar of 6/4, I think. Because it's in a strange time signature, it sounds much more complicated than it actually is: you put in an extra beat and everybody throws their hands up. Actually, it's rounding it off—it's making what should be in common time [5+5+6 = 16: the same number of beats as four bars of 4/4]. It rounds it off in the right place, which gives it a closure, and although you're not counting, you feel the closure.

On "Shibuya Bop"

Shibuya is an area of Tokyo, full of kids and loud music and shops with pinball machines. Very vibrant. I was walking past this shop with a really hard techno track coming out. It was the very intense, claustrophobic feeling about the rhythm—it didn't let you go. I thought it would be interesting to write a rock riff that, just as you thought it was going to give up, turned a corner and carried on. It was incessant, fast, hard, and not very bluesy.

The rock 'n' roll koto solo has more of a Spanish scale—the Phrygian. But you can change the character of a scale by accentuating a different interval in the scale.

On "The Thunderthief"

That one's much more of a blues scale. It has a strong tritone going from the A to the E♭, with a C in between. The riff is structured so as not to have it going on at the same time as the words. It's almost like a confirmation of the lyric—it's like, *Okay, think of the lyric for a bit while I play the riff.* Another example of this would be [Berry Gordy's] "Money."

On playing riffs in a band

I usually think of any riff in terms of the rhythm section—how it's going to sound with the drums. So, occasionally, if I want the snare to be a feature—like an offbeat to pop out—I'll leave a space for it, and likewise the kick drum. Sometimes it's good to have the bass drum kicking the riff along.

Sometimes you can stop the riff and let the kick drum go another beat. Or have an accent. It gives texture to the riff and makes it much more interesting. Like [Led Zeppelin's] "The Wanton Song," where the snare is isolated between the octaves—whereas in "The Immigrant Song" there isn't a gap like that, because the whole point about the "Immigrant" riff is the kick down: *Dum da da da dum* [emphasizing the second beat].

You've got to think like an arranger, look at the whole picture. Think rhythmically and spatially. Often, I would stop in any complicated riff, work out what the dynamic of the riff is, and let the drums do it—otherwise, if you're both playing at the same time, the whole thing becomes weak. Which, to me, is where a lot of the metal bands go wrong, because if you're all playing at the same time, it's not heavier—it's weaker. It's much stronger to get constituent parts of a riff to work so the whole thing pushes and pulls, and the tensions are on a micro-level, not a macro-level. It's the same thinking that says you need a stack of guitar amplifiers when in fact you can get much more out of a small amp with good mics. And the more times you multitrack a riff, the more you lose all the grain.

Everybody's got to listen. If you choose a note, there's got to be a reason for it. Does it help the harmony, does it help the rhythm? If you're just playing it for no reason, then you'd be better off not playing it.

Postscript 2010: Them Crooked Riffs

Them Crooked Vultures vividly demonstrates that there is plenty of mileage left in riff-based rock, especially if you have the combined instrumental prowess and imagination of members of Led Zeppelin, Nirvana and the Foo Fighters, and Queens of the Stone Age. Across 13 tracks and over 66 minutes, John Paul Jones, Dave Grohl, and Joshua Homme deliver something of a textbook in writing and arranging riffs, frequently leading the musical structures into unexpected territory. Many of the types of riff described in this book appear on the album.

Familiar pentatonic minor or blues minor third riffs feature on tracks like "New Fang." Its first riff is based on B pentatonic minor, but with the note G added toward its end. The riff takes four bars to play and then functions as the verse. The coda of the song features another B pentatonic riff.

"Scumbag Blues" takes as its starting point a very '60s blues-rock riff on the pentatonic A minor scale, with three strong beats on A, before the run down to D, and then a run back up in the second bar of the riff. It also has a small rhythm variation and the addition of a chromatic G–G♯–A run. It ends with a Hendrix-like high bent C dropping an octave to the C below that. The high vocal sounds like Jack Bruce and Cream, until a funky clavinet comes in on the left suggesting "Trampled Underfoot."

"Caligulove" has a first riff based on D pentatonic minor in fifths. "Warsaw or the First Breath You Take After You Give Up" has a heavily detuned pentatonic riff with a galumphing chromatic scale extension. It's a riff with an inbuilt sense of humor and a swing feel that becomes more noticeable as the song speeds up. "Gunman" opens with octaves, a drop D tuning, a wah effect on the riff, and a scale based on D pentatonic minor, with strong octave leaps. "Dead End Friends" constructs an exotic-sounding riff on the scale of C♯ natural minor, with a brief upward snaking figure of G♯–A–B–C♯.

The pentatonic minor scale tends to produce far more rock riffs than its major equivalent, but *Them Crooked Vultures* has a powerful example of the latter. "Mind Eraser, No Chaser" opens with a riff based on A pentatonic major with a flattened third note added, the whole riff colored by a demented wah-wah effect. Listen in particular for a significant arrangement touch: the note Jones leaves out at the end of each riff, allowing the drums to come through the space.

Several tracks have motifs colored by modes. "Caligulove" has a second riff, based on the notes D–E♭ at 0:45, which is Phrygian and sounds very Queens of the Stone Age. "Elephants" opens with a scale riff based on the mode of G Dorian, with three phrases ending an octave plus a fifth above the G it started on. After four plays, this suddenly increases in speed and turns into a second riff on a G pentatonic minor variation reminiscent of the Led Zeppelin track "Wearing and Tearing." Further on in the song is a classic 3+1 phrased riff, finished by a six-note "slam phrase" with snare hits to each note.

The technique of transposition—playing a riff from a higher or lower note than when it was first heard—features too. There's a riff transposed up a fourth from A to D at 4:37 in "No One Loves Me and Neither Do I." In "New Fang," at 2:07, the riff shifts up a tone to C♯ and becomes a simpler variant; riff 1 then returns on B.

Elsewhere on the album, there are interesting uses of intervals. The main riff of "Bandoliers" is an A–C–Dm chord-change riff, in itself noteworthy because putting the IVm chord (Dm instead of D) into a riff is unusual. These chords are varied by adding notes to give Dm6, and also the inversion A/C♯ in verse two. A second riff appears at 3:04, in the guise of a figure derived from the E–F chord change used for the chorus. It features compound thirds (i.e., an octave plus a third); the notes are G♯B moving to EG♯, then FA moving to DF. The main riff of "Spinning in Daffodils" has a G bass note with rapidly moving thirds above it (B♭D to AC♯). In the main riff of "Dead End Friends," a fifth on F♯ opens out into a sixth of F♯D. Around the five-minute mark in "Spinning in Daffodils," there's a new figure that has octaves moving over an open-E pedal on string six.

There are many fine arrangement touches: "Bandoliers" sounds like it has ended at 4:18, but two seconds later the band hit the main riff but only with drums and bass—a clever device for getting a different tone into the song. "Caligulove" turns into a mandolin hoedown in its mid-section. There are several unexpected instrumental codas.

One of the best riffs drives the album's opener, "No One Loves Me and Neither Do I"—a track that exemplifies much of what the band achieve. The first riff mixes consecutive fourths with a splash of an Am7 chord at the fifth fret and the strong contrast of ascending and descending phrases. Around 2:20, a second riff appears, as fast fifths slide back and forth a tone. At 2:44, riff 3 comes in, bolstered by the bass. It has a strong minor third (AC), with a chromatic G–G#–A in octaves.

This riff has some odd accents and a couple of strange interpolations, including a chromatic run that almost derails the riff. There must have been a lot of beat-counting in rehearsals to get this impressively tight. The conclusion is that a riff can always be developed and adapted, melodically, harmonically, or rhythmically.

example riffs

To illustrate the types of riff described in the text, this book also includes 56 specially recorded audio tracks. Tracks 1–16 illustrate the tutorial section of the book. Tracks 17–46 correspond, in sequence, to the 30 riff types described in sections 1–3. An additional 10 riffs demonstrate how a single riff might mix ideas from those 30 riff types.

This section contains the music notation for these riffs, so you can play along, and a commentary giving details about how each riff is constructed, plus some of the arrangement approaches used on the recording (as discussed in section 4). Unless otherwise noted, each track has a four-beat count-in and features a single-coil-pickup guitar on the left channel and a double-coil-pickup guitar on the right.

TRACK 17 semitone (half step)

Rather than use a traditional rock 'n' roll or punk semitone riff, this track elects to do something less predictable by fretting the semitone below each of the open strings. Each semitone pair has a slightly different "color" because of the changing chords (especially as the G♯m and Bm chords are unexpected in what sounds like a blues-inflected E major in the first two bars).

The form of the riff here is a1+a2+a3+b, where "a" is the first eight quavers (eighth notes), which have three different final phrases. For "b" (bars 7–8), further use is made of the semitone by adding bends. The arrangement has a single guitar track recorded in stereo.

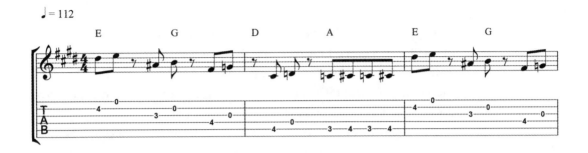

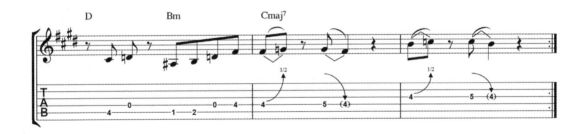

TRACK 18 **tone (whole step)**

Usually, a tone riff will move on to the root note. Track 18 does this in bar 4, but in bars 1–3 it moves off the root note. A 16th-note rhythm is used throughout, giving a rock/funk hybrid feel. Notice that bars 1–3 are not rhythmically identical; small variations make things more interesting. Like track 17, this riff could also be described as having an a1+a2+a3+b form.

The arrangement features bass playing the riff, with the two guitars heard in bar 1 on the left and right. In bar 2, another guitar enters, playing a third above; in bar 3, a fourth guitar enters, playing a fifth above the root notes. With all three parts sounding in bar 4, triad chords result.

TRACK 19 **octaves**

Here's a typically "bouncy" octave riff, where the bass plays along with the guitar. Notice the semitone movement from the bottom E onto F in the middle of bars 1–3 (which could only sound like this in this key), and the powerful, accented 16ths of bar 4. The attack of bar 4 complements the slinky quality of bars 1–3.

TRACK 20 **fifths**

This riff uses a descending run of fifths in G minor. The form is a1 (bars 1–2) + a2 (bars 3–4). There are small changes in the length of some of the notes, and the run at the end of each phrase is one note shorter in bar 2. Listen for the sinister effect of the guitar on the right, which puts the riff through a wah-wah pedal. A piano sketches in the major and minor chords that the bare guitar fifths don't make explicit.

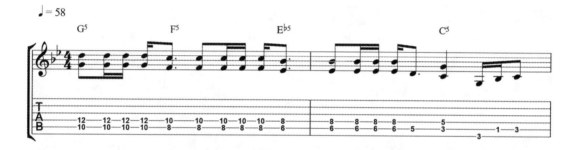

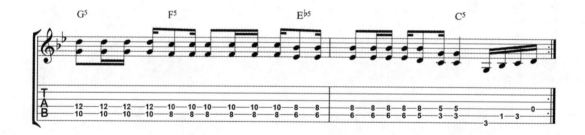

TRACK 21 **fourths**

Two bars of the so-called "Hendrix" chord act as an intro for this riff, which uses fourths on the lower and middle strings in a two-bar phrase that falls and then rises. Notice the tie across the middle of bar 3 and the second quaver rest in bar 4—both mean there are no notes on beat 3, creating a distinctive "pull." This riff would lend itself easily to transposition up the neck for variety.

TRACK 22 **tritones**

Tritones often work best in a riff made of other elements. They function like the addition of hot spices to a meal. This riff uses drop D tuning and a D Mixolydian scale (D E F♯ G A B C) with the addition of F, the blues ♭III (flattened third). Like the previous track, it's a two-bar form with different endings. In bar 1, a tritone can be heard on the last beat. The expected A5 (AE) is replaced with a more unsettling tritone (AE♭). A second tritone occurs in bar 2 as FB. The B is bent up a semitone to C, and momentarily the tritone becomes a fifth.

One arrangement trick to highlight different parts of a riff is to overdub guitars playing only part of the riff. On this track, two guitars, left and right, play the whole riff. In the center of the mix, a third guitar doubles the tritones only, and on the third repeat a fourth guitar doubles the first-beat 16th notes (of which there are four) an octave higher.

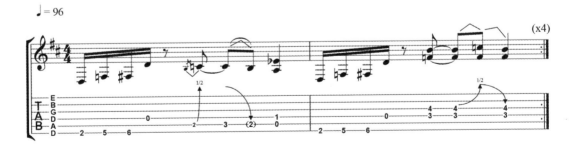

TRACK 23 **thirds**

This riff brings out something of the "sweet" sound of thirds over a major-key sequence. Unlike a riff in fifths, thirds strongly emphasize the major/minor harmony. As is often the case, the thirds are combined with other intervals such as fourths, some coming from open-string combinations. The form of the riff could be described as a four-bar phrase with two different endings (bars 4 and 8). This type of riff requires less distortion on the guitars.

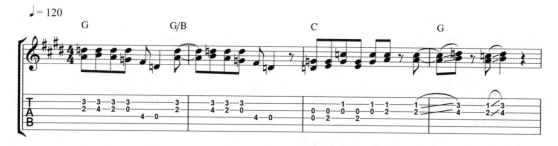

TRACK 24 **sixths**

The structure of this riff in sixths is a1 (bars 1–2) + a2 (3–4) + b (5–6) + a3 (7–8). The "a" sections each have a different final two beats. The purpose of the "b" section is to create contrast, which it does by a change of rhythm and the unexpected introduction of a couple of fifths. Their "bare" neutral quality contrasts with the harmonically explicit sixths.

Another important feature is the fact that the a1 run of sixths is mostly heard over A minor, whereas a2 and a3 are heard over F. This shows that the same riff can be harmonized with more than one chord and will consequently sound different.

TRACK 25 **mixed intervals**

This mixed-interval riff combines sixths, fifths, and fourths in bars 1–3 and 5. In bar 4, the fifth is supported by two open strings. Some of these fifths are not even built on the root note of the chord over which they are played; for example, in bar 1, G#D# is sounded against an Emaj7 chord. This works because Emaj7 is EG#BD#. Only in bar 5 does this fifth actually sit on the root note of the chord, which is then G#m.

This riff is a good example of asymmetry because it's five bars long, not the expected four, and bar 5 is rhythmically dramatic. The overall effect is of an unexpected and passionate outburst before the music can return to bar 1. The structure can be described as a+a+a+b+c.

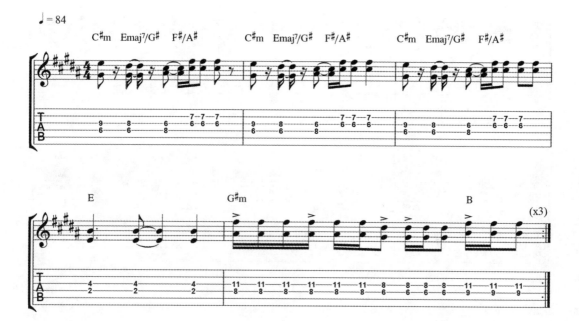

TRACK 26 **pentatonic minor**

Here's a typical pentatonic minor riff in C, with rock syncopations every other bar, a tone transposition in bar 5 (from C to D), and one additional passing note in the B and C♯, which occur in bars 2 and 6. Bass and guitar play the same notes. Listen for the guitar overdub the second time through, which doubles the riff an octave higher. Unlike track 25, which is rich with chords, track 26 has no supporting harmony (hence the NC: "No Chords")—which partly accounts for its classic hard rock sound.

TRACK 27 **blues scale**

This riff draws on the E blues scale: E G A B♭ B D. The blues flattened fifth (♭V) makes its appearance in bar 2 in a traditional bend/pull-off figure. It wouldn't make sense to try to copy this on the bass because it's too fast, so the bass is free to play other ideas. This blues lick is replaced in bar 4 by a stark fourth (DG) with a passing tritone (C♯G). The BE fourth throughout is '50s rock 'n' roll or '70s glam—however you hear it.

TRACK 28 **pentatonic major**

This two-bar riff is another '50s-influenced idea, but with a twist. The main notes are taken from E pentatonic major (E F♯ G♯ B C♯), but where G♯m appears, the note C♯ is bent a tone to D♯. D♯ is one of the notes of G♯m, and also the seventh note of the scale of E major—so on both accounts it fits perfectly. It's still a surprise, though, because that C♯ would normally be bent only a semitone to D, the blues flattened seventh (as can be heard on track 23).

TRACK 29 **major scale**

The normal seventh of the major scale is also the determining factor in the riff here. This two-bar riff in G major is based on a common 1950s rock 'n' roll idea—notice the flattened third (B♭) and natural third (B) next to each other— but with one significant difference. With the jump of a major seventh from G, the riff reaches not the expected F natural (the blues flattened seventh) but F♯—the seventh of the major scale. Notice also that the bass guitar does not double the whole of the riff, but only the last five notes.

This idea of emphasizing the usual seventh of a major key is then adapted for the verse section. Instead of putting the riff under the vocal, it is simplified into a rhythmic figure that implies Gmaj7 instead of the more usual G7. After four bars, we get the predictable chord change to C—but it's Cmaj7, not C7. This verse has used eight bars of a 12-bar blues sequence, but not the chords you would normally hear. The swing feel of this track is created by using 12/8 time.

TRACK 30 **mixolydian**

This is the first of our examples to start with an incomplete bar, on the third offbeat. This shifts the rhythmic shape of the riff, which ends halfway through bar 7. C Mixolydian (C D E F G A B♭) supplies most of the notes. This is reinforced by the implied C7 chord of bars 1 and 2, and the B♭ ♭VII chord in bar 4.

Notice how the rhythm pattern changes in bar 4. Bars 5 and 6 make an unexpected shift of harmony to E♭ (a blues ♭III chord), and then to the exotic B♭m. This chord change is linked by the transposition of bar 5 down a tone to bar 6. The predictable blues harmony of the Mixolydian opening has been taken somewhere new. The sequence ends with a strong tone shift from C to B♭. Listen for the 12-string guitar (on the right), playing the riff throughout.

TRACK 31 **minor/aeolian**

Back to the swing of 12/8—but very, very slow. The E Aeolian scale (E F♯ G A
B C D) is pressed into doomy service for a clearly scale-based climbing riff. The
form is a1+a2, with two contrasting endings to the two-bar phrase. In bar 2, a full
Am7 contrasts dramatically with the single notes that surround it. In bar 4, the
C–B notes are transformed by brief arpeggios based on the chords of C and G/B.
Throughout, the bass guitar sticks to the basic scale and root notes.

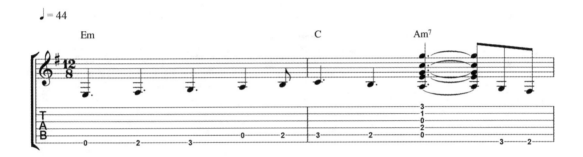

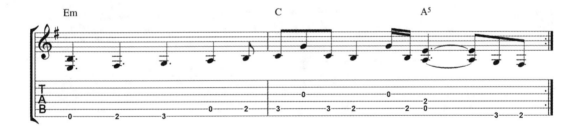

TRACK 32 **dorian**

This Dorian riff in single notes is structured a1+a2+a3+b, each section lasting two bars. The scale of A Dorian (A B C D E F♯ G) is supplemented by a flattened fifth (E♭) note in bar 7. The Dorian flavor is created by the emphasis on F♯. The first part of a1, a2, and a3 is a phrase that ends on this note. Notice how the riff uses rising and falling phrases. Listen for the guitar overdub in bars 5–8, which doubles the riff an octave higher.

TRACK 33 **phrygian**

The "signature" note of the Phrygian mode on A is B♭, the flattened second. This riff emphasizes that note in the way track 16 emphasized F♯, the Dorian sixth. The track begins on the fourth beat of the bar. An initial 16th-note phrase is played four times with variations. At bar 5, the riff turns into chords. The note B♭ is heard in the A7sus4/♭9 chord (where it is the flattened ninth), and in Gm and B♭. Choice of chord helps to retain the flavor of the mode.

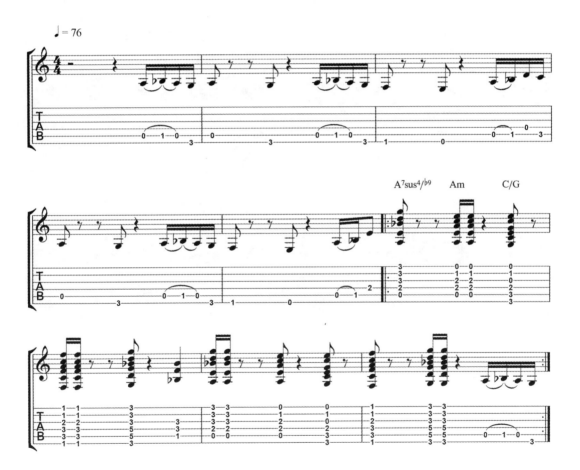

TRACK 34 **lydian**

F major normally has a B♭ in its scale (F G A B♭ C D E). This means that the chords G and Cmaj7 (both of which contain a B natural) would not normally occur in this key. However, the Lydian mode on F gives F G A B C D E, so the chords of G and Cmaj7 are possible.

Apart from the scale-like passages in this riff, there are also arpeggio-based ideas, as in bar 2. Listen for the 12-string guitar on the left side. Remember that a 12-string guitar overdub is an easy way of doubling the riff an octave higher.

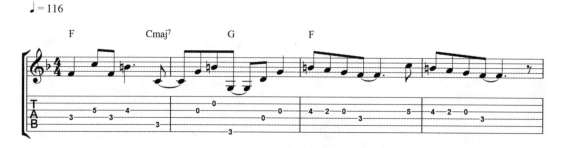

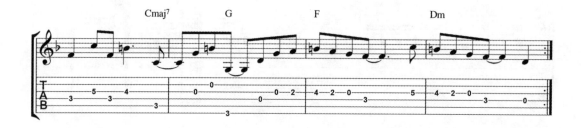

TRACK 35 **locrian**

This riff in F♯ Locrian (F♯ G A B C D E) is played entirely in fifths, as might be expected in a heavy rock style. Of all the modes, the Locrian is the most asymmetrical, because of its flattened fifth note (C), resulting in chord I being a diminished triad rather than a major or minor. A fifth on the root note F♯ should be a flattened fifth (F♯C) or tritone, but in practice bands turn this into a perfect fifth (F♯C♯).

The asymmetry of this mode is enhanced by the use of an asymmetrical time signature—5/4—and the fact that 5/4 and 6/4 bars alternate. The absence of a regular pulse has almost as unsettling an effect as the mode itself.

TRACK 36 **chromatic**

Chromatic riffs are characterized by stepwise movement, as track 36 illustrates in a funky style. The key is D major (D E F# G A B C#), but to these notes are added F, C, E♭, and B♭. Bar 2 transposes bar 1 down a tone, so the riff structure is a1+a2+b1+b2. Listen for the creeping movement back to the keynote in bar 4. The bass plays the same notes as the guitars. Notice the "jumpy" effect of the dotted 8th/16th-note pairing in bars 1–3.

TRACK 37 **pedal note**

The pedal note itself is D, and the scale played on string three is D Mixolydian (obvious because of its C instead of C#). Notice the semitone bend in bar 2. A 12-string guitar plays the riff on the right. The significant element to this riff is the arrangement: the first time, the riff is supported by slight percussion; the second time, the drums enter properly; on the third time through, bass and organ clearly change chords, altering the sound of the riff even though the riff is the same. Remember that new light can be cast on a riff by reharmonizing it.

TRACK 38 **drone note**

To play this riff, a new tuning is required: EADF#BC#, with alterations to the first and third strings. All the played strings are allowed to ring, so be careful not to accidentally damp them. This riff looks complicated on paper, but it's based on the shape of a fifth, moving up the lower strings. The drone notes are the top three strings.

Listen for the entry of the 12-string guitar overdub. A further overdub has a guitar in standard tuning just playing fifths, to strengthen the bass frequencies. Notice also that this riff is grouped in three four-bar phrases instead of the more common four. Four repeats give a 12-bar verse, instead of the usual 16-bar verse.

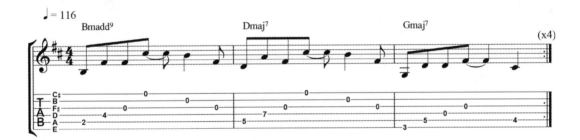

TRACK 39 **arpeggio**

Back to the '50s swing feel of 12/8 time for this riff in E, which uses some traditional arpeggio figures on E7 and A7. As before, a twist is given to the ideas by the semitone bend from C# to D (implying a tritone against the G blues chord), which is harmonized in sixths on its second and third appearances. The same thing happens to the A7 riff: when the C chord appears in the last bar, another tritone (F#) is created against it by the offkey sixths.

TRACK 40 major chords

Here's a typically meaty chord riff in E major, using a I–IV–V–IV–♭VII sequence, then repeated with the last chord replaced by a ♭III G. Although all the chords except the Dsus2 are straight majors, the scale degrees of ♭VII and ♭III (D and G) complicate the picture slightly, giving a harder blues edge. Even with only two guitars playing, there isn't much room left in the sonic picture for more rhythm overdubs.

TRACK 41 **mixolydian chords**

Sometimes, a riff can be created simply by holding a chord and lifting a finger on and off a string. The chord in question here is a familiar D7, made to yield a rock riff by taking the fingers off the first and third strings to get the sense of something happening. The "dominant seventh" chord—here formed on the first of the scale, D, in true blues fashion—naturally occurs as chord I of the Mixolydian mode. The ♭VII of that mode is also heard in the descending run which ends each of the riff's phrases, though one has an F and the other an F♯. Notice how the single notes of the riff's ending contrast with its chordal bars.

TRACK 42 **minor chords**

Minor chord riffs lend themselves to less rocky material. In B minor, the three main chords would be Bm, Em, and F#m. They are supplemented here by the more exotic Gm6. On the arrangement, one cleanish electric guitar is joined by an acoustic guitar.

TRACK 43 **suspended chords**

The tension of a suspended chord is exploited in track 43 by the heavy accenting of A7sus4, G7sus4, Esus4, and Fsus2 chords. Notice the unexpected Chuck Berryish double-stop bend in bars 1 and 3, and the shift to a higher register for the G7sus4 up at the seventh fret. The structure of the riff is a1 + a2 (on A) + b (on E).

TRACK 44 **triads**

This triad riff has a slight soul feel because of the 16th-note rhythm patterns. The triads are in D and move up the top three strings. Extra harmonic color is created by additional tones such as the sus4 in bar 2, the add9 in bar 3, and the minor add9 in bar 4. Notice that the rhythm pattern is fairly constant in each bar; the chords change against this.

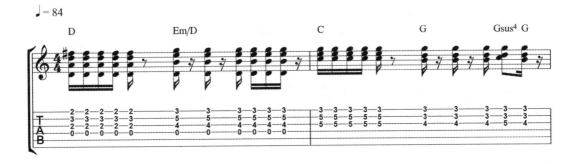

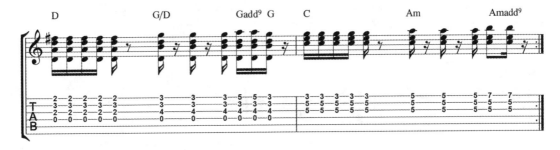

TRACK 45 **inverted chords**

The logical way to make a riff with inverted chords is to construct them on a bass line that is moving in steps up or down. Track 45 features a rising bass line of E–F♯–G–A–B–C–D–E. After the initial root E, those bass notes are harmonized with a sequence of inversions that goes: first, second, second, first, first, first, culminating in another root E. The bass guitar strengthens the sound of the inversions by also following this line—if it played the root note of each chord, the effect of the guitar inversions would be weaker. In bars 8–9, two more inversions appear, putting a new slant on an old chord progression.

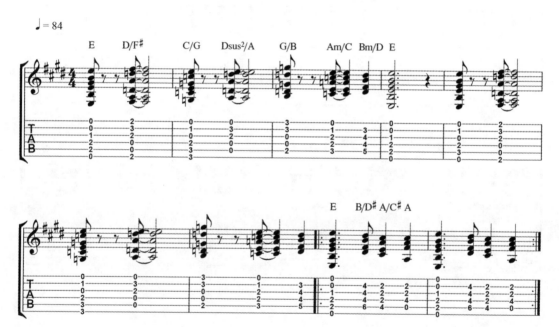

TRACK 46 **unusual chords**

Here's a riff that brings together several musical elements. The asymmetrical, unsettling effect of the 5/4 time signature is enhanced by the unusual chords. The tone-shift first beat of bar 1 would not normally be followed by an Am6 chord (since Am is foreign to the key of B major); the F♯7 chord would not normally have an add11 in it; and such a hard rock riff would be unlikely to have a G♯m chord.

The riff is then developed. In bars 3–6, the music goes into 4/4. The first beat is retained, but more common ♭III (Dsus2) and IV (E5) chords are added—only to then be trumped by the wholly unexpected Gm6 and first-inversion Dmaj9. A climbing low bass phrase leads to a further development of the opening riff, which is in 6/4, and dropped a tone to be based around A (although it is not an exact transposition). In the song from which this example is taken, the 6/4 riff does not occur until a verse and chorus have passed. In a real musical context, it would be too much to put these three riffs next to each other, but this has been done here for the sake of illustration.

Remember that development is a technique hardly used in rock, so there's an opportunity here to do something out of the ordinary now and again. Instead of repeating the same riff throughout a track, why not write a variation on it that can be slipped in at certain points to add extra interest? Track 46 shows how a single idea can mutate in and out of different time signatures and pitches.

Continued on next page.

TRACK 46 *continued*

TRACK 47

This riff develops its basic rhythm and chord basis as it proceeds. Bars 1–2 are mostly the rhythmic strike of an A5 chord, with a fragment of a Mixolydian descending scale at the end of bar 2. When this idea repeats in bars 3–4, a minor third C natural is added. In bars 5–6 and 7–8, that C becomes a ♭III chord over the A note pedal, instead of just a single note. The short run down in bar 6 is thickened into intervals of a fifth and sixth.

TRACK 48

This riff in E draws from the Mixolydian scale. A powerful octave leap from the sixth-string open E initiates a descending sequence featuring D (a leap of a minor seventh) and C♯ (a leap of a major sixth)—a sequence that's punctuated by a sudden C5–B5 change. This interruption in bar 2 has its variant in bar 4, with an A5–B5 change, but is heard again in bar 6. In bars 5–6, during the third playing of the riff, the upper E, D, and C♯ are harmonized by thirds.

If this riff was played by two guitars, they could perform this harmonization by taking one note each, but if there is only one guitar, it is easy enough to play the thirds alone. Using the 3+1 formula, bars 7 and 8 do something different. The riff is rounded off by a two-chord stab of E9, and then a more ornate descending E pentatonic minor phrase, with hammer-ons and pull-offs.

TRACK 49

You can sometimes write different-sounding riffs if you put down your pick and play with your fingers. A change of hand technique created this riff, which has high plucked thirds alternating with an offbeat bass note A played with the thumb.

Notice how variations of the initial two-bar idea keep it fresh. The last two thirds in bar 2, which are a sort of answer to the opening thirds, answer differently at the end of bar 4 where there is a distinct shift of harmony to a D chord. Instead of simply repeating bars 1–2 at this point, what were thirds in those bars turn into triads in bars 5–6, with a mildly jazz-blues effect of Am–Bm–Cm–Bm triads over the A pedal. Notated as versions of the underlying A harmony, these triads imply Am–A13–A7♯9♭5. The riff is completed with a Gsus4 triad, given color by the bass guitar moving to an E, implying the chord change Gsus4–G–Em7add13.

TRACK 50

Here's a riff developed from a simple arpeggio of Bm7 (B–D–F♯–A). When the riff has been heard three times, a variation comes in with the changing of the last note from A to G♯. The G♯ gives the arpeggio an edgy quality. It implies the scale of B Dorian (B C♯ D E F♯ G♯ A), since in B minor we would expect the sixth note to be a G. The Dorian mode, coupled with the rhythm, gives the riff a Latin flavor.

In a song, this riff would constitute a verse. Another variation is the addition of fourths on some of the notes. Listen for the way the bass guitar's move to E and then A colors the riff just before what would be the chorus. A new riff appears, made of a descending offbeat chromatic scale figure on the chords B–A. After three, the chords C♯ and F♯ are implied by the guitar notes, before the first riff returns.

TRACK 51

This is a chunky riff in G, developed through a 12-bar-based sequence. In bars 1–2, we have the first idea—a G7 chord with a bouncy leap from a low G up a minor seventh to the F. This has the effect of accentuating the angular nature of the seventh chord. Instead of playing this riff as a single-note idea, the open second and third strings are also hit, adding some grunge. A few descending notes lead the riff back down to its starting point. The initial riff is transposed up a fourth onto C7 for four bars, before the progression returns to the G7 riff. The progression might have ended with a version of the riff on D7, but instead the music has an F chord (♭VII in G) going to a D/F♯, so that the lowest guitar notes creep back by a semitone to the riff's low G.

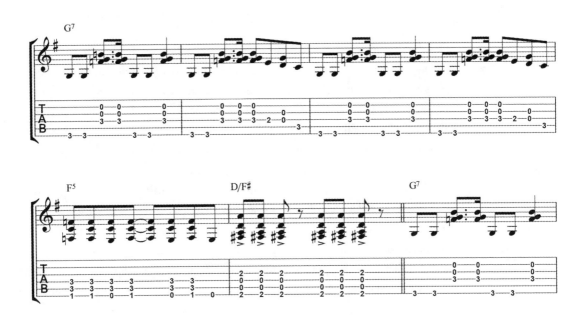

TRACK 52

This book has often stressed the importance of leaving spaces in riffs, but sometimes you just want to let rip with a headlong rush that doesn't let up. This riff is almost entirely eighth notes, with the occasional tied note across a bar line, or a quarter-note at the end of a phrase to draw breath. It can be thought of as two riffs, each with small variations.

Riff 1 is built from the scale of A pentatonic minor, and has two different endings—the first in bar 4 is a descending phrase, the second in bar 8 ascends. Riff 2 is centered on E and implies an E Mixolydian scale as its climbs upward, ending first on a flat seventh (D) and second on a descending E pentatonic minor phrase. On the repeat, this last phrase is replaced by one drawn from riff 1 to take the music back to that.

Both riffs are very guitar-oriented in their shape and fingering, making use of the instrument's two lowest open strings with pull-offs to increase the flow of the notes. They also make a good test of the accuracy of your picking.

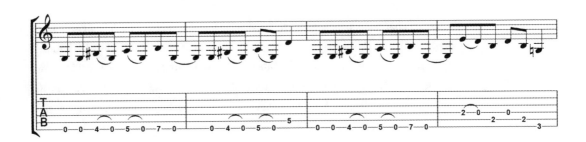

D.C. al fine

TRACK 53

There's a change of time signature for this slow riff in 12/8. The overall character might be labelled "bluesy," but there are some unexpected touches of harmony that prevent this being a straight blues riff. The main figure is in E minor, and implies the chords Em–G–A–C. In bar 3, the next time this is played, the C arpeggio on the fourth beat becomes a Cmaj7, which is quite startling in this musical context. In bar 7, the A5 becomes an Am, and a D5 takes the place of the C chord. Each two-bar riff is finished either with an E pentatonic minor scale idea (as in bar 2) or an E blues-scale run (in bar 4).

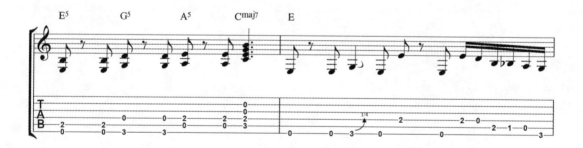

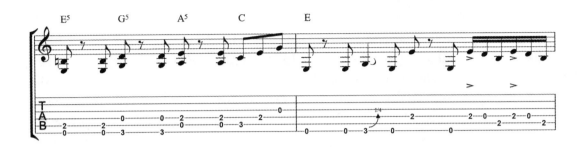

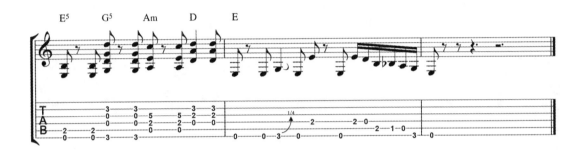

TRACK 54

This is a simple but effective riff using an interval with an open-E drone. The riff consists of three sixths in the key of A major, played on strings 2 and 4. When it is first played, the bass is only providing a pedal note of A. In the verse, the bass guitar moves from A to E to D and back to E, which makes the riff imply the chords of A, E, and Dadd9. Their harmonic value is further extended by the changing notes of the bass and the chords from the rhythm guitar. The chords of F#m and Bm are heard, distinctly altering the color of the riff. There is much that can be found creatively by seeing how a riff might be varied not by changing its notes but by changing the context in which it is heard.

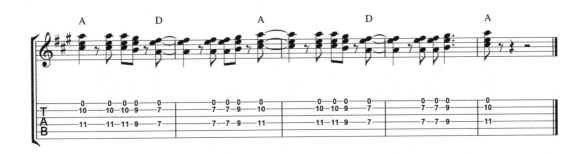

TRACK 55

This riff in D uses drop D, in which string six is detuned by a tone. The progression of the riff is laid out on a 12-bar pattern, but with an additional eight bars. The basic riff on D (bars 1–2) features a flat third/major third idea, with a higher interval that implies a dominant seventh chord (D7 and G7). The riff is transposed to G and eventually to A. Thereafter, there's a change of rhythm, as the eighth notes are replaced by a descending, syncopated, dotted-quarter-note idea. The second phrase has a couple of extra thirds and a different ending (in fifths). Each phrase is answered by the D riff.

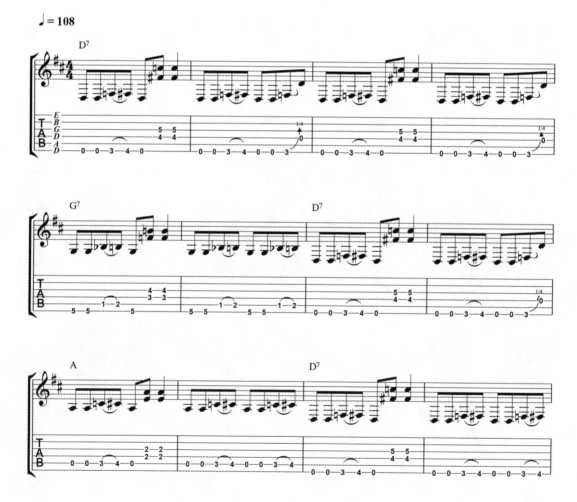

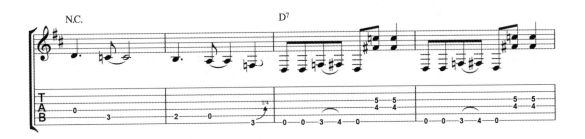

TRACK 56

Like track 53, this is a riff in 12/8. In contrast to that slow bluesy riff, this one is a perky, chromatic riff with the swing that a faster 12/8 tempo can give. It is unusual also for being pitched in the key of C, which is not a popular key for guitar riffs. The structure of the riff is a classic a+b+a+c form. Bars 1–2 and 5–6 match; bars 3–4 are a variation, and bars 7–8 contrast the main riff's ascending direction with a descending idea. The notes for the riff are drawn from a C major scale (C E F F♯ G) with a chromatic sharpened fourth and a C blues scale (C E♭ G♭ G B♭). Listen for the contrast in timbre between the G open string in bar 1 and the fretted G in bar 2.

♩. = 126

index of songs

index of artists

acknowledgments

A special thanks to John Paul Jones for giving his time to be interviewed for the first edition of the book. For their involvement in the preparation of this and previous editions, I would like to thank Tom Seabrook, Nigel Osborne, Tony Bacon, John Morrish, and Mark Brend. The audio was mastered by Tim Turan of Tim Turan Audio, Oxford, UK. My guitars are maintained by Dave Smart of Smart Guitars UK. Thanks go to my guitar and songwriting students Ella Tallyn, Alan Swain, Richard Hartwell, William Henry, David Guerro, and Conor Lumsden, who highlighted various riffs and stimulated my thinking on various relevant musical themes.

about the author

Rikky Rooksby is a guitar teacher, songwriter/composer, and writer on music. He is the author of *How to Write Songs on Guitar* (2000; revised 2009, 2020), *Inside Classic Rock Tracks* (2001), *How to Write Guitar Riffs* (2002; revised 2010, 2021), *The Songwriting Sourcebook* (2003; revised 2011), *Chord Master* (2004; revised 2016), *Melody* (2004), *Songwriting Secrets: Bruce Springsteen* (2005), *How to Write Songs on Keyboards* (2005), *How to Write Lyrics* (2006; revised 2021), *Arranging Songs* (2007), *How to Write Songs in Altered Guitar Tunings* (2010), and *Songs and Solos* (2014). He contributed to *Albums: 50 Years of Great Recordings, Classic Guitars of the Fifties, The Guitar: The Complete Guide for the Player*, and *Roadhouse Blues* (2003). He is also the author of *The Guitarist's Guide to the Capo* (Artemis, 2003), *The Complete Guide to the Music of Fleetwood Mac* (revised ed. 2004), *Play Great Guitar* (Infinite Ideas, 2008), 14 Fastforward guitar tutor books, and has transcribed and arranged over 40 chord songbooks of music, including *The Complete Beatles*. His entries for many rock musicians appear in the new *Dictionary of National Biography* (Oxford University Press), and his published interviews, reviews, articles, and transcriptions in *Guitar Techniques, Total Guitar, Guitarist, Bassist, Bass Guitar Magazine, The Band, Record Collector, Sound on Sound, Shindig!*, and *Making Music*. His memberships include the Society of Authors, Sibelius One, and the Vaughan Williams Society. Visit his website at www.rikkyrooksby.com for more information.